SO-BVN-580

A Canadian Social Psychology
of Ethnic Relations

Contributors

Frances E. Aboud
John W. Berry
Jean Burnet
Robert C. Gardner
Fred Genesee
Rudolf Kalin
Wallace E. Lambert
Marlene Mackie
Lise Simard
Donald M. Taylor
G. Richard Tucker

A Canadian Social Psychology of Ethnic Relations

Edited by
Robert C. Gardner,
University of Western Ontario

and

Rudolf Kalin,
Queen's University

⟨ⅅ⟩ **Methuen**

Toronto   New York   London   Sydney   Auckland

Copyright © 1981 by Methuen Publications
A division of the Carswell Company Limited

All rights reserved. No part of this publication may
be reproduced, stored in a retrieval system or
transmitted in any form or by any means, electronic,
mechanical, photocopying, recording or otherwise,
without the prior written permission of Methuen
Publications, 2330 Midland Avenue, Agincourt,
Ontario, Canada.

Canadian Cataloguing in Publication Data
    Main entry under title:
    A Canadian social psychology of ethnic relations

    Includes index.

    ISBN 0-458-94590-0 pa.

    1. Ethnic relations. 2. Canada—Ethnic relations.
    3. Ethnicity. 4. Social psychology—Canada.
    I. Gardner, Robert C., 1934-   II. Kalin, Rudolf.

    ✓ FC104.C36   305.8'00971   C80-094772-X
    F1035.A1C36

48, 318

Printed and bound in Canada

1 2 3 4 5   81   86 85 84 83 82

Contents

CAMROSE LUTHERAN COLLEGE
LIBRARY

Preface

Plans for this book first started taking shape in 1976 when both editors were on sabbatical leave at the University of Bristol. Its impetus was a discussion of the role of culture in social science and the recognition that the social milieu not only influences the types of problems investigated, but also the theoretical concepts and empirical approaches used. One example initially discussed was the matched guise technique (see Chapters 7 and 8) developed in Canada in 1960 to study stereotyped reactions to speakers of French and English. It seemed somehow peculiarly Canadian that research on ethnic relations would use speech as the stimulus, that it would focus on French/English relations, and that the original study would include as a secondary issue reactions to different varieties of French (European *vs.* Canadian) but not English. The significance of the cultural context becomes apparent when the way in which this technique is used in other societies is examined. In the United States, this procedure has been used mostly to study ethnically accented English; in Great Britain it has been used primarily to study regional accents and status related variations in accents.

This discussion gave rise to the proposition that a truly international social psychology course concerned with general principles of social behaviour should make use of textbooks from a number of different cultural settings and examine directly the resulting assumptions, concepts and approaches. To provide a Canadian contribution, we contacted social psychologists and sociologists with clear research programs on Canadian problems to invite them to contribute a chapter to this book. The major criterion for selecting authors was that they be active contributors to the research literature. Furthermore, it was not sufficient that the research be conducted in Canada—it had to be distinctively Canadian. A second criterion for inclusion was that chapters present comprehensive discussions of topic areas rather than detailed and specific research reports. A third criterion, admittedly added after an initial survey, was that the topic matter involve ethnic relations or a clearly related topic. This limitation was not our original intent but became necessary by the nature of much of the social psychological research being conducted. Distinctly Canadian research does exist in sub-areas other than ethnic relations, but it could not easily be integrated into a common theme which could serve as the nucleus for a course in social psychology.

The book is organized into four sections. Section I, *Conceptual and Historical Background*, provides the cultural and historical context for the study of ethnic relations in Canada. Section II, *Social Development*, focuses on the formation of identity in children. Given the theme of ethnic relations, primary attention is devoted to factors influencing the development of ethnic identity. Section III, *The Language Issue*, centres on the basic linguistic duality of Canada and considers the social pyschological implications of the official bilingual nature of this country. Section IV, *Intergroup Relations*, looks at social psychological processes involved in relations between groups.

When using this book we recommend that instructors encourage students to consider carefully the sociocultural basis of the material presented. Students should ask themselves how, or even whether, a particular research problem or approach is uniquely Canadian, and how it would be conceptualized in some other cultural setting. When looked at in this light, this book serves not only as a summary of much Canadian research on ethnic relations but also can act as the impetus to question and examine the cultural basis of social scientific research.

Section I
Conceptual and Historical Background

Chapter 1

The Cultural Context of Social Psychology

Rudolf Kalin, Department of Psychology, Queen's University
R.C. Gardner, Department of Psychology, University of Western Ontario

The title of this book contains the phrase "Canadian Social Psychology" as opposed to "Social Psychology in Canada." Canadian social psychology is used to refer to social psychology which is instigated by and dependent upon the Canadian physical and social context. It may make use of methods and concepts common to social psychology in general or it may necessitate developments unique to Canada, but it is characterized by its direct relation to the social problems, issues and cultural make-up of Canada. Social psychology in Canada, on the other hand, refers to the investigation of social psychological problems in Canada. Examples would be studies in conformity, attitude change, altruism, aggression, or group dynamics, that happen to be conducted in Canada but could be carried out anywhere. A similar distinction has been made by Berry (1978b) who called it psychology *in* Canada and *of* Canada.

The major basis for the distinction between Canadian social psychology and social psychology in Canada rests on the importance of the Canadian context to the investigation. The position adopted here is that Canadian social psychology derives from issues important to the Canadian context, though not necessarily unique to it. For this reason, studies examining the applicability of a given concept or generalization to the Canadian context, or investigations conducted to provide cross-cultural contrasts would be classified as "social psychology in Canada" because the Canadian setting did not instigate them. In making this distinction, we would also argue that both types of social psychology have merit, in that each can serve to broaden and reinforce the scientific base of the discipline. There is no intention here to denigrate either. The focus in this book might be taken by some to represent merely a nationalistic stance. Nothing could be further from the truth. Instead it represents an attempt to highlight the universal nature of social psychology by emphasizing the role played by the culture of investigators in determining the types of problems they study and the concepts they use.

Social Psychology and Culture
The Nature of Social Psychology

A universally accepted definition of social psychology is not available; Allport (1968), however, defines it as *"an attempt to understand and explain how the thought, feeling and behavior of individuals are influenced by the actual, imagined, or implied presence of others"* (p.3).

Social psychology is basically the study of social influence. Not answered by the definition are two important questions: (1) who investigates and determines the social influence? and (2) who are the individuals being influenced? From the point of view of social psychology, these questions are of great significance.

The Influence of Culture on Social Psychology

Psychologists have long argued that the way people perceive the world and how they organize it is in part a function of the cultural context in which they live. Wilhelm Wundt (1832-1921), considered by many to be the founder of modern psychology, proposed that our thinking is heavily conditioned by language, custom, and by myth. Wundt's nineteenth century idea that perception and thinking are influenced by the cultural context is generally accepted in modern psychology and anthropology.

Unlike other scientists, psychologists do not stand truly apart from the phenomena they study. They are subject to the same influences as other humans. Their own cultural background and personal history influence the way they perceive and construe the world. It is therefore likely that the personal and cultural characteristics of psychological investigators influence their assumptions about human nature, the problems and hypotheses they study, the methods they select and the interpretations they place on their results. Crutchfeld and Krech (1963) concisely summarize the dynamic link between psychologists and their culture when they state that ". . . the scientist—like every person—is a member and product of his society. Certainly no psychologist can escape this influence, no matter what his experimental problem, and no matter how thick and sound-proof are the walls of his laboratory cubicle" (p.12).

Does it matter what people social psychologists study? In reports of psychological investigations, individuals being investigated are called "subjects"; but are they just subjects? It is now widely recognized that generalizations about one group of subjects may not apply to another . In many earlier psychological investigations, for example, mention of the gender of research subjects was omitted. The assumption was that what applies to one sex also applies to another. We are now aware that there are important sex differences in psychological characteristics (e.g., males are more aggressive than females, Maccoby & Jacklin, 1974). Besides gender there are, of course, many characteristics of individuals that might make them behave differently. There is a vast research literature concerned with the question of how cultural background affects people's behaviour. There is in fact a sub-discipline within psychology, called cross-cultural psychology, that deals precisely with this question. From cross-cultural studies it is apparent that generalizations about human behaviour derived from the study of individuals in one particular culture do not necessarily apply universally.

Cultural Origins of Social Psychology

The failure to specify who studies whom in social psychology would not necessarily be a problem, if social psychologists from many cultures studied individuals from many cultures and came up with similar descriptions of human behaviour. The fact is, however, that modern social psychology comes primarily from one culture, the United States. The textbooks widely used throughout the world are American, as are the research and the theories they present.

Given the current American influence on social psychology, it is important to ask whether it has always been this way. The origin of social psychology is difficult to pinpoint. The originators and significant figures were not all Americans. The year 1908 saw the publication of the first two general texts in the English language with the titles *Social Psychology*. The first of the two was written by the American sociologist E.A. Ross, the second by William McDougall, who was British.

Germany might have rivalled the United States in developing social psychology. Germans were busy at the beginning of the twentieth century studying experimentally the question of individual versus group performance, a problem which also received wide attention in the Untied States. But the possibility of later free academic inquiry was severely impeded by Germany's involvement in two world wars. Many of the German psychologists from the period emigrated to the United States. The most significant of these for social psychology was Kurt Lewin. He developed field theory and initiated the study of group dynamics. Many of the American social psychologists who were to lead the discipline in the 1950s and 1960s were students or associates of Lewin.

A true understanding of modern social psychology requires an understanding of Anglo-American intellectual traditions. Allport (1955) has argued that the thinking of the English philosopher, John Locke, particularly has influenced American psychology. Locke conceived of the mind as a *tabula rasa* (blank tablet), a passive thing acquiring content and structure only through the impact of sensations and through the association of such sensations. Allport describes the Lockean tradition,as it became part of American psychology, as consisting of the following five presuppositions: (1) the external is more important than the internal; (2) what happens between stimulus and response is not important; (3) the small, molecular is more important than the large and molar; elements are more important than patterns; (4) various species are equivalent; (5) early development is more important than later development.

In contrast to the Lockean tradition that has characterized Anglo-American psychology, Allport has suggested that the Leibnitzian tradition (after the German philosopher Leibnitz) has guided European psychology. In this tradition the person is the source of acts. Behaviour is purposive and concerned with self-preservation and self-affirmation. The human mind is active, not passive.

While it cannot be argued that the Lockean tradition characterizes all of American psychology, certain aspects of this psychology fit the Lockean blueprint: the concern with manipulation of situations and behaviour; the emphasis on situationism; the study of the molecular rather than the molar.

The Cultural Distinctiveness of Canada

The history of North America shows interesting similarities and differences between the United States and Canada. Although both cultures are rooted in British thought, that of the United States developed out of the colonies' revolution against King George III. This revolutionary origin gives further clues about its current intellectual character, particularly in contrast to its neighbour, Canada. The Declaration of Independence. promised Americans life, liberty and the pursuit of happiness; the British North America Act pledged Canadians peace, order and good government.

There are other similarities and differences. Both countries were inhabited by the native peoples (Amerindians and Inuit, the original immigrants to North America) before the advent of Europeans in the sixteenth century. While three great colonial powers, England, France and Spain, established settlements in the land-area that is now the United States, the English dominated and eventually became the exclusive colonial power. Canada was first settled by the French, and became the colony of New France. The treaty of Utrecht in 1713 gave the British Hudson Bay, Newfoundland and Acadia (present-day Nova Scotia). Still, New France flourished along the St. Lawrence through the Great Lakes and down the Mississippi until the British Conquest in 1760. The Treaty of Paris in 1763 ended New France; however, the conquest by Britain did not end the cultural existence of the French in North America. In the Quebec Act of 1774, Britain granted French Canadians the right to have the laws, government and religion they wanted. Civil law was to be French and criminal law English. Since then, French Canadian society has developed alongside English more or less peacefully. Thus a basic duality has characterized Canada from her beginning. It is now recognized that both the British and French are "charter-groups" (Porter, 1965) of today's Canada.

During the nineteenth century many people whose background was neither British nor French emigrated to North America. While the policy dealing with immigrants was originally one of Anglo-domination in both countries, it shifted to a melting pot ideal in the United States. In Canada, on the other hand, a policy of cultural pluralism became the accepted way to accommodate immigrants. Immigrant groups could retain their old ways and customs and were not obliged to assimilate. The resulting picture has been called an ethnic mosaic, in contrast to the melting pot. In 1971, multiculturalism became the official policy of the Government of Canada.

Societal and Universal Social Psychology

Any differences which exist between countries could be relatively unimportant to the discipline of social psychology if it were truly a universal science. But is it? As indicated earlier, culture influences science; it is therefore important to consider the societal basis of social psychology. Until recently, however, this has not been done. Most social psychologists have simply conducted their research on the assumption that it was universally applicable. Authors of textbooks in social psychology have generally ignored the cultural origin and location of the studies they discuss. Most social psychological research reported in textbooks has been conducted in the United States, yet often the findings and their explanations have been presented as if they were universal. Recently, writers from a number of countries have questioned this assumption. The French social psychologist Moscovici (1972) has argued that research problems are likely to be congruent with societal ideologies. He states (p.19) that American social psychology "took for its theme of research and for the contents of its theories the issues of *its own* society." Similar arguments have been presented by the British social psychologist Billig (1976). From a Canadian perspective, Berry (1978a) has raised the issue of the societal vs. universal nature of social psychology. He starts with the premise that social psychology is rooted in a social system. It is therefore *"desirable* and *possible* to: (a) make these societal bases explicit in order to better match the science with reality, and (b) analyze communalities comparatively in order to generate a more universal science of human behaviour" (p.93). A failure to make explicit the societal basis of social science may create the illusion of having established universal truths. Making it explicit involves two separate steps, according to Berry (1978a). The first is to acknowledge that much of modern social psychology has its origin in the society of the United States. Because American social psychology may be different in content and approach to what a Canadian social psychology might be, Berry has likened American social psychology to a blueprint which may not fit the Canadian machine. When machine and blueprint don't match, there is a danger of changing the machine to match the blueprint. This danger calls for the second step: developing a blueprint to describe the machine as it is. From the point of view of Canada, this requires the development of a Canadian social psychology from a Canadian perspective. From a universal point of view, this requires the development of a social psychology which explicitly recognizes its local origin.

There is a danger, of course, in developing a local social psychology, which is as serious as the unquestioned import of a social psychology developed elsewhere. The danger is ethnocentrism (Sumner, 1906; Adorno, Frenkel-Brunswik, Levinson & Sanford, 1950; LeVine and Campbell, 1972). Ethnocentrism may lead to a distortion of reality in that one's own culture-bound perspective is taken as universally appropriate. Campbell (1961) has addressed the problem of how ethnocentric distortion may be reduced and eliminated. A particular phenomenon must be studied not only by members of a particular society, but also by outsiders. Berry (1978a) has made a convincing point that the results of studies by "insiders" and "outsiders" must be subjected to a comparative analysis. It is this comparative analysis that will eventually lead to a universal science of human behaviour.

The present book was written, in part, with such an objective in mind. The universal nature of social psychology can be stressed by focussing on national topics. Consider the international flavour of a social psychology course which used textbooks from a number of different national contexts. The availability of books with similar orientations written in England, Europe, and the United States and other cultural communities, would be a step toward a truly universal social psychology.

Learning and Teaching Social Psychology

Learning Social Psychology

Social psychology represents information which can serve several ends. Learning about the state of the art of modern social psychology may be a step in becoming an educated person. Learning about social problems and issues of one's country makes students more knowledgeable citizens. Social psychology also presents new concepts useful for explaining social behaviour. This knowledge can influence the way students perceive social reality and think about social issues.

In addition to acquiring information, students may also be influenced in their values$\frac{1}{2}$ from a social psychology course. Knowledge is seldom value free. Values emphasizing human dignity, freedom, equality, and open-mindedness and decrying bigotry, narrow-mindedness, and coercion underlie the work of many social psychologists. By learning their discipline, students are likely to acquire many of their values.

Teaching Social Psychology

Teaching social psychology is a considerable problem, particularly in the Canadian context. Sadava (1978a, 1978b), Berry (1978b), and Alcock (1978) have recently addressed this issue. Because of the possible ethnocentric nature of a social psychology developed in one country, instructors and students ideally would like a text with universal applicability. Concepts, theories and empirical generalizations should be relevant inside and outside the country of origin. This ideal is currently not possible as most texts are American in origin. Since the United States is a major force in social psychology, it would be meaningless and foolhardy to suggest that students should not become familiar with the research, concepts and theories coming from there. They should, however, be encouraged to recognize their source, and continually question their applicability to their own cultural context. The point being made here goes beyond the simple issue of the empirical illustrations contained in many texts, and includes the nature of the concepts and theoretical formulations, as well as the potential generalizations made.

Many of these issues have been raised by Canadian instructors using American-based texts. Alcock (1978) has pointed out that police brutality, race riots, and the hippie movement are, or were, significant social problems south of the border. In Canada they are of much less significance. In American texts the coverage of inter-ethnic attitudes, prejudice and discrimination is usually in the context of black white relations. This emphasis is reasonable, given the large number of blacks in the United States and the melting pot ideal. In Canada on the other hand, there are relatively few blacks and their origin and history are different. And instead of the melting pot ideal, Canada favours multiculturalism. Transporting the pre-eminence of black white relations and the emphasis on desegregation into the Canadian classroom fails to do justice to Canadian social reality.

There are, of course, many similarities between Canada and the United States, and considerable interchange between them so that it is easy for Canadian students to identify with American texts. To a visitor from abroad, Canadians and Americans may well look very much the same. They speak the same language. They watch the same TV shows, buy similar consumer products, and drive the same types of cars. After all, how could you tell Raymond Massey, Lorne Greene, Rich Little and Morley Safer from Americans? It is perhaps not unreasonable, therefore, that Canadian students adopt American issues as their own. This is clearly demonstrated by Black (1969) who examined a large number of sociology essays submitted by Canadian students. Almost half the essays written on race relations dealt with the problem of American blacks. Very few addressed distinctly Canadian racial problems. Black concludes that "the most devastating blow . . . was the fact that several Canadian students used the term my, ours, us when they were actually referring to the United States" (p.111, quoted in Alcock, 1978). Sadava (1978b) adds a further note of concern. In evaluating his social psychology course at Brock University, he asked students whether it bothered them that all the texts used in the course were American. A majority (60 per cent) were not concerned; only 3 per cent were "often" bothered by this fact. One wonders whether this is a typical Canadian reaction from individuals who watch American television shows, use American products, and keep up to date with American news almost as much as Americans. Or would this be true of students in most countries?

Authors of texts also contribute, often unwittingly, to the fusion of Canadian and American social issues and problems. The excellent and popular text by Wrightsman (1977) serves as an example. After recognizing the dangers of an ethnocentric perspective he attempts to extend the applicability of his text by including Canadian examples. Sadava (1978a) has carefully examined Wrightsman's text and pointed out eight examples where Canada and the United States have been paired as if they were one "conceptual package." Sadava indicates that French Canadians moving into English schools are not the equivalent of the United States school integration problem, or that separatist demonstrations cannot be coupled with black civil rights demonstrations. Alcock (1978) has also questioned Wrightsman's equating the problems of Amerindians in Canada and the United States. Although Wrightsman's text has borne the brunt of recent criticisms, it should be applauded, because it has at least recognized that Canada exists separately from the United States.

In addition to reinforcing cultural equations which might not really exist, failure to consider closely the cultural setting can lead to the importation of the value system associated with the knowledge. Students may not only begin to consider social issues of another country as their own, but they may also adopt as their own the values underlying the social science of the other country. In the case of Canadian students using American-based texts this means simply the acceptance of the values which serve as the foundation of American social psychology. Obviously it is important for students to be aware of and to appreciate these values. However, Canadian students should not adopt them automatically without a careful examination of their appropriateness for the Canadian context.

In addition to containing much non-Canadian material, texts written in other countries also fail to deal with Canadian problems and consequently often neglect the considerable amount of relevant Canadian research literature. In an attempt to make up for this omission, instructors sometimes make use of books of Canadian readings (such as Berry & Wilde, 1972; Driedger, 1978; Koulak & Perlman, 1973; Goldstein & Bienvenue, 1980), but these are at best ancillary. They do not provide systematic overviews of those problems that ideally deserve treatment in a Canadian course on social psychology. The nature of these problems, particularly those that have been extensively researched, is described in the next section.

Social Psychology of Ethnic Relations
The size of Canada, its sparse, yet highly urbanized population, with its substantial geographic variations create problems deserving of attention by social psychologists. Regional disparity and rivalries have psychological components, and there are many other distinctly Canadian problems that are waiting to be tackled. Consider, for example, the social psychological implications of royalism vs. republicanism, continentalism, outside economic and cultural influences on Canada, Canadian indentity, and

energy conservation. It was recognized as long as twenty-five years ago that some of these problems provide a fertile ground for psychological inquiry. After a four-year review of psychology in Canada, MacLeod (1955, p. 55-56) concluded that the social situation here provided a unique laboratory to investigate such phenomena as bilingualism, the learning of languages at different age levels, the effects of language on thought, social psychological factors associated with living in remote areas with cultural inbreeding, the effect of low temperatures, different diets, and seclusion from society.

In 1955, when MacLeod presented his assessment of Canadian psychology, he came to the conclusion that at that time, there was no distinctively Canadian psychology. He suggested, however, that such a psychology may develop because of Canada's singular problems.

Were he to assess the state of psychology in Canada today, his conclusions might be somewhat less bleak. Yet, to a considerable extent, MacLeod's conclusions remain accurate. There are many Canadian psychologists making significant contributions to the advancement of their science, but few are fully exploiting the resources of their country. Even in the area of social psychology, where attention to societal problems is particularly warranted, many social psychologists pay no attention to them.

In a recent assessment of Canadian content in psychology, Symons (1975) in his *Report of the Commission on Canadian Studies* urges that psychology pay greater attention to Canadian problems. This advice by the Commission received no national support. Symons reports that "it was frequently rebuked by some of those working in the discipline and by others who asked, often with some acerbity: What possible role has psychology in the field of Canadian studies?" (p. 102). To answer this question, the Commission listed nine areas for psychological inquiry that had been suggested by Berry, Kalin, & Wilde (1973) and were based on Berry (1974). Among these areas were northern development, bilingualism, French/English relations, isolation, multiple intergroup relations, immigration, communication, and cultural relativity in job selection and placement.

Most of these problems involve some aspect of ethnicity. It is likely that the importance of ethnicity in Canada is the major reason why social psychologists have tended to focus their attention on ethnic relations and have at times developed highly unique research programs. There may, however, be another pragmatic reason for this interest. The considerable American influence in Canadian social psychology may have led to the focus on ethnic relations when searching out a Canadian problem. Though different in many respects, the United States also has a profound interest in ethnic relations, and Canadian social psychologists can find in this problem an issue with immense value to their country yet one which maintains their association with mainstream social psychology.

Psychology in Canada

Although social psychology is a sub-discipline of both psychology and sociology, the focus in this historical perspective concentrates on psychology. There are two reasons for this. First, the authors of this chapter, like the majority of authors in this book, identify with the discipline of psychology, and hence are simply more aware of its history. Second, many of the historical incidents described with reference to psychology are equally appropriate to sociology, and it would seem redundant to state them twice. A reading of Clark's (1975) "Sociology in Canada: an historical overview" will reveal many parallels in the developments of the two disciplines in Canada.

Development of Psychology in North America

The birth of academic psychology is often placed at 1879 to correspond with the establishment of Wundt's laboratory in Leipzig. It would be equally reasonable to identify its beginnings in various countries with the establishment of national associations concerned with psychology. According to this criterion, psychology in the United States dates to 1892, the founding of the American Psychological Association. The same year could be used as the birth of psychology in Canada since the American Psychological Association was "established as a 'continental' rather than a national organization" (Wright, 1974, p. 113). The Canadian Psychological Association was not established until 1938. Such dates are useful in estimating the age of psychology, but psychology had been taught in universities for a much longer time. Myers (1965) reports that psychology was first taught in Canada in 1843 by a University of Toronto Professor of Philosophy; he also credits the University of Toronto with establishing the first Chair of Psychology in Canada. The year was 1889; the appointee was "an able young American by the name of James Mark Baldwin" (Myers, 1965, p. 6). The appointment of an American to the first Chair of Psychology in Canada is somehow typically Canadian. Baldwin was an able and influential psychologist. In 1890 he established the first psychological laboratory in Canada. He was one of twenty-six charter members of the American Psychological Association in 1892. He left Toronto in 1893 and in his subsequent life he is credited with establishing two more psychological laboratories (Princeton, 1893; and Johns Hopkins, 1903), and became president of the American Psychological Association in 1897.

The non-Canadian influence on Canadian psychology has a long tradition. Wright (1974) points out that in 1938 only twenty of the forty academic psychologists in Canada had obtained their highest degrees from Canadian universities; eleven were American trained, eight were educated in the United Kingdom, and one in Germany. Although such numbers might simply reflect the educational opportunities available at that time, the trend seems to have continued. In 1955, MacLeod observed (p. 30) "the foreign influence is still strong. More than half of the senior psychologists in Canadian universities received their advanced training outside Canada, most of these in the United States." And this obviously continued for some time. Wright (1969, p. 242) states that "... by 1966, more than half the psychologists with Ph.D. degrees in Canada were either American citizens or Canadians who had received their training in the United States." A similar state of affairs also characterized sociology. Clark (1975, p. 225) states "not only have Canadian universities recruited their sociology staffs from the United States, but most of the Canadians we have had teaching sociology in this country have acquired their training across the border."

In the case of pyschology this Americanization was fostered even though there were a number of graduate psychology programs in Canada. Wright (1969), for example, indicates that graduate programs in psychology departments were established before 1929 at the University of Toronto and McGill, and before 1949 at the Universities of British Columbia, Western Ontario, Ottawa, Montreal, Manitoba, Dalhousie and Acadia. Not all of these departments granted Ph.D. degrees, but at least the Universities of Toronto, McGill and Ottawa did grant such degrees before 1949 (Wright, 1978). The important point to be made, however, is either that Canadian universities felt it unnecessary to produce a sufficient number of Ph.D. graduates or that despite the production, better qualified staff could be obtained from outside Canada.

The American influence on psychology is not restricted to Canada. Berlyne (1968) states, for example, that European psychologists must travel to American universities if they are to be experts in psychology. Given the propinquity of Canada to the United States, and the rather favoured (until recently) position Americans had in Canadian immigration, the relatively large number of American psychologists in Canadian universities is not surprising. Wright (1969) claims that to some extent Canada gained prestige by being the largest colony of American psychologists, and that Canadian departments profited from the fact that these new faculty members brought with them the "drive which has made American psychology productive" (p. 242). Wright also cites disadvantages. These include her perception that American psychologists are not likely to assimilate or identify with their new-found home, and that not only do they tend to retain their American citizenship, but more importantly, their professional ties tend to remain American. Canadians trained in American schools, similarly retain their professional connections with the United States.

Research Funding in Psychology

Like many countries, Canada was motivated to support psychological research because of the world wars. MacLeod (1955, p. 13) states that "it was World War I that brought Canadian psychology fully to life." This claim was based on the observation that during World War I, Canadian psychologists were involved in the rehabilitation of military personnel. They had demonstrated their usefulness so that at the beginning of World War II it was understandable that they should be called on by the Canadian government. In 1939, The Canadian Psychological Association was given the first of a number of small grants from the National Research Council to aid in war-related research (Myers, 1965). It wasn't, however, until 1948 that the National Research Council established an Associate Committee on Psychology and invited applications for grants-in-aid of research. "In 1949, NRC's grant support in psychology amounted to $12,000." (Myers, 1965, p. 18). It was at about the same time that research monies became available from two other sources. In 1947, the Defence Research Board of Canada established a research panel representing four areas of psychology, "social, physiological and experimental, clinical, and education." (Wright, 1974, p. 125). In 1948, the Department of National Health and Welfare established a fund for mental health research. It is quite evident from these dates that the history of research funding has not been a long one. Nor has it ever been overly abundant. Myers (1965, p. 18) reports for example that in 1964, the National Research Council provided just over $200,000 in funds to support psychological research, and that the other two bodies had "each reached a level of support which is about half that of NRC." (Myers, 1965, p. 18).

The relatively short history of grant support and the generally inadequate funds for psychological research help explain the rather late development of Canadian psychology. There are other factors which seem important particularly with respect to the development of Canadian social psychology. For many years, Canadian psychologists were heavily dependent upon the generosity of American granting bodies—and they were generous indeed! Myers (1965) reports that a 1957 survey conducted by the Canadian Psychological Association revealed that approximately 40 per cent of the grant support for psychological research in Canada came from American sources. Wright (1969) reveals that this increased to approximately 50 per cent in the early 1960s and fell to about 30 per cent by 1966. Given such reliance on outside support it is perhaps understandable that there was not a great interest in social problems indigenous to Canada.

Perhaps, however, the greatest reason for the relatively slow development of social psychology in Canada rests on the fact that it is only comparatively recently that a granting body was established to support specifically social psychological research. Although the National Research Council, Defence Research Board and the Department of National Health and Welfare began supporting psychological research before 1950, it was not until 1966 that The Canada Council assumed the task of providing funds for research on social psychological problems. In 1978, this function was taken over by the Social Sciences and Humanities Research Council.

Emphasis on Basic vs. Applied Research

The earliest research in psychology in Canada had a definite applied orientation (Myers, 1965), thus it may appear inconsistent to suggest that the relative infancy of Canadian social psychology may also be due, in part, to an anti-applied orientation of early Canadian psychologists (and retained, in many quarters, by psychologists today). Such a bias was apparent in statements made by MacLeod (1947) to the effect that *basic* research was required to bring about an understanding of man.

It seems quite likely that an avoidance of practical problems represented a reasonable position at that time since there seemed to be a fear that applied research might carry with it some form of control by granting agencies over the type of research done and the results which might be reported. Wright (1974) indicates that when the National Research Council was considering the establishment of grant funds for psychological research, a number of government bodies, including the Department of Labour, and the Secretary of State, were approached to outline concrete proposals of needed research. Many government agencies responded, but when their enthusiasm was reported at the following meetings of the Canadian Psychological Association, it was met by considerable protest. Wright (1974, p. 122) states "there was genuine fear that psychologists might be forced to engage in a kind of 'contract research' in order to obtain funds." In fact, in 1947 the Canadian Psychological Association passed a motion at their annual meeting which stated in part that "the primary task of psychological research is to investigate freely the basic problems of our field. . . ." (Wright, 1974, p. 123).

This motion may only have been a reaction against possible intervention by granting agencies and an assertion of the right to pursue basic research. But its tone suggests more. By calling basic research the primary task of psychologists, applied endeavours by implication become secondary, and psychologists with interests in applied problems become suspect. Inasmuch as social psychology frequently addresses social (applied) problems, it is not difficult to see why its development has been retarded. The emphasis on basic research by the psychological establishment was not conducive to the scientific investigation of problems in society.

Social Psychology in Canada Today

Given the various factors that may have impeded the development of a distinctly Canadian social psychology, the reader may be curious about the extent of social psychology in Canada today. This is difficult to determine directly; however, some rough estimates can be made. In 1978, the Canadian Psychological Association issued a new Directory of Members. Members were asked to indicate in order of importance up to three areas of psychology with which they identified. They were instructed to add areas that were not among the seventy presented. We examined the identifications of those members who indicated an area of interest to determine the frequency with which they selected social psychology. Imagine our surprise when social psychology received only three selections! Although this might be taken as evidence of the virtual absence of social psychologists in Canada, it must be noted that social psychology was not included in the original list. Of course this might say something about the prestige accorded social psychology in Canada.

Because of the absence of "social psychology" as a given category, interest areas were identified which could signify a commitment to social psychology (e.g., interpersonal relations, minority groups). A count was made of the number of individuals who selected one of them as their first choice. The result was that ninety-five members of CPA identified themselves as social psychologists. If the order of selection is ignored, and all individuals who selected at least one of these areas are counted, 306 individuals would be identified as being involved in social psychology. These figures should not be taken too seriously, as the methods used to arrive at them are somewhat arbitrary. Nonetheless, the numbers suggest that there is a substantial nucleus for a Canadian social psychology.

Another indication of the awakening of an interest in social psychology in Canada can be seen in recent attempts of such a group to organize. *The Canadian Compendium of Social Psychology* (Thorngate, 1979) published a list of 205 individuals describing their major interests in social psychology. The list was entitled "What Canadian Social Psychologists are Doing." These figures, like those given above indicate that there is a substantial number of psychologists in Canada who identify themselves as social psychologists. Another sign that psychology may be coming of age in Canada is the fact that the President of the Canadian Psychological Association for 1979-1980 was John G. Adair, a social psychologist. A Texan by birth, he has been a strong supporter of the development of psychology within Canada. Perhaps the time is right to prepare a book focussing on at least a branch of Canadian social psychology.

REFERENCES

Adorno, T.W., Frenkel-Brunswik, E., Levinson, D.J. and Sanford, R.N. *The Authoritarian Personality.* New York: Harper & Row, 1950.

Alcock, J.E. *Social psychology and the importation of values.* Paper presented at C.P.A. Annual Conference. Ottawa, 1978.

Allport, G.W. *Becoming: Basic Considerations for a Psychology of Personality.* New Haven: Yale University Press, 1955.

Allport, G.W. The historical background of modern social psychology. In G. Lindzey and E. Aronson (eds.), *Handbook of Social Psychology* (Vol. 1) (2nd Ed.) Reading: Addison-Wesley, 1968, pp. 1-80.

Berlyne, D.E. American and European psychology. *American Psychologist*, 1968, *23*, 447-452.

Berry, J.W. Canadian psychology: some social and applied emphases. *The Canadian Psychologist*, 1974, *15*, 132-139.

Berry, J.W. Social psychology: comparative, societal and universal. *Canadian Psychological Review*, 1978, *19*, 93-104 (a).

Berry, J.W. *Teaching Social Psychology IN and OF Canada*. Paper presented at C.P.A. Annual Conference, Ottawa, 1978(b).

Berry, J.W. and Wilde, G.J.S. *Social Psychology: The Canadian Context*. Toronto: McClelland and Stewart, 1972.

Berry, J.W., Kalin, R. & Wilde, G.J.S. *Brief to Commission on Canadian Studies*. Canadian Psychological Association: Subcommittee of the Scientific Affairs Committee, 1973.

Billig, M. *Social Psychology and Intergroup Relations*. London: Academic Press, 1976.

Black, J.L. Americans in Canadian Universities. *Laurentian University Review*, 1969, *2*, 111.

Campbell, D.T. The mutual methodological relevance of anthropology and psychology. In F.L.K. Hsu (ed.), *Psychological Anthropology*. Homewood: Dorsey, 1961.

Clark, S.D. Sociology in Canada: an historical overview. *Canadian Journal of Sociology*, 1975, *1*, 225-234.

Crutchfield, R.S. and Krech, D. Some guides to the understanding of the history of psychology. In Postman, L. (ed.), *Psychology in the Making*. New York: Knopf, 1962.

Driedger, L. *The Canadian Ethnic Mosaic: A Quest for Identity*. Toronto: McClelland and Stewart, 1978.

Goldstein, J.E., & Bienvenue, R.M. *Ethnicity and Ethnic Relations in Canada: A Book of Readings*, Toronto: Butterworths, 1980.

Koulak, D. and Perlman, D. (eds.) *Readings in Social Psychology: Focus on Canada*. Toronto: Wiley, 1973.

LeVine, R.A. and Campbell, D.T. *Ethnocentrism: Theories of Conflict, Ethnic Attitudes and Group Behaviour*. Toronto: Wiley, 1972.

Maccoby, E.M. and Jacklin, C.N. *Psychology of Sex Differences*. Stanford: Stanford University Press, 1974.

MacLeod, R.B. Can psychological research be planned on a national scale? *Canadian Journal of Psychology*, 1947, *1*, 177-191.

MacLeod, R.B. *Psychology in Canadian universities and colleges: A report to the Canadian Social Science Research Council*, Ottawa, 1955.

Moscovici, S. Society and theory in social psychology. In I. Israel and H. Tajfel (eds.), *The Context of Social Psychology*. London: Academic Press, 1972.

Myers, C.R. Notes on the history of psychology in Canada. *Canadian Psychologist*, 1965, *6*, 4-19.

Porter, J. *The Vertical Mosaic*. Toronto: University of Toronto Press, 1965.

Sadava. S.W. Teaching social psychology: a Canadian dilemma. *Canadian Psychological Review*, 1978, *19*, 145-151(a).

Sadava, S.W. *From the outside looking in: The experience of the instructor and student of social psychology in Canada*. Paper presented at C.P.A. Annual Meeting, Ottawa, 1978(b).

Sumner, W.G. *Folkways*. New York: Ginn, 1906.

Symons, T.H.B. *To know ourselves. The report of the Commission on Canadian studies*. Ottawa: Association of Universities and Colleges of Canada, 1975.

Thorngate, W. *The Canadian Compendium of Social Psychology*. Edmonton: University of Alberta, 1979.

Wright, M.J. Canadian psychology comes of age. *Canadian Psychologist,* 1969, *10,* 229-253.

Wright, M.J. CPA: The first ten years. *Canadian Psychologist,* 1974,*15,* 112-131.

Wright, M.J. A sketch of some of the history of psychology in Canada. U.W.O. Colloquium, November, 1978.

Wrightsman, L.S. *Social Psychology* (2nd ed.).Monterey: Brooks/Cole, 1977.

Chapter 2

The Social and Historical
Context of Ethnic Relations

Jean Burnet, Department of Sociology, Glendon College, York University

Canada has from the beginning been characterized by an ethnically, culturally, and linguistically diverse population. The vast and varied territory that is now Canada was at the time of first contact with Europeans inhabited by heterogeneous peoples; the Europeans added at first a few and later a considerable number of new elements; as time passed recruitment of population widened to include all peoples of the globe. What is relatively recent is not diversity, but recognition of diversity, and recognition also of diversity not as a temporary phenomenon but as likely to endure.

Ethnic Groups and the Census

According to the 1971 census, the Canadian population was 21,500,000. The number of ethnic groups making up the population and the size of each are impossible to determine with precision. An ethnic group is characterized by a sense of peoplehood (Gordon, 1964, pp.23-24): its members believe that they have a common ancestry, whether in fact they do or do not; they have memories of a shared past; and they have certain badges, physical or cultural or both, which enable them to identify one another and to exclude outsiders (Schermerhorn, 1970, p. 12). Because it involves subjective factors, ethnicity is hard to gauge. Further, ethnic identity is not fixed and certain. Ethnic group membership used to be considered ascribed at birth. "If it is easy to resign from the group it is not truly an ethnic group," wrote Hughes in an article published in 1948. Now it is recognized

Table 2.1
Population by Ethnic Origin, 1951, 1961 and 1971

Ethnic origin	1951		1961		1971	
category	No.	%	No.	%	No.	%
British Isles	6,709,685	47.9	7,996,669	43.8	9,624,115	44.6
English	3,630,344	25.9	4,195,175	23.0		
Irish	1,439,635	10.3	1,753,351	9.6		
Scottish	1,547,470	11.0	1,902,302	10.4		
Welsh and other	92,236	0.7	145,841	0.8		
French	4,319,167	30.8	5,540,346	30.4	6,180,120	28.7
Other European	2,553,722	18.2	4,116,849	22.6	4,959,680	23.0
Austrian	32,231	0.2	106,535	0.6	42,120	0.2
Belgian	35,148	0.2	61,382	0.3	51,135	0.2
Czech and Slovak	63,959	0.5	73,061	0.4	81,870	0.4
Danish	42,671	0.3	85,473	0.5	75,725	0.4
Finnish	43,745	0.3	59,436	0.3	59,215	0.3
German	619,995	4.4	1,049,599	5.8	1,317,200	6.1
Greek	13,966	0.1	56,475	0.3	124,475	0.6
Hungarian	60,460	0.4	126,220	0.7	131,890	0.6
Icelandic	23,307	0.2	30,623	0.2	27,905	0.1
Italian	152,245	1.1	450,351	2.5	730,820	3.4
Jewish	181,670	1.3	173,344	1.0	296,945	1.4
Lithuanian	16,224	0.1	27,629	0.2	24,535	0.1
Netherlands	264,267	1.9	429,679	2.4	425,945	2.0
Norwegian	119,266	0.8	148,681	0.8	179,290	0.8
Polish	219,845	1.6	323,517	1.8	316,425	1.5
Portuguese	..	..	..	..	96,875	0.4
Romanian	23,601	0.2	43,805	0.2	27,375	0.1
Russian	91,279	0.7	119,168	0.7	64,475	0.3
Spanish	..	..	..	..	27,515	0.1
Swedish	97,780	0.7	121,757	0.6	101,870	0.5
Ukrainian	395,043	2.8	473,337	2.6	580,660	2.7
Yugoslavic	21,404	0.2	68,587	0.4	104,950	0.5
Other	35,616	0.2	88,190	0.5	70,460	0.3
Asiatic	72,827	0.5	121,753	0.7	285,540	1.3
Chinese	32,528	0.2	58,197	0.3	118,815	0.6
Japanese	21,663	0.2	29,157	0.2	37,260	0.2
Other	18,636	0.1	34,399	0.2	129,460	0.6
Other	354,028	2.5	462,630	2.5	518,850	2.4
Eskimo	9,733	0.1	11,835	0.1	17,550	0.1
Native Indian	155,874	1.1	208,286	1.1	295,215	1.4
Negro	18,020	0.1	32,127	0.2	34,445	0.2
West Indian	..	..	..	..	28,025	0.1
Other and not stated	170,401	1.2	210,382	1.2	143,620	0.7
Total	14,009,429	100.0	18,238,247	100.0	21,568,310	100.0

Source: *Canada Year Book 1976-77*, Table 4.19, p. 192-3. Reproduced by permission of the Minister of Supply and Services Canada.

that ethnic identity can change, although not easily, and an individual can also at the same time or over a period of time identify with more than one ethnic group, depending upon the particular situations in which he finds himself. A Guyanese Canadian student has reported that among her former countrymen now in Canada are a folksinger who identifies himself with Canadian Indians; people of Chinese origin who deny their Guyanese background and identify with Chinese Canadians, and still others of East Indian stock who, after preserving their cultural heritage sedulously in Guyana, now identify with blacks in order to avoid being called "Pakis."

The Canadian census has from the beginning been concerned with the origins of the population. It has not asked people their ethnic self-identification, but rather their ethnic origin, and from 1901 to 1971 has indicated that they should trace their roots through the male line. The wording of the question asked by the census has varied over time, partly in response to criticism (for example, the term "racial" was used until 1941 but was dropped in 1951); and the results have by no means been precise or "scientific" (Ryder, 1955; Kralt, 1978). However, the ethnic origin figures from the census have been the index most often used in estimating the size of various groups. Table 2.1 gives the population by ethnic origin category for 1951, 1961, and 1971; figures for earlier census years may be found in book 4 of the Report of the Royal Commission on Bilingualism and Biculturalism (1970). Figure 2.1 indicates the proportions of the population of French, Anglo-Celtic and other origins from 1871 to 1971.

It is impossible likewise to be precise about the number and strength of the various cultures represented in Canada. Culture is concerned with the organized system of understandings shared by a people; it includes beliefs, values, institutions, rituals, and manners. The boundaries between cultures in the modern world are hard to determine; indeed, some people talk of the

Figure 2.1
Ethnic Origin of the Canadian Population from 1871 to 1971

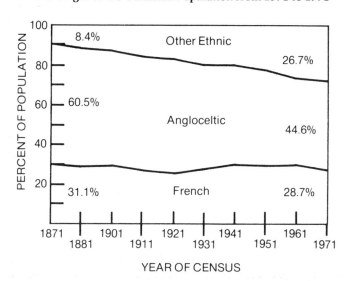

Source: The figure was drawn on the basis of information contained in Warren E. Kalbach, Growth and Distribution of Canada's Ethnic Populations, 1871-1971. In Leo Driedger, ed., *The Canadian Ethnic Mosaic.* (Toronto: McClelland and Stewart, 1978), pp. 86-87. Reprinted by permission.

convergence of cultures, or say that culture has become a myth (Porter, 1965, 1969, 1972, 1975). Ethnic groups are frequently thought of as the bearers of cultures, but ethnic groups unless territorially isolated do not have totally distinct systems of institutions, beliefs, and values but, rather, partial or truncated cultures; they do have symbols of their ethnic identity or peoplehood, such as the Scot's kilt and bagpipes, the German's sauerkraut and Oktoberfest, the Pole's polka and the Ukrainian's decorated Easter eggs.

Language is part of culture, and often—though not always—the most cherished badge of ethnic identity. Some ethnic groups, like Canadians, Americans, and Australians, do not have a distinct language, and some, like the Dutch, place more emphasis on another cultural trait, such as religion, than they do on language. Language does, however, provide another objective index that census-takers can use. In addition to knowledge of the official languages of Canada, English and French, the Canadian census records mother tongue, that is, the first language learned in childhood and still understood, and recorded also for the first time in 1971 language used in the home.

Classification of Canadian Ethnic Groups

The peoples of Canada may be classified according to the time and circumstances of their immigration as:

1. Native peoples: Amerindian and Inuit
2. Colonizers: French and British
3. Other ethnic groups.

The native peoples are the descendants of the people who were living in the northern part of North America when Europeans first arrived on this continent. The French claimed much of the territory by right of exploration and established colonies of settlement in the sixteenth and seventeenth centuries, but were forced to capitulate to the British in 1760. The French and the British are described in the terms of reference of the Report of the Royal Commission on Bilingualism and Culturalism as the two founding peoples.[1] They are also considered to be charter-member groups, in the sense that they in turn set up political structures and established political boundaries, of a sort that the native peoples did not know. They still retain a special status. Other ethnic groups could be called immigrant ethnic groups because they are not native and did not come as representatives of a colonizing power. The term "immigrant ethnic groups" is unsatisfactory, however, since among them are descendants of people who came in the seventeenth and eighteenth centuries, and in many cases a substantial portion are Canadian born; for example, at the time of the 1971 census 82 per cent of those of Ukrainian ethnic origin had been born in Canada. For these reasons the term "other ethnic" is used to designate persons of non-British, non-French, and non-native descent.

Regional Differences

The vastness of Canada, its geographical and climatic variety, and the length of time over which its settlement has taken place have meant that the various regions of Canada have recruited their populations from different ethnic groups, and that the ethnic groups have evolved in different ways within the country. The oldest parts of the country have the lowest proportion of population of origins other than British, French, Amerindian and Inuit; they also have the lowest proportion of foreign born. In Nova Scotia, the ethnic groups whose interrelations have shaped and are shaping the social life of the province are chiefly English, Irish, Scottish, and French; the Germans, Dutch, Scandinavians, and blacks are long established but numerically small origin categories, and Syrians, Lebanese, and Chinese are all recently arrived and relatively few (Campbell, 1978). The British entered in part directly, after the territory was ceded to the British in 1713, and in part by way of New England in the early 1760s and as Loyalists in the 1780s. Quebec is the only province in which the numerical majority and the politically and socially dominant group is French Canadian; political dominance is being used at present to wrest economic power from the English, who have held it since the Conquest. The British are still the largest minority, but substantial and important Jewish and Italian groups exist, and others are emerging as a result of recent immigration. All of the non-French and non-native groups tend to be concentrated in Montreal. Ontario, which like the Maritimes received many United Empire Loyalists, was long regarded as basically British. However, since the mid-nineteenth century there have been French Canadians in the Windsor area, and later French Canadians settled and even became the numerical majority in Eastern Ontario and parts of Northern Ontario. In addition, over the years Germans have settled in the Bay of Quinté and the Kitchener-Waterloo areas, Finns and Italians in Northern Ontario, and Jewish immigrants in Toronto. Since World War II over half the immigrant population to Canada has settled in Ontario and as a result, a third of the population is of other ethnic origins, and a substantial portion of foreign birth. The Prairies are usually considered the most ethnically heterogeneous part of Canada, because they were settled during the massive wave of immigration before World War I (see chapter 11 for further details). They do in fact have the greatest proportion of population belonging to the other ethnic groups, and of foreign born who belong to ethnic groups which immigrated before 1946. However, of the three provinces only Alberta has drawn many post–World War II immigrants. British Columbia has a substantial British and Scandinavian population, and because of its location on the Pacific has long held more persons of Asian origin than any other region. The Yukon and Northwest Territories, until recently the domain of Inuit and Amerindians, has a small but growing population of European origin.

The Native Peoples

The first immigrants to Canada, who had lived in the territory for thousands of years, were themselves heterogeneous. At the time of contact with Europeans, they numbered from 250,000 to 300,000, and constituted about fifty different societies, belonging to a dozen linguistic groups. They varied in socio-political organization from loosely knit nomadic bands of hunters and gatherers to highly structured chiefdoms of sedentary fishers and cultivators of the soil. The different peoples, although thinly scattered, entered into a variety of relations with each other, including trade and war. One classification groups them into seven categories: Inuit or Eskimo; Beothuks; Algonquins; Huron-Iroquois; Sioux; Mountain Tribes, and Pacific Coast Indians (Lacoursière, Provencher, and Vaugeois, 1976, pp. 16-19).

The Indians, whose ancestors came from Asia about 15,000 years ago, entered into contact with European fishermen and explorers on the east coast of North America as early as the tenth century. Contacts became frequent in the sixteenth and seventeenth centuries as European settlements were established (Jaenen, 1976). Some Indians were taken to Europe for exhibit as curiosities. Others served the early explorers and settlers as mentors in coping with the environment, as trading partners, allies in war, and potential converts to Christianity; a few were made slaves (Trudel, 1960). With the advance of settlement some Indian peoples, notably the Beothuks of Newfoundland, were exterminated;[2] others were ravaged by diseases introduced by the newcomers, or were killed in warfare by the lethal weapons introduced by Europeans. Most became progressively cut off from one another, and were pushed back into remote areas or onto reservations. Treaties were made with some of the Indians, whereby they relinquished their claims to various territories in return for reserve lands and such benefits as treaty money and educational and medical services. Since Confederation, under the Indian Acts of 1876 and 1951, a department of the federal government has been responsible for carrying out policy with regard to Indians; in 1980 it is the Department of Indian Affairs and Northern Development. The Indians have become dependent and pauperized; however, their numbers, which at first had declined, began to recover about 1900 and have continued to increase ever since.

Through the years some of the old lines of distinction between Indian peoples have become blurred as a result of the general label Indian, common treatment by other Canadians, and, especially with the formation of the National Indian Brotherhood in 1969, association for united action. The signing of treaties has however led to a new line of demarcation, between registered or banded or status Indians and others. According to the Indian Act, an Indian is "a person who pursuant to this Act is registered as an Indian or is entitled to be registered as an Indian," and only such persons are legally members of bands, with the right to live on reserves and participate in various programs of the Department of Indian Affairs and Northern Development. Non-registered Indians have surrendered Indian status, usually for monetary considerations, or have forfeited it, in the case of a woman by marrying someone other than a registered Indian; but non-registered Indians may still consider themselves to be Indians and may still be treated by others as Indians, except in regard to eligibility for federal services (Nagler, 1970, pp. 3-4).

In the late eighteenth and early nineteenth centuries a new people, the Métis, emerged as a result of unions between Amerindians and Europeans. The Europeans were mainly French; descendants of Indian and British— usually Scottish—unions were ordinarily called half-breeds rather than Métis. Métis were chiefly confined to the Prairie Provinces and the North West Territories. At first voyageurs, hunters and trappers, the Métis later became farmers. Their sense of identity was strengthened by their part in the struggle between the North West Company and the Hudson's Bay Company, the Battle of Seven Oaks in 1816, and the two Riel rebellions of 1869 and 1885 (Woodcock, 1976). Lacking the legal status of registered Indians, they are among the most deprived of the native peoples.

The Inuit or Eskimo, who are thought to have come to North America about 3,500 years ago, were for a long time sheltered from Europeans by their location in the far north. Their ties were rather with their kin in Siberia, Greenland and Alaska. Their first contacts with Europeans were with explorers, missionaries of various denominations, whalers, traders, and Royal Canadian Mounted Police. Lately, however, their land has been invaded by seekers for gas and oil, and by surveyors and builders of pipelines. They were not mentioned in the British North America Act, and do not come under the Indian Act. The administration of their land was allocated in 1953 to the Department of Northern Affairs and National Resources, now the Department of Indian Affairs and Northern Development.

In the 1970s there were, according to official statistics, between 15,000 and 20,000 Inuit in Canada, and nearly 300,000 registered Indians; there were probably also about 750,000 non-status Indians and Métis. Their birth rates were high, although their death rates and especially their infant mortality rates were also extreme, and, in addition, in recent years some people have come to claim Indian or Métis identity who previously did not.

Of late the Indians, Métis and Inuit are increasingly being drawn into modern western industrial society, as they move into towns and cities or as industry moves outward, particularly into the North. The moving of the Indians is precipitated by the overpopulation and dire poverty of many reserves. In the process, the native peoples have come to form new concepts of themselves and their identity (Sawchuk, 1978) and to organize to press for their goals, influenced to some extent by the example of other ethnic groups and by the example, and sometimes the aid, of native peoples elsewhere. For example, the system of the communal representation in the government of New Zealand Maori has been advocated for Canada by some Indian spokesmen. Those whose rights were not extinguished by treaty have demanded that those rights be recognized; some of those who come under treaties have denounced the terms and demanded renegotiation. Notable are the emergence in the North West Territories of the Dene nation, and the James Bay Agreement of November 11, 1975. The Dene in 1975 issued a declaration insisting upon their recognition as a nation with the right to independence and self-determination within the country of Canada, and have since reiterated their claims. By the James Bay Agreement natives of northern Quebec whose land was being devastated by a gigantic hydro project renounced their claims to collective land title in return for guarantees of exclusive hunting, fishing, and trapping rights in certain lands, a considerable degree of self-government, and a sum of money (Richardson, 1975).

As for governmental policy, it could be characterized in the past as paternal and protective, but with an assimilationist strain. The zenith of the assimilationist emphasis was the White Paper of 1969, which proposed the phasing out of protective measures—the repeal of the Indian Act, the transfer of matters from federal to provincial jurisdiction, and the phasing out of the Indian Affairs Branch—in the interests of integration. The strong opposition of Indian organizations led the government not to proceed with the steps it had contemplated. The rallying cry of the native peoples, to the extent that they are united, has been adopted from a report commissioned by the federal government: "citizens plus." It signifies that the native peoples feel entitled to all the rights of Canadian citizens, and in addition to special consideration as the first inhabitants of the land.

Colonizers

The French Canadians
The first colonizers of what is now Canada, the French, settled in the St. Lawrence lowlands and in the Bay of Fundy area of the Atlantic region from the early years of the seventeenth century. The descendants of the first French settlers in the Atlantic regions, the Acadians, became a subordinate ethnic group in 1713, when, by the Treaty of Utrecht their territory passed into the possession of the English; Cape Breton and Prince Edward Island, however, remained in French hands. In 1755 many of the Acadians were expelled from their lands for refusal to take an oath of allegiance to Britain and settled in Louisiana, or went to France, England, or New England; those who remained and those who later returned are the ancestors of much of the considerable Acadian population in the region today. They have been joined in New Brunswick by some French Canadians from Quebec.

The French of the St. Lawrence lowlands in turn became a subordinate group after the Conquest in 1760. Numerically the majority in what was to be Quebec, the French Canadians were dominated economically and socially by the British.[3] In the nineteenth century, they were largely rural, devoutly Catholic, highly familial, and preoccupied with survival. Although they were reinforced by few French-speaking immigrants, they assimilated some Irish, Scots, English, and others who settled among them. This and their very high birth rate enabled them to increase their number, and despite heavy emigration in the latter half of the nineteenth century to remain as approximately 30 per cent of the Canadian population.

In the twentieth century the French Canadians have rapidly entered the modern industrial urban world, but their self-image and the picture others had of them evolved slowly to take account of their changing situation. It was in the 1960s, against a background of ethnic movements throughout the world, that the French Canadians in Quebec began to redefine themselves as a dominant or majority group in their own province and as a charter-member group in the Canadian federation. The term Québécois came into vogue to designate a French Canadian who views himself as a member of the majority in the province or—better—the state of Quebec (Rioux, 1974).

After the death of the long-time Premier of Quebec, Maurice Duplessis, a Liberal government elected in 1960, with Jean Lesage as premier, tried to adapt to the new social and economic order in the Quiet Revolution. This was a period of rapid change, during which economic planning began, private electric power companies were nationalized, social security was extended, and the educational system transformed. More importantly, the French Canadians gained a new conception of themselves and their potential, and of the role of the Quebec government in social and economic development (Posgate and McRoberts, 1976, chap. 6). By the time of the Liberal defeat in 1966, many French Canadians expressed their new self-confidence and orientation by calling themselves Québécois. Meanwhile, separatism gathered strength, and terrorism in support of separatism flared briefly from 1963 to 1970. The federal government set up a Royal Commission on Bilingualism and Biculturalism in 1963 to recommend what steps should be taken to develop the Canadian confederation on the basis of an equal partnership between the two founding peoples; as one of its early responses to the Commission's findings the government passed the Official Languages Act of 1969. However, French-speaking Quebecers continued to experience economic domination; their incomes remained below those of several other groups, although their position improved and the gap between Francophones and Anglophones narrowed considerably between 1961 and 1971.

Since the Quiet Revolution the government of Quebec has been attempting to use its powers to improve the position of the French majority, and also to enlarge its powers against those of the federal government for the same purpose. Its particular concern has been language. In 1974 the Quebec government proclaimed French as its official language in Bill 22; in 1977 the recently elected Parti Québécois government of Quebec introduced a more stringent language bill as Bill 1, and eventually adopted it as Bill 101. The provisions of this Bill in the late 1970s are coming into force in the schools and in the working world.

The pressure of French Canadian nationalism has put severe strains on Canadian unity. There seem to be two main conflicting views. One, expressed in the General Introduction to the Report of the Royal Commission on Bilingualism and Biculturalism (1967), is that there is a Canadian society composed of two linguistic communities, each of which is nurtured by many cultures, and the problem is to bring about greater equality between the two linguistic communities. The other view is that there are two nations, English Canada and Quebec or French Canada, and each nation should be sovereign within its own territory although linked with the other in some form of association. Confrontation between these two stands is now at the centre of the unity crisis in Canada.

The one million Canadians of French origin living outside of Quebec have been subject to linguistic assimilation, and their disappearance has been predicted (Joy, 1972, 1978). With the changes in Quebec, some members of the Francophone groups have become active and vocal in seeking governmental and community support. In New Brunswick the formation of the Acadian Party and in Ontario agitation for French schools are among the manifestations of a new militancy among the Francophones outside Quebec.

The British
The second of the colonizing groups is heterogeneous in that it includes English, Irish, Scots, and Welsh. Its numbers rapidly increased after the Conquest in 1760, and especially after the American Revolution. The British were favoured by the immigration policy until the 1960s, and still a considerable proportion of immigrants are of British origin, coming either from Great Britain or the United States. However, those in the British ethnic origin category, unlike the native peoples and the French Canadians, steadily declined as a proportion of the total Canadian population from 60.6 per cent in 1871 to 43.9 per cent in 1961. That they then increased to 44.6 per cent in 1971 may be attributed to the change to self-enumeration in the method of census-taking and to English as the first answer category in the census questionnaire (Kralt, 1978).

The British received favourable treatment within Canada as well as at entry. For example, as late as 1977, under the Canadian Citizenship Act of 1947, a British subject could become a Canadian citizen more easily than another alien. He did not have to answer questions about the duties and privileges of citizenship, submit to a linguistic test, or appear before a judge to take the oath of allegiance. The new Citizenship Act that came into effect in 1977 has placed all applicants for citizenship on the same footing for the first time. Previously, British subjects could also vote after one year's residence in Canada; they can no longer do so in federal elections.

In spite of the decline in the British proportion of the population, the dominance of the British in the economic elite and to a slightly lesser extent in the political and bureaucratic elites was clearly shown by Porter (1965) and confirmed by Clement and Olsen (1974).

Assimilation of native peoples and other ethnic groups into the British group is suggested by the fact that the number of Canadians who have English as their mother tongue is much higher than the number who are of British ethnic origin, and the number for whom English is the language most used in the home is substantially greater than the number who claim English as their mother tongue. While in some other cases the number claiming a given language as mother tongue is greater than the number of the appropriate ethnic origin, in all cases the number claiming a language as mother tongue is greater than and often several times as large as the number claiming it as the language most used in the home. The fact that linguistic transfer does not necessarily signify assimilation in other regards, especially in the first generation, should of course be kept in mind.

Because of their dominance, the attitudes of the British towards members of other groups hold particular interest. Although insufficient research has been done on the subject of British-Canadian attitudes (see chapter 8 of this book), there is ample evidence that in the past the dominant ethnic group manifested considerable prejudice, and enshrined much of it in discriminatory legislation, directed in some measure against all but northern European peoples. During the nineteenth and early twentieth centuries the British had a strong belief in the superiority of their institutions and their stock, tempered only occasionally by some doubt about the quality of British working class or pauper immigrants. Other ethnic groups were ranked as desirable in proportion to their similarity to the British, and hence their presumed assimilability. The preference for the British governed immigration policy, and also treatment of immigrants and members of ethnic groups within the country. Anglo-conformity was the model that guided school curricula, public opinion and hiring practices (Palmer, 1976).

The Other Ethnic Groups

Although individuals and small groups of immigrants not belonging to the native peoples or the British or French groups have settled in Canada since the beginning of European settlement, their numbers were small until the beginning of the twentieth century. In part this was a result of remigration to the United States. In 1871 they were 8 per cent of the population; in 1901 they were 10 per cent. But with the inauguration of a vigorous immigration policy by Clifford Sifton, Minister of the Interior from 1896 to 1905, their numbers, and the proportion they constituted of the population, increased greatly. Until the outbreak of World War I in 1914, Germans, Dutch, Scandinavians, Ukrainians, Poles, Hungarians, Russians, Italians, Jews, Chinese, Japanese and South Asians poured into the prairie west (see chapter 11), the construction, mining, and lumbering camps of the north, the cities of Ontario and Quebec, and British Columbia. In the 1920s, most of these groups increased, except the Asians, whose immigration was severely restricted. There was a sharp decline in immigration during the Great Depression of the 1930s and World War II, but in the late 1940s it resumed. At first it came chiefly from traditional sources, but in the 1960s Portugal and Greece became important sources, as did the West Indies and Asia in the 1970s; South America also has become increasingly important in the 1970s. As a result by 1971 the proportion of the population of non-native, non-British, and non-French origins had reached 25 per cent.

One of the determinants of the numbers of immigrants is the country's immigration policy. From Confederation until 1895 it was completely open; from 1896 until the 1960s, it favoured immigrants from Great Britain, the United States, and to a slightly lesser degree other northern and western Europeans. France, concerned with maintaining its population, did not permit recruiting of immigrants until after World War II, at which time France was placed on equal footing with Great Britain. Eastern and central Europeans were encouraged during the Sifton regime as the best settlers for the second best land in the West, and otherwise tolerated; such sects as Mennonites, Doukhobors and Hutterites were at first welcomed and then discouraged; Asians and blacks were consistently discouraged, and at times excluded entirely, as the Chinese were between 1923 and 1947. After World War II a trend towards the elimination of racial and ethnic discrimination in immigration began, culminating in the point system of 1967 and the Immigration Act of 1977 (replacing the 1952 Act), in which universalism and nondiscrimination were enshrined as principles.

That governmental policy is not the sole regulator of immigration is apparent from the fact that there has always been considerable illegal immigration, especially when the Canadian economy is expanding. Periodic amnesties, the latest in 1973, have not succeeded in persuading all illegal immigrants to rectify their situation. Estimates in the mid-1970s run from 200,000 to 500,000 illegal immigrants (Anderson, 1974).

Emigration and remigration have also affected the ethnic composition of the Canadian population. It is difficult to estimate their role, since Canadian statistics concerning them are not kept. From Lord Durham onwards, however, it has been recognized that for many Canada has been a way-station for those intending to enter the United States. It is also being increasingly recognized that many immigrants have always returned and still return home, and others, though reckoned as immigrants, are part of an internationally mobile labour force (Richmond, 1967, p. 252).

Members of the other ethnic groups are few at the highest level of the economic structure and no other ethnic group is so disadvantaged as the native peoples. Otherwise they are to be found throughout the structure of the country. First-generation immigrants of non-British, non-French origin have been described as occupying positions that Canadians do not have the skills or training to qualify for on the one hand and positions that Canadians do not want on the other, such as domestic service and unskilled jobs in construction. Legal immigrants recently have had a higher educational level on the average than the Canadian-born or immigrants that arrived before World War II, although there are wide variations from ethnic group to ethnic group (Kalbach, 1970, pp. 187-200). They have settled mainly in the three largest metropolitan areas of Canada, Toronto, Vancouver and Montreal. Their intended occupations have been predominantly in the manufacturing, professional and technical, and service and recreational categories. Illegal immigrants probably on the average comprise lower educational levels, are located in the same metropolitan areas, and occupy lower occupational categories.

The Policy of Multiculturalism within a Bilingual Framework

In the past, the assumption of the dominant British group in Canada has been that immigrants admitted to the country or their descendants would assimilate to the British group. The reason for the isolation of the native peoples on reserves and for the restriction or exclusion of blacks and Asians was that they were considered unassimilable; the south and central European groups whose admission was grudging were thought to be assimilable but only with difficulty. Anglo-conformity in time became unfashionable, and was replaced in discussions by references to the Canadian mosaic, that is, a theory that ethnic groups contributed and should contribute to Canadian society and culture by retention of their ancestral culture and traditions. However, although the mosaic was extolled in the speeches of politicians and other dignitaries, public policy continued to be governed by the notion of Anglo-conformity.

In the 1960s, with heightened concern about human rights and the emergence of ethnicity as a dominant theme in many parts of the world, the awakening of ethnic consciousness among the native peoples in Canada, and the tumultuous nationalism of Quebec, the other ethnic groups showed a new assertiveness. Efforts were made, led mainly by Ukrainian Canadians, to create a "Third Force,"capable of playing a mediating role between English and French Canadians. The strength of the Third Force was usually estimated as being at least equal to all those listed in the census as being of non-French and non-British origins. On the other hand, Porter in his widely acclaimed work, *The Vertical Mosaic* (1965), was at the same time insisting that ethnic and cultural differences should be ignored, in the interests of equality. To Porter, the vaunted mosaic was simply a division of labour by means of which the British maintained a privileged position. However, his readers were more impressed by his data showing the ranking of various ethnic origin categories in the occupational and income hierarchies than by his prescription. In response to the situation the federal government rapidly abandoned the term bilingualism and biculturalism in favour of the term bilingualism and multiculturalism, and the Royal Commission on Bilingualism and Biculturalism devoted Book 4 of its Report to "the other ethnic groups."

On October 8, 1971, the federal government, in answer to Book 4 of the Report of the Royal Commission on Bilingualism and Biculturalism, proclaimed a policy of multiculturalism within a bilingual framework.

> First, resources permitting, the government will seek to assist all Canadian cultural groups that have demonstrated a desire and effort to continue to develop a capacity to grow and contribute to Canada, and a clear need for assistance, the small and weak groups no less than the strong and highly organized.
>
> Second, the government will assist members of all cultural groups to overcome cultural barriers to full participation in Canadian society.
>
> Third, the government will promote creative encounters and interchange among all Canadian cultural groups in the interest of national unity.
>
> Fourth, the government will continue to assist immigrants to acquire at least one of Canada's official languages in order to become full participants in Canadian society.
>
> (House of Commons Debates, 1971)

The proclamation was no empty gesture. A minister of state responsible for multiculturalism was appointed in 1972, and the following year the Canadian Consultative Council on Multiculturalism was set up to advise him. The Council has been active on both national and regional levels. The Multiculturalism Directorate was established within the Department of the Secretary of State, and among other things it has carried on liaison activities with ethnic communities and with the ethnic press; sponsored research, including major projects on non-official languages and ethnic attitudes to multiculturalism, and a series of histories of ethnic groups; aided the development of the Canadian Ethnic Studies Association; supported activities in the performing and the visual arts; and assisted programs of linguistic instruction. The four provinces of Ontario, Manitoba Saskatchewan, and Alberta have also proclaimed policies of multiculturalism, and have taken initiatives in the spheres under their jurisdiction, notably education.

Criticisms of the Policy

The policy has been greeted with acclaim by some Canadians, and has aroused considerable interest abroad. However, it has also been the object of suspicion and dissatisfaction. Apart from Porter, who has continued to inveigh against multiculturalism on the grounds that culture is on the one hand retrograde and on the other nearly or entirely mythical (1967, 1969, 1972, 1975), there are at least three categories of critics. The first is composed largely of French Canadians, and includes some of the leading intellectuals in Quebec, notably Guy Rocher and Claude Ryan. They have looked upon the policy of multiculturalism as destructive to the hard-won status of the French Canadians as one of two charter-member groups in the Canadian federation, and as conducive to independence. Rocher (1973, 1976) has argued that the policy puts the future of bilingualism in jeopardy, by removing all bases for it except convenience; that it robs bilingualism of any cultural connotation; that it destroys the foundation for national unity that biculturalism could afford, and that it is a backward step for the Francophone community.

The second category of critics is made up of spokesmen for some ethnic associations who regard the policy as insufficient. For them as for the French Canadians, language and culture are inseparable. Hence they have derived a program that provides grants for folk arts and supplementary schools, but fails to give massive aid for the maintenance of language and culture in public schools, colleges and universities, public broadcasting, and the press, and they have rejected the idea of cultural interchange as destructive to cultures (Canadian Consultative Council on Multiculturalism, 1975, p. 20). They have seen the policy of multiculturalism as static, supporting museum cultures rather than cultural coexistence of a significant kind.

The third and possibly the largest category consists of those who regard the policy of multiculturalism as "first and foremost a political program with very definite political aims along with the means to accomplish these aims" (Peter, 1978, p. 2). They have argued that the Liberals had long enjoyed much support from the other ethnic groups; the influx of conservative newcomers after World War II and the bid for their favour by John Diefenbaker had destroyed some of the advantage the Liberals had over the Progressive Conservatives; and the policy of multiculturalism was a Liberal bid to recapture "the ethnic vote." Critics in this category have refused to believe any claims that the policy was motivated by a vision of a more egalitarian Canadian society and a conviction that it could best be achieved by recognizing and extolling ethnic differences rather than by denying them. They have also not addressed the fact that whereas it was a Liberal government that introduced multiculturalism federally, Conservative and New Democratic governments introduced it provincially.

Much of the criticism of multiculturalism has to do with ambiguities and lack of clarity in the statement of the policy and in the objectives of ethnic groups. The term multiculturalism suggests the maintenance of the distinctive values, customs, and institutions of the many groups that are part of the Canadian population. Such maintenance would be impossible in a new environment; it could be approximated only in conditions of isolation, as it is, for example, among the Hutterites and a few other sects. Yet the prime minister, in proclaiming the policy, spoke not only of cultural retention and development but also of full participation in Canadian society and creative encounters and interchange. Furthermore, cultural maintenance is impossible without the use of the appropriate language in all spheres of life (Brazeau, 1958), yet multiculturalism was to be within a bilingual framework. It seems therefore that the government's intent was to help all Canadians to share certain structures and values in either the English or the French linguistic community and at the same time retain some cultural symbols related to their ethnic background or affiliation. That the policy of multiculturalism within a bilingual framework, if understood in this way, would not have aroused fear and hostility in French Canada is suggested by the fact that it is very similar to the policy for Quebec outlined by Camille Laurin (1978). It might not have occasioned disappointment among ethnic spokesmen if the name and the initial statement of the policy had been precise and unequivocal and had not raised unrealistic expectations.

It needs to be said also that ethnic groups often have incompatible objectives. They want to maintain distinct cultures, or distinct social structures, or both, but they also want to be full and equal participants in Canadian society. The maintenance of distinctiveness requires, however, that participation in the larger society be restricted; indeed it is best achieved when a group is geographically isolated (Burnet, 1977).

The Future of Multiculturalism
In spite of the declarations of the government that multiculturalism is a permanent part of its policy and of the statements of leaders of opposition parties that they also favour multiculturalism, the policy's fate depends on the sensitivity and flexibility with which it is administered. So far those responsible have been sensitive and flexible. They have introduced changes to adapt their programs to new insights and new developments in Canadian society.

For example, the programs at first were focussed on the other ethnic groups, since other government policies dealt with French-English relations and with native peoples. It soon became apparent that restriction of the programs to part of the Canadian people was unnecessary and undesirable. Hence it has become accepted that all ethnic groups, including the British, French and native peoples, should be direct beneficiaries of the policy.

Also, in the early years support was directed primarily towards folklore activities and the maintenance of ancestral languages. This did not take into adequate account the situation of new immigrants, and especially immigrants belonging to the "visible minorities," such as the West Indians and South and East Asians, whose numbers have been increasing rapidly since the changes in immigration regulations in 1967 (Burnet, 1975). For them, cultural survival was of less immediate concern than the overcoming of discrimination. In November 1975 the minister then responsible for multiculturalism, the Hon. John Munro, announced that emphasis was to be transferred from the maintenance of language and culture to group understanding. The announcement met with vituperation from a number of ethnic leaders, but since the announcement the number of projects having to do with the analysis and the combatting of discrimination has increased.

The policy of multiculturalism is built upon the recognition of the diversity of the Canadian population, which has existed since the beginning of the country's recorded history and has showed no tendency to diminish. It is therefore likely to continue, although not necessarily in its present form. As it lasts, it will cease to be regarded as faddish and opportunistic and will win increasing acceptance.

FOOTNOTES

[1] The term used in the English version of the terms of reference is founding races; however, the French terms of reference speak of *peuples.*

[2] The Beothuks, whose custom of decorating their bodies with red ochre led to their being called Red Indians, are said to have offended Europeans by pilfering, and were hunted down and killed. Nearly all were exterminated during the eighteenth century; the last survivor died in 1829 (Price, 1979, 76-7; Such, 1978, chaps. 6-9).

[3] They were, however, treated with generosity unusual at the time, partly, it is often held, because of British fears that otherwise they might assist the rebellious Thirteen Colonies. The Quebec Act of 1774, which has been called "la charte de la population canadienne française,"extended the boundaries of Quebec, authorized the tithe and opened the way for Roman Catholics to hold public office, and re-established French civil law (although English criminal law, more liberal than French criminal law, was retained). (Neatby, 1966, 1972.)

REFERENCES

Anderson, G.M. *Networks of Contact.* Waterloo: Wilfrid Laurier University Publications, 1974.
Brazeau, E.J. Language Differences and Occupational Experience. *Canadian Journal of Economics and Political Science,* 1958, 24, 532-40.

Burnet, J. Multiculturalism, Immigration and Racism. *Canadian Ethnic Studies*, 1975, 7, 35-39.

Burnet, J. Separate or Equal. Paper presented at symposium on the social sciences in Canada, University of Calgary, Calgary, Alberta, 1977.

Campbell, D.F., ed. *Banked Fires—The Ethnics of Nova Scotia*. Port Credit, Ontario: The Scribbler's Press, 1978.

Canadian Consultative Council on Multiculturalism. *First Annual Report*. Ottawa: Information Canada, 1975.

Clement, W. and Olsen, D. The Ethnic Composition of Canada's Elites, 1951 to 1973. Report submitted to the Secretary of State, 1974.

Gordon, M.M. *Assimilation in American Life*. New York: Oxford University Press, 1964.

House of Commons Debates. Statement of P.E. Trudeau, October 8, 1971.

Hughes, E.C. The Study of Ethnic Relations. First published, 1948, reprinted in *The Sociological Eye: Selected Papers*. Chicago: Aldine-Atherton, 1971, pp. 153-158.

Jaenen, C.J. *Friend and Foe*. Toronto: McClelland and Stewart, 1976.

Joy, R.J. *Languages in Conflict*. Toronto: McClelland and Stewart, 1972.

Joy, R.J. *Canada's Official-Language Minorities*. Montreal: C.D. Howe Research Institute, 1978.

Kalbach, W.E. *The Impact of Immigration on Canada's Population*. Ottawa: Dominion Bureau of Statistics, 1970.

Kralt, J. Ethnic Origin in the Canadian Census. Paper presented at Conference on Social Trends among Ukrainian Canadians, University of Ottawa, Ottawa, 1978, Sept. 15-16.

Lacoursière, J., Provencher, J., and Vaugeois, D. *Canada-Quebec: synthèse historique*. Montreal: Edition du Renouveau Pédagogique, 1976.

Laurin, C. Ethnic Minorities and the New Quebec. *Canadian Ethnic Studies*, 1978, *10*, 5-11.

Nagler, M. *Indians in the City*. Ottawa: Canadian Research Centre for Anthropology, 1970.

Neatby, H. *Quebec: The Revolutionary Age, 1760-1791*. Toronto: McClelland and Stewart, 1966.

Neatby, H. *The Quebec Act: Protest and Policy*. Scarborough, Ontario: Prentice-Hall, 1972.

Palmer, H. Reluctant Hosts. *Report of the Second Canadian Conference on Multiculturalism*. Ottawa: Canadian Consultative Council on Multiculturalism, 1976, 81-118.

Peter, K. Multi-Cultural Politics, Money and the Conduct of Canadian Ethnic Studies. *Canadian Ethnic Studies Association Bulletin*. 1978, 5, 2-3.

Porter, J. *The Vertical Mosaic*. Toronto: University of Toronto Press, 1965.

Porter, J. Bilingualism and the myths of culture. *Canadian Review of Sociology and Anthropology*, 1969, 6, 111-119.

Porter, J. Dilemmas and contradictions of a multi-ethnic society. Paper presented to Section II, The Royal Society of Canada, St. John's, Newfoundland, 1972.

Porter, J. Ethnic Pluralism in Canadian perspective. In Glazer and Moynihan, eds., *Ethnicity: Theory and Experience*. Cambridge, Mass.: Harvard University Press, 1975, 267-304.

Posgate, D., and McRoberts, K. *Quebec: Social Change and Political Crisis*. Toronto: McClelland and Stewart, 1976.

Price, J.A. *Indians of Canada*. Scarborough, Ontario: Prentice-Hall, 1979.

Richardson, B. *Strangers Devour the Land*. Toronto: Macmillan, 1975.

Richmond, A.H. *Post-war Immigrants in Canada.* Toronto: University of Toronto Press, 1967.

Rioux, M. *Les Québécois.* France: Editions du Seuil, 1974.

Rocher, G. Les ambiguités d'un Canada bilingue et multiculturel. In *Le Québec en mutation.* Montréal: Hurtubise, HMH, 1973, 117-126.

Rocher, G. Multiculturalism: The Doubts of a Francophone. *Report of the Second Canadian Conference on Multiculturalism.* Ottawa: Canadian Consultative Council on Multiculturalism, 1976, 47-53.

Royal Commission on Bilingualism and Biculturalism. *Report: General Introduction.* Ottawa: Queen's Printer, 1967.

Royal Commission on Bilingualism and Biculturalism. *Report: Book 4, The Cultural Contribution of the Other Ethnic Groups.* Ottawa: Queen's Printer, 1970.

Ryder, N.B. The interpretation of origin statistics. *Canadian Journal of Economics and Political Science,* 1955, 21, 466-479.

Sawchuk, J. *The Métis of Manitoba.* Toronto: Peter Martin Associates, 1978.

Schermerhorn, R.A. *Comparative Ethnic Relations.* New York: Random House, 1970.

Such, P. *Vanished Peoples.* Toronto: NC Press, 1978.

Trudel, M. *L'esclavage au Canada français.* Quebec: Les Presses de l'Université Laval, 1960.

Woodcock, G. *Gabriel Dumont.* Edmonton: Hurtig, 1976.

Section II
Social Development

Chapter 3

Ethnic Self-Identity

Frances E. Aboud, Department of Psychology, McGill University

The Meaning of Ethnic Self-Identity

The meaning of *ethnic self-identity* that came to your mind upon reading the title of this chapter was probably something like: the way I describe my ethnic background. This definition is adequate in that the chapter does deal with ethnicity as it is used to identify oneself. It will soon become clear, however, that the meaning of ethnicity and the meaning of self-identity are complex to psychologists. Only by examining each of these concepts separately will we understand fully the meaning of ethnic self-identity.

To begin, let us consider the terms self and self-identity. Psychologists have used the term self to refer to at least three distinctly different entities: (1) the total person or personality, (2), the consciousness which knows the personality, or (3) the part of the personality which is known to the person. We will be using the last meaning: the self as the object of one's knowledge, the thoughts one has about oneself—in other words, one's self-cognitions. These cognitions or ideas may be based on the attitudes one holds about oneself, on the perceptions one has of one's appearance or behaviour, or on the self-reflections common to most adults. Therefore, we will include in our definition of self anything which is part of "me" or "I" and which I can know.

To possess a self-identity is to possess self-cognitions which allow one to identify oneself. At least four features of self-cognitions are relevant for identifying oneself:

1. They deal with attributes which describe oneself;
2. They deal with attributes which are distinctive to oneself;
3. They deal with attributes which are essential for being oneself.

Attributes which describe oneself or describe aspects of oneself are, in a sense, the elements from which one constructs a self-identity. One of these attributes may be your name *Samantha Jones*, and another *Canadian*, and another *friendly*. Of course, you will know many more of your attributes and they can all be used to identify yourself. Some of these attributes or their combination will distinguish you from other people. Your name, for one, is an attribute which makes you distinctive. Psychologists believe that people rely on their distinctive attributes when identifying themselves (McGuire & Padawer-Singer, 1976). Thinking of oneself as a unique individual is therefore part of having a self-identity. Moreover, certain attributes will be considered important or essential for being oneself. For example, our respondent, Samantha, might feel that being friendly is very important for being herself; she would feel radically altered if she were an unfriendly or a shy person. Thus, people focus on their important or essential attributes when identifying themselves (Rorty, 1976; Sampson, 1978). Finally, people tend to organize these attributes into a network of interrelated elements. Some attributes are basically similar to one another (e.g. friendly and sociable) and others are different (e.g. friendly and critical). Yet they are related to one another by virtue of being part of the same personality. The extent to which people organize their attributes into a differentiated yet integrated whole affects their self-identity (Markus, 1977; Scott, 1974). Research into these four features of self-cognitions has greatly enhanced our understanding of the structure and the functions of self-identity, one of the major components of ethnic self-identity.

The second major component of ethnic self-identity is ethnicity. Our phenomenological definition of ethnicity is thoughts one has about one's own ethnic group, or ethnic cognitions. The chapter on stereotypes (Chapter 9) is relevant here since ethnic stereotypes are basically cognitions about particular ethnic groups. However, in the present chapter we will focus on cognitions about one's own ethnic group since they are most useful for identifying oneself.

What is the relationship between ethnicity and self-identity? The schematic representation of self and ethnicity, as seen in Figure 3.1, illustrates the relationship. Self and ethnicity are parallel structures.

The self, labelled *me* consists of cognitions about attributes, some of which are essential (represented by A's) and some of which are less important yet still descriptive (represented by a's). Likewise, an ethnicity, labelled X Canadian, consists of cognitions about attributes, some of which are essential for being an X Canadian (E's) and some of which are less

Figure 3.1
Schematic Representation of Self and Ethnicity

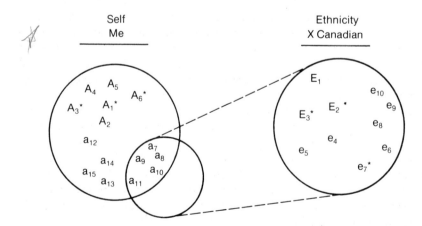

important (e's). Both self and an ethnicity include some attributes which are distinctive to those entities (marked with an *) and others which are shared with many other selves or ethnicities respectively (no *). Finally, both self and an ethnicity are organized. Attributes which are similar to one another are closely associated in one's thoughts, in that when you think of one, you often think of the other (attributes represented in close proximity to one another). Attributes which are different from one another are not closely associated in one's thoughts (attributes represented as distant from one another). Thus it is possible to conceive of self and ethnicity as comparable structures. Identifying an ethnic group is facilitated by the same features of cognitions as identifying oneself.

However, when one or more of the self-attributes corresponds with the attributes of an ethnicity, we have ethnic self-identity. In Figure 3.1, five of the ethnic attributes correspond to five self-attributes ($E_1 = a_7$, $E_2 = a_8$, $E_3 = a_9$, $e_4 = a_{10}$, $e_5 = a_{11}$). Perhaps one of these, E_1, is the name or label of that particular ethnic group. Other ethnic attributes may be the language spoken by that group, being raised by parents of that ethnic background, celebrating certain occasions, and so on. Ethnic self-identity, therefore, means knowing that oneself is defined in part by attributes which are in turn used to define an ethnicity.

The study of ethnic self-identity has continued to be of major interest to Canadian social psychologists since the early 1960s when Lambert and his colleagues (see Lambert & Tucker, 1972) assessed the self-identity of English and French Canadian children. The children were asked to describe themselves with respect to a list of traits such as smart, friendly, and so on. Their profiles were then matched against their descriptions of English Canadians and of French Canadians with respect to the same list of traits. A child whose self-cognitions matched his or her cognitions about English Canadians more than those about French Canadians was assumed to possess an English Canadian identity. A child whose self-cognitions matched his or her cognitions about French Canadians more than those about English Canadians was said to possess a French Canadian identity. The meaning of identity here is slightly different from the one we propose to use in this chapter, since there is no indication that the children *knew* that they were English Canadian or French Canadian, or *knew* that their self profile was similar to their ethnic group profile. Nonetheless, this formative work provided a framework for the study of ethnic self-identity which continues to be valuable. Our discussion of the four features of self-cognitions and ethnic cognitions which contribute to an ethnic self-identity will proceed therefore in terms of this framework. Whenever research permits, the relevant literature on self-cognitions will be presented first and then the literature on ethnic cognitions and their relationship to the self. For ease of presentation, the first line of research will be referred to as self-identity research, and the second as ethnic self-identity or simply ethnic identity research.

Attributes: The Elements of Ethnic Self-Identity

Self-Attributes and the Place of Ethnicity Among Them

What do people know about themselves? When a person pauses to think about himself or herself as a person, what is the content of those thoughts? Psychologists have elicited self-cognitions by having people ask themselves the question, "Who am I?" or "What kind of a person am I?" The words or phrases typically given by university students in answer to these questions (Gordon, 1868) can then be classified as: *external* meaning observable (appearance, behaviour, age), *role* meaning a socially defined category (student, friend, son), or *internal* meaning covert (traits, beliefs, preferences, values). Students have been found to use an average of fourteen attributes to describe themselves, at least half of which are internal (Aboud, 1979). Thus young adults seem to think of themselves mostly in terms of subjective, psychological qualities, the attributes we usually think of when we talk about a person's personality. However, social roles and external features also appear in most self-descriptions (Sampson, 1978), though they tend to be excluded from most self-concept inventories using adjective lists. Ethnicity is classified as a social role comparable to one's occupational or family role. In a Canadian sample, approximately 30 per cent referred to their ethnicity (Aboud, 1979), though this would be expected to vary from one region to another.

Clearly this is not the whole picture. We would expect people to know more about themselves than they convey in these spontaneous descriptions. For example, most people think about how good or acceptable they are; they evaluate their opinions and abilities. But in fact the record shows only infrequent references to self-evaluation (Ickes, Layden & Barnes, 1978, McGuire & Padawer-Singer, 1976). Likewise, we would expect more than 30 per cent of a sample to know their ethnic affiliation. Why, then, do people not describe what they know of themselves? The problem is rooted in the context of inquiry. When describing yourself to a new-found friend, you focus on what you think is important: your interests, your opinions, your activities, and your genial nature. Assuming that your companion is inquiring about you as a potential friend, you select accordingly. Likewise, when a pyschologist says, "Tell me about yourself," you are likely to mention those qualities which you think would be informative to a strange adult. Keeping in mind that these qualities have to be put into words, you limit yourself to the ones you can articulate verbally.

Knowing these constraints, psychologists have tried to arrange a context that would maximize the expression of self-knowledge. The most frequently used, and probably the best method is to pose a self-directed question such as, "Who am I?" or "What kind of a person am I?" and to emphasize that the respondent should do this in dialogue with himself or herself rather than with the experimenter (Ickes, Layden & Barnes, 1978).

The question should be answered in a relaxed and private atmosphere. Most of the studies which report spontaneous self-descriptions do not provide conditions for maximizing the expression of self-knowledge. Consequently, it is very likely that the respondents know more about themselves than what they report. The descriptions do, however, tell us something about the self-cognitions which are most available or salient, most easily verbalized, and considered most informative to a strange adult. Ethnicity, for the most part, does not appear to meet these criteria.

The most popular alternative method is to provide a context wherein the dimension of interest is made salient. For example, a self-esteem questionnaire would ask how competent one felt at various intellectual, social, and physical activities. An ethnic identity questionnaire would likewise provide various ethnic labels and ask you to describe yourself with one. For example, Meisel (1975) posed the following question to a sample of Canadians in 1968: "People may think of themselves as English Canadians, French Canadians, German, Italian, or Irish Canadians, or in some other way. How do you prefer to think of yourself?" Even after being provided with an ethnic context, 80 per cent of the English speakers said they were simply "Canadian." This was also true of a survey reported by Berry, Kalin and Taylor (1977). Most of the people who described their father's ancestral country as Britain used the label Canadian rather than English Canadian to identify themselves. Among these people, ones who preferred the national over the ethnic label had generally more tolerant attitudes toward outgroups (Kalin & Berry, 1979). But there are several negative effects of the exclusive use of the national label and of minimizing the importance of ethnic labels. One is that minority group members may get the impression that Canadian is synonymous with English Canadian. This has been documented in studies of ethnic perception among Chinese and Greek Canadian children (Aboud & Christian, 1979). These children assume that they cannot be "real" Canadians because they are not English Canadians. The other negative consequence occurs when those who call themselves Canadian insist that others shed their hyphenated identity (Ward, 1978). Many people believe that to encourage the use of ethnic or hyphenated identity is to foster ethnocentrism (negative outgroup attitudes). As we will discover shortly, ethnic identity and ingroup preference do not produce ethnocentric attitudes among minority Canadians.

Those of French ancestry possess a strikingly different ethnic identity from English Canadians. Half referred to themselves as Canadien français and 23 per cent as Québécois (Berry et al., 1977). Only one-quarter used the term Canadien. This French-English difference reveals an important feature of ethnic identity that is often overlooked: the way you think of yourself in ethnic terms is not based solely on your actual ethnic background. People who call themselves Canadien français may do so because they speak French and live as other French Canadians, not because their ancestors came from France. In fact some of these families came originally from Ireland. But for one reason or another the more important part of their identity is defined as French Canadian.

Of those whose ancestors came from neither England nor France, 60 per cent said they were simply Canadian and 25 per cent said ethnic Canadian (e.g., Italian Canadian). Those who identified themselves in ethnic terms tended to be first or second generation Canadians, to have learned a language other than English as children, and to have married a member of their ethnic group. They were also younger. Unlike those of British ancestry, Canadians of other-ethnic background who had a hyphenated identity were found to be as tolerant of others as those with an unhyphenated Canadian identity (see Kalin & Berry, 1979). This is a fortunate finding in light of the government's support of ethnic identification and ethnic development through its multiculturalism policy. The financial and institutional support made available to Canadian cultural groups have spawned a revival of ethnic pride among second- and third-generation Canadians. Personal accounts of this new awareness reveal a painful but constructive process through which conflicting identities become integrated (Kostash, 1977). Children's picture books depicting the experiences of, for example, a Canadian Indian boy or a Canadian Mennonite girl are now becoming available. Although we have not yet evaluated their impact, the mere presence of such books conveys to a child that non-white, non-English-speaking people are worth writing about.

It has probably become apparent by now that what people think they are may be slightly different from what they are "officially" or objectively. This is not so puzzling when we remember that self-identity is a subjective, psychological phenomenon. The discrepancy between a person's objective and subjective identity is therefore of great interest to psychologists because it allows us to examine the role of factors other than ancestry. One such factor is age or the level of cognitive development which in turn affects the use of internal, role, and external attributes for self-decription. If university students are preoccupied with their internal attributes, then they are not likely to think about their ethnic role. Is there a point in one's self-identity development when ethnicity is important?

Development of Ethnic Self-Identity
If we were to ask a five-year-old the question, "Who are you?" or "What are you?" he or she may mention approximately two to five attributes (Keller, Ford & Meacham, 1978). Part of their difficulty is in focussing on themselves or making themselves the objects of their own attention. So rather than think about themselves they tend to look at themselves or form an image of themselves. Perhaps because of their perceptual orientation young

children describe themselves most often in terms of observable attributes: behaviours, possessions, and appearance (Aboud, 1979; Keller, Ford & Meacham, 1978). The first subjective or internal characteristic to appear in children's self-descriptions is preference for certain possessions or activities (e.g., I like playing with my toys).

Children may describe themselves in terms of external features associated with their ethnicity (language, appearance, school) long before they think of ethnicity itself as an attribute, so it is not a simple matter to determine the exact age of the first ethnic self-identification. The spontaneous use of an ethnic attribute when describing oneself may occur as early as five years of age in some children and never in others. Once again, however, we must interpret spontaneous self-descriptions with caution; they do not fully represent everything children know about themselves. The children may forget to mention their ethnicity but recognize it immediately once someone has provided a label or a photograph. For a more accurate picture, we must look at the research in which children are offered various ethnic descriptors and asked to identify themselves.

One technique which has been successful in measuring the reactions of preschoolers makes use of picture books. The main character of each book belongs to one of five ethnic Canadian groups (Aboud, 1977, 1980). The investigator points to one book character at a time and says something like, "This is Normie, a Canadian Indian. Are you a Canadian Indian?" The other ethnic characters in this study were labelled black, white (or English), Chinese, and Eskimo Canadian. Chinese, white, black, and Indian children from preschool and Grade 1 classes have been tested with these books. A larger proportion of white children as compared to non-white children chose the correct label for themselves. By Grade 1 almost all the white children were accurate whereas only three-quarters of the Indian and black children were. Children younger than this were much less likely to pick the correct label—anywhere from half to two-thirds of them were incorrect. More often than not this was a result of their answering "no" to all five ethnic labels. We inferred from this that many preschoolers did not seem to understand the concept of ethnicity as expressed by a label.

In conjunction with this pattern of non-identification or misidentification, young children from non-white ethnic groups do not always show the usual ingroup preference or ingroup perceptions of similarity. That is, when photographs are presented without any ethnic label, black and Indian youngsters often feel more positive toward and similar to the white child than to the black or Indian child (Crooks, 1970; George & Hoppe, 1979). Thus, three critical features of the identification process—perceived similarity, preference, and knowledge of the ethnic label—may be at odds with one another. The resulting conflict may explain why non-white children were less likely than whites to choose the correct ethnic label.

This overview of the child research raises a number of questions about the forces which facilitate and impede the development of ethnic identification. These forces are both experiential and maturational. They include such experiences as perceiving differences in appearance, hearing parents and teachers apply the ethnic label to themselves and to the child, and being associated with ingroup members and events which subsequently acquire an ethnic meaning. Maturational forces of a cognitive nature, such as the ability to use abstract concepts, are also critical. However, the ethnic minority child also associates negative feelings with his or her self-identification experiences. Thus despite having all the typical self-identification experiences and cognitive abilities, minority children are less likely to express their ethnic affiliation for self-esteem reasons. The link between ethnic self-identification and self-esteem has been demonstrated recently in a study by George and Hoppe (1979). Positive self-esteem facilitated ethnic self-identification among Grade 2 Indian children; by Grade 6 self-esteem was less influential. Perhaps knowledge of the ethnic label and perceptions of similarity were so strong in the older group that they identified themselves as Indian even though they still felt negatively about it.

Distinctive Self and Ethnic Attributes
Having attributes that one considers distinctive or different contributes to a person's self-identity in two ways. First, the differences ensure that one will be distinguishable from other people, and therefore identifiable in a social context. In a certain sense we are all unique in that we are each only one of a kind. However, those who have a strong need to be unique usually think of themselves as different from others in all respects. Your answer to the question, "If you were in every respect (or in many respects) exactly like your friend X, could you still be yourself?" might be a simple way of finding out whether uniqueness is important to your self-identity. Although most people want to feel somewhat special, the need to be unique seems to be greater in some individuals (Snyder & Fromkin, 1977). This need may be heightened by, for example, finding out that many other people hold an opinion which is similiar to one's own. In this case, the aroused need for uniqueness would motivate one to change one's opinion in order to be different. This is a rather extreme reaction, but a prevalent one among Fromkin's university subjects. Thus distinctive attributes enhance one's sense of being a unique individual, identifiable in a social context.

Secondly, differences serve an informational, as opposed to a motivational, function. They allow one to describe oneself through contrast. For example, when a student says, "People at this university are so competitive" the implication is, "I am not competitive." In such a competitive setting, one's own uncompetitiveness becomes salient. Research in the area of person perception suggests that distinctive attributes contribute greatly to impressions formed about people generally (Schneider, Hastorf & Ellsworth, 1979). Their importance tends to be exaggerated perhaps because they "stand out" or are salient and available to one's thoughts. Thus distinctive attributes contribute to self-identity simply by enhancing the availability of information about oneself.

Perceived Self-Other Differences

The most direct way of finding out which attributes make a person feel distinctive is to ask, "What are you that others are not?" McGuire, McGuire, Child and Fujioka (1978) asked a similar question of their Grades 1 to 11 students who were instructed to "Tell us what you are not." Their answers were compared with answers given by another set of children who were told, "Tell us about yourself." The only attribute analyzed in this study was ethnicity; it was found that 6 per cent mentioned an ethnicity they were *not* (in response to the former request), whereas 3 per cent described the ethnicity they were (in response to the latter request). The authors concluded that "people are more likely to think of other's ethnicity as something they are not than of own ethnicity as something that they are." (p. 519). As a postscript to this study, we should add that these subjects were unlikely to think about ethnicity at all, given such low percentages. However, other studies conducted by McGuire demonstrate that people tend to describe themselves in terms of physical features or social roles which distinguish them from others in the immediate social milieu.

Other techniques, used particularly with children, involve asking the question, "In what ways are you the same as other people? In what ways are you different from other people?" (Rosenberg, 1979) and "What would you have to change about yourself for you to become your best friend?" (Mohr, 1978). When the findings of several studies are integrated, an interesting developmental pattern emerges. Children of all ages, (five to eighteen years) refer to similarities in behaviour and preferences, perhaps because these attributes form the bases of activity groups. Distinctive attributes, on the other hand, develop from being a reflection of the child's social exterior (behaviour, appearance and social roles) to being a representation of the adolescent's psychological interior (traits, emotions, thoughts). Distinctive attributes, then, seem to describe more than shared attributes the important changes in a developing self-identity. In fact, the distinctive attributes are the ones most often mentioned by children when asked, "What is it that someone who knows you best knows about you?" (Rosenberg, 1979). The implication is that distinctive attributes are a significant factor in self-cognitions.

Perceived Ethnic Differences

The questions which have guided research on distinctive self-attributes can also be applied to the study of distinctive ethnic attributes. Do people attend to the differences among ethnic groups more than to their similarities? What attributes are salient when one attends to differences?

Several studies have been conducted in Canada to answer these questions. The procedure, referred to as multidimensional scaling, requires a respondent to judge the dissimilarity between pairs of stimuli such as English Canadian and French Canadian. A series of such judgments are made when many stimuli are used—in fact a judgment is made about each stimulus when paired with every other. These dissimilarity judgments are mathematically integrated to produce a spatial representation of one's cognitions. Stimuli that are perceived to be dissimilar to one another will be represented as spatially distant, and stimuli that are perceived to be similar will be located close to one another (Ramsay, 1978). By examining the clusters of similar stimuli and the distance between dissimilar stimuli, one can infer which attributes underlie judgments of dissimilarity.

Berry, Kalin and Taylor (1977) conducted a large-scale study to determine Canadians' conceptions of ethnic groups using a similar procedure. Looking at the location of various ethnic groups in two-dimensional space, one can interpret the dimensions underlying respondents' judgments and thereby the attributes which contribute to an ethnic group's distinctiveness. Among both English and French Canadian adults sampled, four attributes seemed to be relevant for distinguishing between ethnic groups: established Canadian vs. new Canadian, white vs. non-white, religion, and culture. The clusters of ethnic groups found in the spatial configuration reveal the nature of shared as well as distinctive attributes. One cluster represented Eastern cultures such as Japanese, Chinese, East Indian and Arab; a second cluster included the charter groups Indian, Eskimo, French and English; a third cluster consisted of white, new Canadians such as Polish and Italian; and a fourth very distinctive cluster represented Doukhobors, Hutterites, and Mennonites. Little distinction was made among the non-white groups who tended to be clustered together; whereas a number of non-racial characteristics were used to distinguish between white groups such as English, Hutterite, and Polish. Language was not a critical attribute in this study which involved a nationwide sample.

A comparable study conducted in the United States by Funk, Horowitz, Lipshitz, and Young (1976) found a similar structure of ethnic cognitions. In addition, their respondents rated the ethnic groups in terms of personality traits which were then superimposed on the two-dimensional representation. The traits most useful for distinguishing between American ethnic groups were industrious, patriotic, aggressive, emotional, and activist. Thus, the attributes which people spontaneously use to make distinctions among North American ethnic groups are immigrant status, physical appearance, religion and culture, and these distinctions extend to internal traits as well.

Selected samples of children have been tested with the multidimensional scaling procedure. Their perceptions of distinctive ethnic attributes are strikingly similar regardless of their own ethnic background. Taylor, Bassili and Aboud (1973) found that both French Canadian and English Canadian students in a Quebec high school used language as a way of distinguishing between stimulus persons who were described in terms of three attributes: their ethnicity (French Canadian or English Canadian), their place of residence (home town, Quebec, or Canada), and their language (French speaking or English speaking).

In another study, ethnicity not language emerged as a distinguishing attribute underlying the perceptions of Jewish, Greek, and Chinese Canadian children (Aboud & Christian, 1979). These children were second and fourth graders in Montreal schools where their own group was highly represented. Each stimulus person was described in terms of only one characteristic: ethnicity, language, region, or a personal attribute. One major distinction made by all children was between their own ethnic group and two or three outgroups. The Jewish Canadian children put Chinese and native Indian Canadians in the outgroup category, the Greek Canadian children added French Canadians to this outgroup cluster; the Chinese Canadian children perceived Greek and French Canadians as outgroups. English Canadians were not part of either the ingroup or the outgroup for any of the samples. A second distinction was made between French-related persons (French Canadian, French speaker, Quebecer) and minority ethnic groups (e.g., Chinese, native Indian). The distinctive attribute is difficult to tease out of this dichotomy, but it may be language or majority-minority status in the community.

Perceived Ethnic Self Differences

We have so far discussed distinctive attributes as they appear in self-cognitions (i.e., the ways in which you differ from other people) and as they appear in ethnic cognitions (i.e., the ways in which ethnic groups differ from one another). If self-identity is enhanced by the awareness of self-other differences, then we would expect ethnic self-identity to be enhanced by the awareness of self-other differences in ethnicity. The two functions served by differences, discussed previously, are allowing one to feel unique and providing information about oneself through contrast. Now we will ask, in terms of one's ethnic self-identity, does one feel more individual with members of a different ethnic group? Does one find out more about oneself?

The evidence for a motivational factor underlying the enhancement of self-other ethnic differences is scarce. Giles, Bourhis, and Taylor (1977) refer to evidence of the divergent language strategies used by some ethnic members when communicating with outgroup members, strategies such as exaggerating their unique speech accent. This would serve to make both parties aware of their differences and consequently their separate identities. This phenomenon is explained by a theory of intergroup comparison proposed by Tajfel and Turner (1979). They claim that distinctiveness is a mechanism for restoring positive social identity. Since minority groups often suffer from unfavourable comparisons with the majority group, the way of avoiding such competition is to enhance what is unique about one's group. It is conceivable, then, that differences between one's own and other ethnic groups or between oneself and other ethnic members will be sought to satisfy the need for a unique identity.

The second possible function served by self-other differences in ethnicity is to provide information about oneself. As described previously, knowledge about what one *is not* may strengthen the knowledge of what one *is*. Ethnic and national identity in particular seem to be strengthened through contrasts with members of other ethnic and national groups. In one study, for example, Canadians said they were most keenly aware of being Canadian when visiting foreign countries, when speaking to foreigners in Canada, and when watching Canadian teams compete internationally (Morse, 1977). Not only were their feelings of pride and attachment enhanced, but their knowledge of Canadian lifestyles was probably more clearly articulated as a result of the contrast.

If the distinctive ethnic attributes underlying the perception of self-other differences contribute to ethnic self-identity, and it appears likely that they do, then it is important to find out when such perceptions develop and what the distinctive attributes are. To study the development of perceived difference between oneself and other ethnic members, techniques are used which rely on ratings of dissimilarity (as in the multidimensional scaling procedure) or on forced choice responses to a question such as, "Who is most different from you?" To discover the nature of attributes on which the perceived difference is based, researchers have used the interview techniques which were described in the section on distinctive self-attributes.

The question, "Who is most different from you?" when directed toward a five-year-old child seated in front of pictures of different ethnic members is usually answered correctly; that is, the child usually picks someone who does not belong to his or her own ethnic group (Aboud, 1977). Vaughan (1963) has found that perceptions of similarity develop first (in response to the question, "Who is most like you?") but that perceptions of difference develop shortly thereafter. However, in a Canadian sample of black and white children between the ages of four and eight years, accurate perceptions of both similarity to one's own group and dissimilarity to four other groups increased with age parallel to one another (Aboud, 1980). Unexpectedly, perceived dissimilarity was unrelated to outgroup attitudes among the white children, and positively related to outgroup attitudes among the black children. Other studies have confirmed that both perceived ingroup similarity and outgroup dis-similarity increase throughout middle childhood (Genesee, Tucker & Lambert, 1978), but that ethnocentrism declines (Kalin, 1979). So, rather than serving to arouse prejudice, perceptions of self-other ethnic dif-ferences may contribute to the development of a positive ethnic self-identity and to an ability to cope with different ethnic perspectives.

To discover the attributes used when judging the dissimilarity of other ethnic members, Aboud (1977) asked the children, "In what way is he different from you?" The first grade sample of white children referred to physical appearance (30 per cent), ethnicity (29 per cent), and behaviour (14 per cent) most often. Ethnicity, in other words, the ethnic label, was a salient distinctive attribute. It was much less salient as an attribute that the child shared with an ingroup member; when asked, "In what way is he the same as you?" only 14 per cent of the children mentioned ethnicity. You will remember that the McGuire et al. (1978) study, described previously, reached a similar conclusion using a different method. However, both of these methods suffer in that they ask the respondent to focus on the attribute of another person who is different, rather than on the attribute that he or she possesses and others do not. Distinctive attributes that are actually possessed by the respondent are more likely to be remembered and therefore to contribute to self-identity than are attributes not possessed (Kuiper & Rogers, 1979). A question such as, "What are you that he (of a different ethnicity) is not?" would be better suited to elicit distinctive ethnic attributes which are part of the respondent's self-cognitions.

Essential Self and Ethnic Attributes

People describe themselves in terms of many attributes, but they usually consider some of these to be more important than others. The ones that are most important for self-identity are the ones that are considered essential for being oneself and without which one could no longer be oneself (Rorty, 1976). Essential attributes thus define the so-called "core" of a person's self; self-cognitions about essential attributes may therefore contribute to this feeling of having a core self. Essential attributes may also provide a sense of constancy. As long as a person can think about a few essential attributes that remain constant over time and context, then many other attributes can change without disrupting self-identity (Aboud, 1979). Our concerns in the present section will be whether or not people consider attributes in terms of varying degrees of importance, and what the essential attributes are.

Essential Self-Attributes

Three procedures have been used to determine the order of importance of a person's self-attributes. Gordon (1968) simply asked students to rank order the list of fifteen attributes they had previously given in answer to the question, "Who am I?" It seemed that the most important attributes came from the end of the list. Perhaps the important ones take more thought because they are internal attributes or because they are less common.

Using a second procedure, Morse (1977) presented students at the University of Saskatchewan with his own list of eight social roles, and asked the students to rate each on a 10-point scale in terms of its importance to their self-identity. The order from most to least important was as follows: Canadian nationality, gender, student, religion, marital status, region, social class, and ethnicity. This order would undoubtedly differ for different samples of the population. Furthermore, when compared with more internal psychological characteristics, these social roles may be relatively unimportant to a person's self-identity. Sampson (1978) tested this idea with a group of university students. There was general agreement that the above mentioned social roles were more "external" to a person than were emotions, thoughts, and values. There were individual differences, however, in whether external or internal attributes were more "important to my sense of who I am."

The third procedure involves proposing the replacement of one attribute possessed by the respondent with another not possessed by him or her, and inquiring whether this would disrupt self-identity. For example, if the respondent had mentioned extroversion as a self-attribute, the question to test the essentialness of being an extrovert would be, "If you were introverted could you still be yourself?" If the respondent answered "no," it would imply that extroversion was considered as an attribute essential for being him or herself. A "yes" answer would mean that extroversion was regarded as a somewhat peripheral attribute, descriptive but not essential.

Aboud (1979) has used this replacement or substitution procedure to assess the number and nature of essential self-attributes and essential ethnic attributes. It was then shown how these attributes contribute to ethnic self-identity. Students from kindergarten, second grade and university were asked to describe themselves in response to the question "Who are you? What kind of person are you?" The first five attributes were then subjected to the essentialness test (i.e. "If you were _____ could you still be yourself?") Of these five most salient or available self-attributes, an average of 3.00 was essential to university students, 1.60 to second graders, and .70 to kindergarteners. When attributes were coded as external, role, or internal, it became clear why the number of essential attributes increased with age. All three grade levels had the same number of external (appearance) and role (ethnicity) essential attributes; but university students mentioned many more internal (abilities) essential attributes. The younger students had initially described themselves in terms of perceptually salient attributes such as appearance and behaviour, yet they knew that those external attributes were not essential for being themselves. It would be possible to discover many attributes considered essential by a young child, attributes such as gender and family, but these were not often mentioned spontaneously, implying that they were not salient. In other words, the attributes which are most salient to a young child and most likely to be generated spontaneously are not regarded as essential.

It was clear that essential self-attributes were not salient to young children; in particular, the spontaneous awareness of internal attributes was lacking. There are times when it helps to have things at the "top of one's head" or readily available for use without having to reflect a great deal. On such occasions, young children would think of themselves mostly in terms of external attributes, ones which they themselves consider peripheral.

When the children were asked to think specifically about their essential attributes, the outcome was not much different. The question was: "What is the most important thing about you, so important that without it you could no longer be yourself?" As difficult as this question appears, half of the kindergarteners and all the second graders were able to propose one essential attribute, which was then validated using the replacement technique. However, only a small proportion of those essential attributes were internal: 20 per cent in the kindergarten sample and 35 per cent in the second grade sample, compared with 95 per cent in the university sample. Young children therefore tended to locate their essential attribute in their physical body or their parents, whereas university students located it in a psychological quality such as intellectual capability, autonomy, feelings, and interpersonal style.

In summary, university students typically describe themselves in terms of attributes which are not only descriptive but also essential. That is, they differentiate between peripheral and essential attributes, and have both types readily available to think about or to communicate. Most of their essential attributes were internal, although role categories such as gender, ethnicity, student, and family members were essential to some people. There are individual and probably cultural/regional differences in the relative importance of internal, role, and external attributes. Developmental differences are also very striking. Very young children may not even differentiate between more and less essential attributes. By second grade, at the latest, children can think about their essential attributes, which are often external or role.

Essential Ethnic Attributes

It is conceivable that people think of ethnic groups in terms of their essential attributes. That is, one may rely on a few characteristics which one considers essential for being a member of an ethnic group to identify a person as a member or non-member. We are not now dealing with the snap judgments that people may make when deciding whether or not to evoke their ethnic stereotype or their prejudice. Rather, we are concerned with the essential attributes of one's own ethnic group and with one's use of these cognitions when identifying oneself as a member of that group.

To determine the number and nature of essential ethnic attributes, Aboud (1979) used the replacement procedure with the same sample of kindergarten, second grade, and university students. This time they were asked to describe an ingroup member instead of the self. Each descriptive attribute was then subjected to the essentialness test, "If a person did not _____ could he be an (ingroup) Canadian?" A "no" answer signified the essentialness of the attribute.

Results indicated that young children produced the same number of essential ingroup as essential self-attributes: kindergarteners had an average of .85, and second graders 1.60. However, university students of the same ethnic background found only 1.20 essential ethnic attributes, much fewer than their essential self-attributes. Once again, the university students thought in terms of internal attributes such as belief system or feeling of pride and attachment; whereas the young children thought that appearance and behaviour (e.g., celebrating certain festivals, going to a particular school) were essential. The number of external attributes peaked in second grade, whereas, the number of internal attributes continued to increase as a function of age.

This pattern of results was replicated when subjects were asked about the essential attributes of an outgroup. One or two of the most salient attributes were considered essential; the number of external attributes was again highest in second grade, and the number of internal attributes was highest among university students. External attributes included such things as language and place of residence; internal attributes included beliefs, attitudes and values. Therefore, relative to essential self-attributes, cognitions about essential ethnic attributes are fewer in number and do not increase with development. They also tend to be more external particularly among second graders. It is conceivable that ethnic cognitions develop later than self-cognitions, and for this reason continue to be based on external attributes in second grade when external self-attributes have begun to decline.

That many adults view their own ethnicity as external became clear in a study reported by Sampson (1978). University students rated various attributes on a 20-point internality scale where 1 meant external or "part of my surroundings" and 20 meant internal or "located within me." Ethnicity was located in the middle toward the external end with an average rating of 9.86. This was slightly more external than their student role for which the rating was 11.58. Sampson's subjects were American from New England.

A sample of McGill psychology undergraduates rated ethnicity at 10.85 (the ratings ranged from 3 to 20), slightly more internal than their student role.

The Interface of Essential Self and Ethnic Attributes

Ethnicity per se was not frequently mentioned as an essential self-attribute. Adults tend to locate ethnicity and self in different sets of non-overlapping attributes: ethnicity is located in more external attributes than self is and in fewer internal attributes than self is. This would lead one to suspect that the two identities function independently. Consequently, adopting the characteristics of a different ethnic group should not interfere with essential self-attributes. If, however, both self and ethnicity are based on the same attributes, external in the case of young children and internal in the case of most adults, then a loss of one should result in a loss of the other.

To test this relationship between self and ethnic attributes, Aboud (1979) proposed six different ethnic identities other than the respondent's own and asked, "Could you be a _____ Canadian and still be yourself?" Students from kindergarten, elementary school (Grades 2 and 4), and university were tested. Respondents identified themselves as Jewish Canadian, so the following six ethnicities were substituted: English Canadian, French Canadian, black Canadian, Chinese Canadian, native Indian, and Eskimo. Across all three samples there was a sharp increase in reported self-identity loss when a non-white ethnicity was proposed: English Canadian 28 per cent, French Canadian 41 per cent, black Canadian 60 per cent, Chinese Canadian 62 per cent, native Indian 59 per cent, Eskimo 64 per cent. The other striking finding was that kindergarteners were more likely to say that they could not be themselves given any of the ethnic substitutions than were elementary school students. The kindergarteners located essential self-attributes externally, which is where they located ethnicity. Thus a change in holidays, in language, in appearance, or in behaviour resulted in a different identity. Second and fourth graders, who were beginning to locate essential self-attributes internally, assumed that they would remain unaffected by the external ethnic change. University students were more variable depending on whether they conceived of ethnicity as internally or externally located.

The implications of this relationship between self and ethnic attributes are striking. Young children may be concerned about losing their self-identity if required to learn a different language, engage in culturally different activities, or even play with other ethnic children. If the child bases his or her self on these particular attributes—language, behaviour, friends—then changes in these attributes brought about by cross-cultural interaction will have negative consequences, negative in that the child will feel a loss of self. There are ways of restoring identity such as by redefining a new set of essential self-attributes to include ones that are more stable and perhaps internal.

The same line of thinking could apply to ethnic self-identity. If, as was found, ethnic membership is based on one or two essential ethnic attributes, and if one of these attributes changes, then we would predict a loss of ethnic self-identity. This was tested with kindergarten and second grade children (Aboud, 1979) who were photographed as they dressed in Eskimo clothing. You will recall that young children typically mentioned external attributes as essential for being a member of their own ethnic ingroup. As predicted, when they looked at the photograph of themselves, they identified themselves as an Eskimo in response to the question, "What are you?" In other words, they identified themselves in terms of their social exterior only. Only those children for whom ethnicity was essential and who thought of their ethnic group in terms of internal attributes identified themselves correctly despite the misleading social exterior. It seems that salient internal attributes can be used to maintain a constant ethnic self-identity, but that few young children have such cognitions readily available.

Concluding Remarks

An important issue reappearing throughout our discussion of ethnic self-identity is the psychological locus of ethnicity. Ethnicity appears in some people as a characteristic internal to themselves, comparable to their beliefs and emotions. Others think of their ethnicity as a surface or external characteristic, comparable to their physical appearance or friendships. An examination of the attributes which contribute most strongly to ethnic identity, namely the distinctive and essential ethnic attributes (E^*) revealed this split in location. They were located both internally and externally. In contrast, the attributes on which self-identity is based (A^*) were typically internal only. To the extent that ethnic and self-identity are located in corresponding attributes, ethnicity will be an important component of self-identity. Studies reported in this chapter indicate that for many people ethnicity is not important to their sense of who they are. In other words, their distinctive and essential ethnic attributes are undistinctive and unessential self-attributes as shown in Figure 1 ($E_2^* \rightarrow a_8$; $E_3^* \rightarrow a_9$). But for others the language and values associated with ethnicity are at the same time distinctive and essential for being themselves. Individual differences in the way one's ethnic schema correspond to one's self-schema provide enough variability to keep psychologists pursuing this issue for many years.

REFERENCES

Aboud, F.E. Interest in ethnic information: A cross-cultural developmental study. *Canadian Journal of Behavioural Science*, 1977, *9*, 134-146.

Aboud, F.E. The development of ethnic identity in relation to self-identity. Paper presented at Canadian Psychological Association meeting, Quebec, 1979.

Aboud, F.E. A test of ethnocentrism with young children. *Canadian Journal of Behavioural Science*, 1980.

Aboud, F.E. & Christian, J.D. Development of ethnic identity. In L. Eckensberger, Y. Poortinga & W.J. Lonner (eds.), *Cross-cultural Contributions to Psychology*. Netherlands: Swets & Zeitlinger, 1979.

Berry, J.W., Kalin, R. & Taylor, D.M. *Multiculturalism and Ethnic Attitudes in Canada*. Ottawa: Ministry of Supply and Services Canada, 1977.

Crooks, R.C. The effects of an interracial preschool program upon racial preference, knowledge of racial differences and racial identification. *Journal of Social Issues*, 1970, *26*, 137-144.

Funk, S.G., Horowitz, A.D., Lipshitz, R. & Young, F.W. The perceived structure of American ethnic groups: The use of multidimensional scaling in stereo-type research. *Sociometry*, 1976, *39*, 116-130.

Genesee, F., Tucker, G.R., & Lambert, W.E. The development of ethnic identity and ethnic role-taking skills in children from different school settings. *International Journal of Psychology*, 1978, *13*, 39-57.

George, D.M. & Hoppe, R.A. Racial identification, preference, and self-concept: Canadian Indian and white schoolchildren. *Journal of Cross-Cultural Psychology*, 1979, *10*, 85-100.

Gordon, C. Self-conceptions: Configurations of content. In C. Gordon & K.J. Gergen (eds.), *The Self in Social Interaction*. New York: Wiley, 1968, 115-136.

Giles, H., Bourhis, R.Y., & Taylor, D.M. Towards a theory of language in ethnic group relations. In H. Giles (ed.), *Language, Ethnicity and Intergroup Relations*. New York: Academic Press, 1977.

Ickes, M., Layden, M.A. & Barnes, R.D. Objective self-awareness and individuation: An empirical link. *Journal of Personality*, 1978, *46*, 146-161.

Kalin, R. Ethnic and multicultural attitudes among children in a Canadian city. *Canadian Ethnic Studies*, 1979, *11*, 69-81.

Kalin, R., & Berry, J.W. Determinants and attitudinal correlates of ethnic identity in Canada. Paper presented at Canadian Psychological Association meeting, Quebec, 1979.

Keller, A., Ford, L.H., & Meacham, J.A. Dimensions of self-concept in preschool children. *Developmental Psychology*, 1978, *14*, 483-489.

Kostash, M. *All of Baba's Children*. Edmonton: Hurtig, 1977.

Kuiper, N.A., & Rogers, T.B. Encoding of person information: Self-other differences. *Journal of Personality & Social Psychology*, 1979, *37*, 499-514.

Lambert, W.E. & Tucker, G.R. *Bilingual Education of Children*. Rowley: Newbury House, 1972.

Markus, H. Self-schemata and processing information about the self. *Journal of Personality & Social Psychology*, 1977, *35*, 63-78.

McGuire, W.J., McGuire, C.V., Child, P., & Fujioka, T. Salience of Ethnicity in the spontaneous self-concept as a function of one's ethnic distinctiveness in the social environment. *Journal of Personality & Social Psychology*, 1978, *36*, 511-520.

McGuire, W.J., & Padawer-Singer, A. Trait salience in the spontaneous self-concept. *Journal of Personality & Social Psychology*, 1976, *33*, 743-754.

Meisel, J. *Working Papers on Canadian Politics*. Montreal: McGill-Queen's Press, 1975.

Mohr, D.M. Development of attributes of person identity. *Developmental Psychology*, 1978, *14*, 427-428.

Morse, S.J. Being a Canadian: Aspects of national identity among a sample of university students in Saskatchewan. *Canadian Journal of Behavioural Science,* 1977, *9,* 265-273.

Ramsay, J.O. *Multiscale: Four programs for multidimensional scaling by the method of maximum likelihood.* Chicago: National Educational Resources, 1978.

Rorty, A.O. *The Identities of Persons.* Berkeley: University of California Press, 1976, 1-15.

Rosenberg, M. *Conceiving the Self.* New York: Basic Books, 1979.

Sampson, E.E. Personality and the location of identity. *Journal of Personality,* 1978, *46,* 552-568.

Schneider, D.J., Hastorf, A.H. & Ellsworth, P.C. *Person Perception.* Reading: Addison-Wesley, 1979.

Scott, W.A. Varieties of cognitive integration. *Journal of Personality & Social Psychology,* 1974, *30,* 563-578.

Snyder, C.R. & Fromkin, H.L. Abnormality as a positive characteristic: The development and validation of a scale measuring need for uniqueness. *Journal of Abnormal Psychology,* 1977, *86,* 518-527.

Taylor, D.M., Bassili, J.N., & Aboud, F.E. Dimensions of ethnic identity: An example from Quebec. *Journal of Social Psychology,* 1973, *89,* 185-192.

Vaughan, G.M. Concept formation and the development of ethnic awareness. *Journal of Genetic Psychology,* 1963, *103,* 93-103.

Ward, P. *White Canada Forever.* Toronto: McGill-Queen's Press, 1978.

Tajfel, H. & Turner, J. An integrative theory of intergroup conflict. In W.G. Austin & S. Worchel (eds.), *The Social Psychology of Intergroup Relations.* Monterey, Calif.: Brooks/Cole, 1979.

Chapter 4

Social Influences on the Child's Development of an Identity

Wallace, E. Lambert, Department of Psychology, McGill University

What I propose to do first in this chapter is describe and illustrate a little understood process that seems to run its course whenever a child develops a notion of who he or she is as a person and as a member of a particular national, linguistic, racial, or ethnic group. This process is basically a form of didactic teaching and learning wherein mental boundaries between ingroups and outgroups are erected in the minds of children by adult socializers. In most cases, the boundaries are ultimately accepted by the children as being real and true, as they are by the adults involved in the process. It seems that young children's ethnic identities take their start in the *contrasts* that children are induced to draw between their "own" ethnic group and various comparison groups. It also seems that "contrast training" is relied upon by adults because it has proven to be a very effective means of fixing group boundaries and thus satisfying children's inquisitiveness about who or what they are. Adult socializers have in their control various ways to approach a child's wonderings about who he or she is. Although most parents don't, they could tone down contrasts that promote ingroup/outgroup thinking and inculcate instead the notion that the child in question is simply a child, a human, or even a primate, rather than a son or daughter of particular parents who belong to a particular family, religious, racial and national group, making them, by implication, quite distinctive and different. Thus, adults play a critical role as contrast trainers and they are responsible for the consequences of instilling either a tight, compartmentalized ingroup/outgroup differentiation, or a loose, open frame of reference for the child. As it turns out, things aren't as compartmentalized and clear as most contrast training might imply. In fact, there may not be that many real or important differences separating ethnic groups—like English Canadians versus French Canadians. Instead, similarities among "cultural groups" may well outweigh differences. But parents and other socializers have difficulty in toning down contrasts because they themselves are already true believers in the contrasts they use with their children, and thus they would feel neglectful and concerned if their children were left adrift and unclear as to what they (the parents) take to be important and obvious ingroup/outgroup boundaries.

This line of thought will be developed in the first part of the chapter. The research base for the discussion will be cross-national in scope, but with an emphasis on the social factors in Canada that influence Canadian children's development of an identity. In the second part of the chapter we explore a different aspect of social influence on identity development—the child-rearing values of parents. To the extent that each ethnic group tries to bring up its children with its own distinctive style of child rearing, children's identities should be shaped accordingly. In part two, we will also rely on cross-national research, and again with the focus on Canadian children both English speaking and French speaking. What is intriguing is that we end up questioning just how "distinctive" these ethnic or national variations in child-rearing values actually are.

Parents as Contrast Trainers

How does a child come to make distinctions between groups, especially his own versus other groups? Early theorists believed that this striving to locate the limits of one's own group was a natural outgrowth of some innate "consciousness of kind," but in more recent times the phenomenon has become somewhat less mysterious and vague (see G. Allport, 1968). At least, the consequences of thinking in own group versus other-group terms are becoming clearer. For example, Piaget and Weil (1951) believe that "the cognitive and affective attitudes associated with loyalty to the homeland and initial contacts with other countries" may form the bases of subsequent international maladjustment (p. 561). Morse and F. Allport (1952) made the same issue the focus of their investigation. They studied the degrees of personal involvement with one's nation and found that an exaggerated loyalty to one's own group was by far the most important single cause of discrimination and exclusion. G. Allport (1954) also recognized the relevance of this issue. As an aid in learning "that human beings are clustered into groups—that there are important distinctions," the child makes use of "the logical generalizations of the sort that mature adults accept"; for example, that certain groups are untrustworthy or uncultured when compared to his own (p. 307f). Allport believes that the child prepares himself for prejudice by learning these generalizations.

If we piece together the ideas available about how own-group/other-group thinking starts, the following picture emerges. At the same time as the preschool child is learning to interact with others, is becoming aware of their distinctiveness, and is developing rudimentary skills in viewing events from their perspectives, he also comes to learn, often painfully, that the private feelings of attachment he has for his own familiar and comfortable settings are not shared by those who belong to other social subgroups within his own nation, and even less so by strangers or by people who live in foreign countries. He comes to realize that these others, those close to home as well as outsiders, are not foreigners when at home where they have their own loyalties to particular places, people, and experiences, and that he himself might well be a foreigner when away from home. He also gradually develops a conception of his own national group through comparisons or contrasts that are made with foreign peoples and places, and through the generalizations he builds up from interpersonal experiences he has had with the strange and different in his own close social environment. Thus, a French Canadian child, for example, comes to understand who he is by having his own group compared and contrasted with other ethnic or national groups and by generalizing or transferring to these supposedly different subsets of people the perceptions and reactions he has already developed towards particular individuals or groups who were different in some essential way from himself and from those with whom he identifies.

One might presume that these reactions are merely transient stages that children pass through in getting to know about the social world, with little long-range significance. The research findings of Morse and F. Allport (1952), however, indicate the contrary—that these early experiences may very well establish basic predispositions toward one's own group and foreign peoples that will manifest themselves throughout life. In their investigation with samples of adult Americans, they discovered three factors that are by far the most important determinants of discrimination and prejudice towards minority group members: (a) "national involvement," meaning a close identification of one's own interests with national interests, a belief that the policies of one's own country are always right, and a glorification of one's own country; (b) a belief in the "racial essence" of the minority group in question, who "have a common racial quality and are different by nature"; and (c) a "differential loyalty" to one's own people, that is, a generalized ingroup versus outgroup feeling" that expresses itself in a differential willingness to help members of one's own national group when they are in trouble, but not foreigners (Morse & F. Allport, 1952).

With these ideas as background, Lambert and Klineberg (1967) conducted a large-scale, cross-national study of children's views of themselves, their national group, and foreign peoples. We wanted to explore in some detail how conceptions of ingroups and outgroups develop from the ages of six to fourteen years, and we wanted to get as large a sample of national groups as was manageable. Our study, therefore, involved three quarter-hour interviews with each child in samples of one hundred six-year-olds, one hundred ten-year-olds and one hundred fourteen-year-olds from large city public schools in each of the following countries: the United States, South Africa (Bantu children only), Brazil, Canada (separate English- and French-speaking groups), France, Germany, Israel, Japan, Lebanon and Turkey. The children selected, fifty boys and fifty girls in each age sample, were of normal intelligence and came from either "working" or "middle" socio-economic backgrounds as defined by specialists in each nation who knew about the country's range of social classes. The interviews were conducted by advanced students or professors of child psychology working in these different nations. The interview started with the question, "What are you?" which led to a probing for the names of people from foreign lands who were considered to be "like us" or "not like us." The children were later asked a standard series of questions about each

CAMROSE LUTHERAN COLLEGE
LIBRARY

foreign group mentioned, for example, in what way are the Brazilians like us (or not like us)? What else do you know about the Brazilian people? Do you like Brazilians? Why do you say that? How do you know about Brazilians? Later the child answered comparable questions about the people of his own country. Finally, he was asked to tell what countries he would most and least like to be from if he didn't have his actual nationality, and to explain his choices.

Among other things, we examined three facets of each child's attitudes toward foreign peoples: his tendency to regard various foreign groups as similar or different, a ratio we refer to as "similarity outlooks," his readiness to express "affection" or disaffection for them, and, for the fourteen-year-old age sample, his general "ethnocentrism" as measured by a separate scale. We compared national and age groups for the patterns formed by the three attitude components for each national group of children. Taking Canadian children as an example, we found that both French Canadian and English Canadian fourteen-year-olds show comparatively little ethnocentrism. With regard to similarity outlooks, the rank positions for Canadian children, relative to those from other nations, fell near the general average at age six and slightly above at age fourteen. The French Canadian children showed a regular decrease from six to fourteen years in the degree of affection shown toward other peoples: at age six they were the most affectionate group, but only average at age fourteen. The English Canadian children also became relatively less affectionate towards foreign people as they moved from ten to fourteen years of age. Thus for both Canadian groups, although they showed relatively little ethnocentrism, they were exclusive about whom they classified as similar, and they showed relative declines in the affection expressed for foreign groups as they progressed into the teens.

But the Canadian children have to be seen in relation to the full array of national groups represented in the study. The national variations in *similarity outlooks* indicated that the Brazilian, Japanese, and Bantu children viewed the world as populated more by peoples who are dissimilar than by peoples who are similar. Thus, they have relatively narrow similarity outlooks when compared to the Israeli, French, American, French Canadian, English Canadian, and Turkish children. We presume that these national differences in breadth of similarity outlooks reflect basic differences in ways of thinking about foreign peoples, and they likely reflect how much children in certain societies come to view themselves as members of distinctive or culturally isolated groups or as people basically similar to most others. We also found that six-year-olds almost universally viewed foreign peoples as different much more frequently than did ten-year-olds. In general, the ten-year-olds considered a much larger array of foreign peoples as similar, and there was little change in similarity outlooks between ten and fourteen.

With regard to *affection for foreign peoples*, children generally were more likely to express affection for people from foreign lands than they were to consider them as being similar. Still, there were large national differences in this regard; the Japanese, Turkish, and Israeli children expressed least affection while the American children expressed most affection for foreign peoples. Again, the six-year-olds were the most reluctant to express affection, and while there was a large increase at age ten, there was not much change from the ten to fourteen-year levels. In several instances, the ten-year age level was the most affectionate. Thus six-year-olds had relatively restricted similarity outlooks and were least prone to express affection for foreign peoples, whether these were thought of as similar or dissimilar. In contrast, the ten-year olds were particularly ready to view foreign peoples as similar and were especially friendly toward them, even those viewed as dissimilar. The fourteen-year-olds in general showed less openness and friendliness than the ten-year-olds; thus, the favourable orientation noted at age ten did not hold up into the teen years.

Such age changes seem to be attributable in part to parallel changes in the way children of different ages define "like us" and "not like us." Typically, six and ten-year-olds rely on clearly observable features to categorize others as different, whereas fourteen-year-olds generally make their judgments according to contrasts in personality and habits, making it more likely that they would dislike foreign groups they consider to be different. This explanation is not the whole story, however, since other factors, apparently cultural ones, play their role, too. For example, the fourteen-year-old American children had broader similarity outlooks and were more affectionate toward foreign peoples than the ten-year-olds; in contrast, the French Canadian and Japanese ten-year-olds were decidedly more friendly toward others than were the fourteen-year-olds.

When national variations in the *ethnocentrism* scores of the fourteen-year-olds were examined, we found the Bantu and Brazilian teenagers had the highest scores, indicating most ethnocentrism, and the American, English Canadian, French Canadian, Japanese, and French had the lowest. The problem comes in interpreting these scores. They suggest that American teenagers in particular are among the least ethnocentric in the world, and this is consistent with other aspects of American reactions to foreign peoples encountered in this study. But from this study alone we do not really know why the Brazilian and Bantu young people show so much ethnocentrism, relatively, or why the American, Canadian and Japanese young people show so little.

Development of a Personal and Ethnic Identity
Once these patterns of attitude components were integrated with the children's descriptions, it became clear that the manner in which the

concept of own group is taught to children and ultimately learned by them has important psychological consequences. In the *first* place, the process of establishing the concept apparently produces an exaggerated and caricatured view of one's own nation and people. Because the child's own group is repeatedly compared with various other groups, the own group becomes the focal point of the developing conception and its salient characteristics are magnified and stereotyped. We make this inference from the finding that the first signs of stereotyped thinking turned up in the descriptions children gave of their own group, not in their descriptions of foreign groups. Even at the six-year age level many different national groups of children made over-generalized statements about the personality traits of their own group while they described foreign peoples in more factual, objective terms. For instance, French children would describe "French people" as being kind, democratic, intelligent at the same time as they would describe "Japanese people" as those with slanting eyes, who eat rice and who worship ancestors. Thus, the stereotyping process itself appears to get its start in the early conceptions children develop of their own group, and it is only much later, from ten years of age on, that they start stereotyping foreign peoples. By the time they are ten and fourteen, young people look at foreign peoples as something more than comparison groups. By that age they have developed a larger repertoire of conceptual categories for thinking about people, have learned the appropriate distinctions among geographical and national units, and they give more diversified descriptions of national groups. We also found that after ten years of age, young people change their interests in people, shifting from comparisons of observable and objective characteristics to more subtle, subjective features such as personality traits and habits. They also change their sources of information—from people to the mass media—to learn about foreign groups. These important changes in interests and information sources are supplemented by other factors working toward a common effect: a heightened awareness of social pressures to think and speak as others do in their peer groups, and a growing realization that they must begin to take on more adult ways of thinking and communicating. These factors in combination appear to play important roles in the development of the teenager's stereotyped, adult-like views of foreign peoples.

In the *second* place, the early training in national contrasts appears to make certain foreign groups outstanding examples of peoples who are different. We noted a strong cross-national tendency for children, even the six-year-olds, to refer spontaneously to the same subset of foreign groups as peoples who are "not like us," suggesting that these particular peoples— blacks, Orientals and Russians—are used for the training in contrasts needed to develop a clear concept of homeland and own group. Our results suggest that the effects of this training persist at least into the teens, and, judging from the work of Isaacs (1958), may well leave durable "scratches on our minds" that will colour our reactions to certain foreign peoples throughout our lives.

Thirdly, the early training in contrasts appears to leave the impression with children that foreign peoples are different, strange, and unfriendly. As mentioned, we found that in contrast to the ten or fourteen-year-olds, the six-year-olds emphasized the differences of foreign peoples much more than the similarities, displayed particularly narrow similarity outlooks, and tended to withhold expressions of affection for foreign peoples, making their overall orientation a very suspicious one. This effect, however, seems to be less permanent than the one previously noted, since for most of the national groups studied the initial orientation became more friendly by the ten-year age level. In fact, fundamental changes take place in children's views of homeland and foreign groups between the ages of six and ten. There is strong cross-national evidence from our study that children are more inquisitive and friendly toward foreign peoples and more prone to see others as similar at the ten-year age level than at either the six or fourteen-year levels. This may be due in part to the fact that ten-year-olds are relatively well adjusted to their social world and without the pressures on them that the teenagers have to prepare themselves to move out and up as the next generation. Thus, the ten-year age period is the most friendly one, relatively, and whether the favourable views of that age level are maintained into the teens or not appears to depend on distinctive socio-cultural events taking place within each national setting.

In the *fourth* place, the early training in national contrasts also affects the child's self-conception. Judging from their self-descriptions, children in certain national settings thought of themselves in racial, religious, or national terms, whereas those from other nations made no mention of these characteristics, emphasizing instead that they were persons, or boys or girls. In other words, the self-concepts of certain groups of children reflect what we presume to be the culturally significant criteria used in training them to make distinctions between their own group and others. Furthermore, there are some indications that these same criteria may become standardized dimensions for categorizing and evaluating people in general, foreigners as well as compatriots.

We have shown that children's attitudes toward foreign peoples vary from one national setting to another. The variations indicate that parents and educators use culturally distinctive ways of teaching their children to differentiate their own group from others. In certain national settings, children develop an inquisitive and friendly attitude toward foreign peoples, seeing them as essentially similar to their own people; in other settings, children see the world as populated mainly by groups who are basically different from themselves and often this outlook is linked with unfriendly attitudes toward foreign peoples and places. It can also happen that parents in particular settings draw contrasts that are not accepted by the children so that the parents' attempt to distinguish among own group and foreigners misses its target or backfires. Thus parents may unintentionally generate in their children dissatisfactions with certain characteristics of their own ways of life, and promote invidious feelings toward foreign peoples who enjoy advantages or styles of comportment the children would like to enjoy themselves. Incidentally, in our study we encountered this type of own-group rejection among the Japanese children.

Overall, then, this study makes it clear that parents and other significant people in the child's social environment transfer their own emotionally toned views of other peoples to the child by assigning specific attributes to members of particular groups during that very period of cognitive development when the child has not differentiated one group from another or his own group from others. By incorporating these views, he learns to distinguish his own group from certain others who are said to be hateworthy, untrustworthy, and so forth. When the assignments are finally mastered, the child will be able to rationalize the generalizations that are commonly made about minority groups at home as well as peoples in foreign lands, and he will be able to use them in adult-like, socially appropriate ways. He has, in G.W. Allport's (1954) terms, been prepared for prejudice and learns how to cope in a prejudice-prone world.

Parents as Child Rearers

The study we have just examined is only a first step toward understanding the complex process of identity formation. It does however demonstrate vividly the powerful role that adult socializers play in the process, and how they arrive at cross nationally common tactics—such as the use of contrast training—to provide children with a multi-dimensional frame of reference for personal and ethnic identity. Long before explicit contrast training begins, these same adult socializers have started another equally important process, that of child rearing. The argument to follow here is that an important part of a child's personal and ethnic identity derives from the particular value templates that adult socializers use in bringing the child up. Just as they draw contrasts between own- and other-groups for their children, with the aim of highlighting own-group distinctiveness, so too parents strive to bring their children up in what they feel to be the appropriate way, a way they believe is both effective and distinctive. Children of course are on the receiving end of these influence attempts, and their ultimate identity is shaped in important ways by the child-rearing plans and hopes of parents.

Is there anything distinctive or unique about child rearing in Canada? And within Canada, are there any real differences between English-speaking and French-speaking Canadian parents in their views of how children should be brought up? To answer questions such as these, we conducted an extensive investigation of the child-rearing values of parents from various nations, including English Canadian and French Canadian parents, one sample representing working-class positions in each of the societies and a second sample representing middle-class positions (Lambert, Hamers & Frasure Smith, 1979). Fathers and mothers of six-year-old children were interviewed in their homes. The interview procedure was novel in that each parent, one at a time, was asked to listen to and then react spontaneously to tape-recorded episodes of a child, one much like their own, in various types of everyday interactions with a parent, with a younger sibling, or with a playmate invited in to play. What the child said and did in each episode was meant to evoke particular types and intensities of reactions from parents, ranging from acquiescence, through "laissez-faire," to outright anger.[1] The parent's task then was to imagine himself or herself as the parental partner in these episodes, either in direct contact with the child or as an observer, and to give spontaneous, first reactions.[2]

What emerges from this investigation, despite the variety of parental values and attitudes toward child rearing in vogue in each of the nations studied, is the interesting fact that the single most important influence on child-rearing values turns out to be the social-class background of parents, not their ethnicity. In Canada, for instance, the effects of social class are extensive and they apply as well for English as for French Canadian parents. Actually, social class plays an important role in all of the nations included in our study, but what is instructive and interesting is that Canada, one of the New World nations where social-class distinctions are often said to be of little real significance, is characterized by such pervasive and important differences in parent-child interactions which can be traced to social-class background. Three other factors play relatively less important roles: the English Canadian–French Canadian ethnicity of parents, the sex of the child, and the sex of the parent. Even so, each has its own distinctive and illuminating influence. We will consider first the role played by ethnicity since that was the basic question that got the research started in the first place, and it is the question most parents, educators and social philosophers might ask first; namely, how different or how similar are English and French Canadian parents in their approaches to child rearing?

Ethnicity of Parents
Being French or English Canadian has a direct effect on how parents deal with children's requests for *help*, their displays of *insolence*, and their requests to have *guests* in to play. In each instance it is the English Canadian relative to French Canadian parents who hold back, in the sense that they are more hesitant to give help, more controlling and harsh on insolence, and more restrictive in extending guest privileges. These contrasts make good social-psychological sense. For instance, English Canadian parents

may tend to withhold help more because they are more anxious to have their children learn to help themselves, to be independent. Such an interpretation is incidentally consonant with the data available on independence training which, according to McClelland (1961), is emphasized more in English Canadian than French Canadian communities, and, according to Rosen (1959), more in Anglo-American than Franco-American communities in the United States.

Similarly, one might develop a convincing argument for the emphasis English Canadian parents place on insolence. English Canadian parents may well feel particularly vulnerable to what seems to be a tendency in the United States for children to break away from adult control and adult direction (see Bronfenbrenner, 1970).

That the French Canadian parents have more of an open-door attitude toward guest privileges for playmates is a surprising and interesting outcome. One possible interpretation is that the French Canadian community, like most ethnic minority communities, may be more inclined to consider other members of the same minority group—including their children's playmates—as extended family members. To have survived as an ethnic group, they perhaps have had to rely on one another to a greater extent and to consider one another as co-habitants of a cultural island. It is also likely that, because of their need for strong ingroup ties, they may have learned to make sharp distinctions between members of the ingroup and members of the various outgroups that "surround" them. The English Canadian parents, in contrast, may try to foster self-sufficiency by discouraging a dependence on playmates as agents of entertainment.

There are other more subtle comparisons that emerge through the various interactions. Of special interest is the flexibility and independence that characterizes the mother role in the English Canadian families studied. The English Canadian mothers are as demanding and harsh as their husbands on matters of help withholding, insolence control and restrictiveness with regard to guest privileges, at the same time as they are more tolerant and lenient in cases of squabbles between siblings, and comfort seeking. In one sense, then, it is the English Canadian mother who plays the more active or flexible role in socializing the child since she, along with the English Canadian father, plays the role of demanding parent in particular domains of interaction and, quite independent of the English Canadian father, the softer, more comforting role in other domains.

The ramifications of this pattern could affect English Canadian children's interpersonal behaviour both within and beyond the family setting. For example, one could trace out an interesting link between attitudes of English Canadian mothers and fathers and the development of achievement motivation in English Canadian children, following the research and theory of McClelland (1961); Rosen (1961); Rosen and D'Andrade (1959); Lambert, Yackley and Hein (1971); and De Koninck and Sirois-Berliss (1978).

There are also potentially important ethnic contrasts in how parents think about sex-role differences. As a group, French Canadian middle-class mothers are particularly attentive to boy-girl differences in styles of conduct suggesting to us that they may be especially concerned about recent social movements that tend to de-emphasize traditional models of comportment for boys and girls.

Our findings also suggest that any social erosion of sex-appropriate behaviour would very likely be a source of concern to certain subgroups of Canadian parents, in particular French Canadian parents of girls and English Canadian parents of boys. What might this intriguing pattern of results mean? Only further research focussed squarely on this issue will give us any substantive answers, but one far-fetched possibility suggests itself. Perhaps in the eyes of English Canadian parents, the English Canadian culture is characterized by its economic and social aggressiveness, traditions that may be considered more masculine than feminine. In contrast, in the perspective of French Canadian parents, the cultural distinctiveness of the French Canadian society may be represented by economic and social non-aggressiveness, traditions that may be more feminine than masculine. There is, in fact, some empirical support for this idea from the work by Aboud and Taylor (1971) who found that the stereotypes held by English Canadians about English Canadians are correlated with their stereotypes of the typical male, while their stereotypes of French Canadians are correlated with stereotypes of the typical female. Thus, French Canadian parents of girls might worry about an erosion of cultural identity that would prompt their daughters to become aggressive. By the same token, English Canadian parents of boys might have similar identity concerns about their sons becoming less aggressive.

There is a parallel comparison at the social class level: working-class parents of boys have much stronger expectations of sex-role differences than do middle-class parents of boys. This contrast suggests that, in the eyes of working-class Canadian parents, boys must be "boys" to succeed in life, whereas middle-class parents are much more liberal on the issue, as though for them, the male's success in the middle-class world calls for something more than "masculine" traits. At the same time, parents of girls from working-class backgrounds are relatively less concerned about their daughters being similar to boys, suggesting that from their perspective girls would find it an advantage too to be able to cope with the harsher side of life. Middle-class parents, in contrast, seem to want their daughters to be different from boys, as though for them femininity was relatively more important and valuable.

Social-Class Background
The influence of social-class background touches parents' relations with children for nearly all of the dimensions we examined, except for *help withholding, attention denial and comfort withholding*. On all other dimensions,

it is the working-class parents—both French and English Canadian—who are the harsher or more demanding socializers. Relative to middle-class parents, they are more inclined to side with the baby and against the child when a dispute breaks out; they control displays of temper, social temper, and insolence more severely; they restrict the child more on guest privileges, side more against the child when he argues with a playmate, control more his bids for autonomy, at the same time as they both expect and perceive greater degrees of sex-role differentiations in the comportment of boys and girls.

The outstanding finding then is that Canadian parents of working-class backgrounds are decidedly more demanding and more punitive than middle-class parents in their child-rearing values. Their relative harshness is limited to provocations by the child that call for discipline and to signs of the child's early moves toward independence or autonomy. With the data available here, we can only speculate about the reasons for these parental differences in outlook. It could well be that working-class parents train their children with more severity and exigence, as a means of preparing them for the world these parents know well, a world where, because of one's lower status in society, one must be prepared to suffer, to be humiliated, and, especially, to be prepared to do what one is told. It is a world, too, where there is little room for arbitrariness about matters of sex-role comportment. Young boys have to be trained to become men, just as young girls must learn to take on the roles of women, although girls should learn to be able to take the bumps of life. Precocious moves toward independence on the part of the child might well worry working-class parents who could lose their child to outside influences before the childhood training has been completed. The training is not all harsh, however, for when aid and nurturance is called for, these discipline-oriented, working-class parents are as ready to help and comfort as anyone else.

The contrasts suggest that *middle*class parents use another world of experience as a reference point. They want their children to face experiences and to learn how to think for themselves, to be able to take care of themselves, and to be prepared to tell others what to do rather than follow directives. Early attempts at autonomy would be encouraged, and any standardized views of what constitutes manly and womanly comportment would be questioned. This contrast jibes nicely with the developmental stages of achievement motivation found by McClelland (1961) and Rosen (1961). Strength of achievement motivation they find is clearly associated with social class, and the middle-class experience not only generates relatively more achievement motivation, but it also seems to provide an earlier foundation for autonomy, for flexibility and for self-reliance.

The middle-class–working-class contrast also takes on another type of significance if one thinks of the effects relatively harsh parental socialization can have on personality development. But we must be clear here about what we mean by the terms "harsh," "demanding," "soft," or "psychological," which we have been using to contrast the approaches of middle-versus working-class Canadian parents. Recently, Guterman (1970) has made a valuable contribution by differentiating parental "punitiveness" from parental "strictness." Guterman was interested in how conscience or superego is developed in children and this of course led him to Freud. In light of research evidence, Freud's belief that severity of training favours the development of a strong superego is *wrong* if by severity he meant parental punitiveness (harsh, fear-provoking treatment), but *right* if he meant parental strictness (consistent and predictable discipline). When we try to apply this important distinction to the Canadian social class differences, we have difficulty deciding whether it is the parents of the middle or the working social class in Canada who are the more punitive or the more strict. As we see it, the Canadian working-class parents are *both* the more strict and the more punitive. They, relative to the middle class, set more definite limits on what the child can or can't do, and they expect more obedience to rules and standards. Thus, Canadian working-class children face *stricter* socialization, which should contribute to the development of a strong conscience, relative to the case of middle-class children. However, the plus of parental firmness and strictness may be offset by the greater degree of working-class parental punitiveness that we found throughout our study: Canadian working-class parents are more inclined to use threat-of-punishment or punishment techniques, while middle-class parents are more inclined to use "psychological" and "reasoning" approaches to discipline, making them more lenient, "soft" and less punitive. Of course, if the non-punitive, non-strict approach is pushed too far, it could become nothing more than the "studied neglect" of children that Bronfenbrenner (1970) worries about.

One wonders what functions are served by this working-class approach to discipline, characterized as it is by its severity in terms of both punitiveness and strictness. If it were dysfunctional we would expect it to change, even though, because of their social-class status, working-class parents may never have the time and energy needed for the more leisurely, drawn-out "psychological" approaches. Would a change in approach bring working-class parents closer to some ideal, or might middle-class parents be well advised to change toward greater strictness? But one wonders what an ideal amount of conscience might be. Too much conscience is debilitating because of the constriction and anxiety it entails. We are left with this important practical question: which social-class group in Canada has the *better* mode of developing ethical standards in children—the middle class with its relatively non-punitive, non-strict approach to child rearing, or the working class with its relatively punitive but strict approach? This question would certainly be worth exploring in future research.

Parents of Boys versus Parents of Girls

There are three instances in the Canadian study where parents of girls are harsher socializers than parents of boys: *social temper* outbursts, bids for *attention,* and *quarrels* between child and playmate. There are no counter-balancing instances where parents of boys are harsher socializers. These three forms of conduct then are particularly annoying to Canadian parents when they originate from girls. If we take into consideration the fact that the taped episodes used in the study were precisely the same in the boy and girl versions, these differences in parental reactions to sons and daughters become doubly interesting. Thus, to the extent that Canadian girls are over-disciplined for social temper displays, for quarrelling with a playmate, and are more thwarted on requests for attention, Canadian boys are relatively underdisciplined and underthwarted, by the same token.

Apparently we are dealing here with a broadly shared point of view in Canada since no ethnic differences emerge in these cases nor are there social-class differences. This means that in general Canadian parents bring girls up so that they will not be socially aggressive or attention seeking. To the extent that social aggressiveness and attention seeking are negative characteristics for Canadian girls, they are relatively positive characteristics for Canadian boys. One can look at this boy-girl contrast as the society's way of developing clear models of what is expected of men and women. There are, however, questions that this contrast brings to mind. Is it valuable or appropriate to differentiate between boys and girls in this fashion from childhood on? If social aggression is a bad trait for girls, how could it be a good trait for boys? It is this matter of training aggression *out* in one case and *in* the other that becomes particularly interesting. If it were a natural proclivity to be socially aggressive, then to discourage it in the case of girls would cause them biological and emotional harm. If it is not a natural tendency and one easy to control, why should boys be encouraged to be aggressive in this already very aggressive world? Apparently Canadian parents feel that to survive in that aggressive world, boys must be given more opportunities than girls to learn to take care of themselves. Perhaps that's why hockey is our national sport!

Mothers versus Fathers

There are two unambiguous instances in the Canadian study of mother-father value differences: one involves *attention* seeking, the other, *disputes* between the child and a playmate. In the case of attention seeking, Canadian fathers are harsher in their reactions than mothers, while in child-playmate disputes, Canadian mothers are harsher than fathers. These contrasts suggest that in Canadian families—whether English or French Canadian—there is a division of socialization responsibilities, and apparently fathers are expected to take a child's nagging or attention-getting ploys as their specialty, while mothers specialize in training the child to behave properly with those outside the family. Since we have no way of explaining why these two particular differences emerge or how the purported division of responsibilities develop, it would be worthwhile to explore further the possibility that Canadian fathers are expected to be more responsible for keeping peace within the family while mothers are expected to be more responsible for smooth relationships with others in the community.

What is noteworthy in the Canadian study is that we found no evidence for cross-sex permissiveness," that is, instances where fathers are differently more permissive with daughters than sons and mothers more permissive with sons than daughters. In their American study, Rothbart and Maccoby (1966) found a large number of examples of cross-sex permissiveness, while we found no cross-sex permissiveness in our Canadian study. Instead we found some examples of "same-sex" permissiveness.

Canadian Child-Rearing Values in a Cross-National Perspective

The Canadian comparisons we have highlighted so far need to be placed in a broader, cross-national framework. In the overall investigation we have drawn on (Lambert, Hamers & Frasure-Smith, 1979) Canadian parents represent two out of ten national groups: Americans, English Canadians, French Canadians, English, French, French Belgians, Flemish Belgians, Italians, Greeks and Portuguese. In each case, information on both working- and middle-class subgroups of parents was available.[3] We can use these as background to see which value features, if any, of a particular group hold as distinctive when viewed from a cross-national perspective and which, if any, hold up for all ten national groups.

What we find is that many of the values that stood out as different and distinctive in the two- or three-nation comparisons level off or disappear on the "wider screen" of a ten-nation comparison. But what is fascinating is that not all narrow-screen contrasts fade away on the wide screen, that is, some national value characteristics hold up as distinctive while others become stable cross-national patterns. The question of interest here, then, is: How distinctive are English Canadian and French Canadian parents' values in this broader context?

The English Canadian Parents

In the ten-nation comparison, our sub-samples of English Canadian parents stand out as relatively severe and demanding and they are clearly the most demanding of the three North American parental groups represented. The way this parental severity or harshness is shown, however, varies with the social-class background of the parents. The English Canadian working-class parents rank as the harshest of all ten working-class subgroups on matters of discipline (composite rank order = 1), but are more lenient on requests for *aid* (requests for help, attention, comfort, autonomy, guest privileges), ranking near the average (composite rank order = 5.5). In contrast, the middle-class English Canadian parents rank among the most lenient groups on the *discipline* issues (composite rank order = 8), but among the most harsh on the *aid* issues (composite rank order = 3). In general, social-class contrasts are large for English Canadian parents on matters of discipline and on the issue of granting the child autonomy, but are less pronounced on the other aid issues. What happens on the aid issues, then, is that the working-class parents are relatively more lenient than they are on discipline matters, while the middle-class parents are relatively less lenient. Apparently there are strong social norms in English Canada that affect parents' modes of disciplining and granting aid to children.

On certain issues, though, English Canadian parents are essentially North American, in the sense that they are similar to Americans and different from Europeans. For instance, like our sub-samples of American parents, they are ready to grant the six-year-old autonomy, and they expect relatively few sex-role differences.

In the ten-nation context, English Canadian parents are also distinctive by their harshness on temper displays, particularly temper directed to things rather than people. On this matter, the English Canadian working class are the most severe of all ten working-class subgroups, and the middle class too are among the three most severe middle-class subgroups. Why so much attention is given to materialistic in contrast to social forms of temper displays in Canada remains a puzzle. It is not an American tendency because American parents are not particularly severe on non-social displays of temper, whereas English Canadian parents of both social classes are. Temper control aside, middle-class English Canadian parents otherwise fall more toward the lenient pole on matters of discipline while working-class English Canadian parents fall clearly near the severe pole. On the aid issues, both working- and middle-class English Canadian parents tend to withhold help and guest privileges relative to other national groups, whereas they are very compliant—and thus very North American—toward a child's requests for autonomy. Like their American counterparts, English Canadian mothers are more ready than English Canadian fathers to extend comfort and to minimize child-baby disputes. Finally, and also like their American counterparts, daughters are treated more harshly on the child-guest quarrel issue than are sons.

The French Canadian Parents

In terms of leniency-harshness, our French Canadian parents are very similar to English Canadian parents on the discipline issues, but different from them on the aid issues. As with English Canadians, social class variations are large on matters of discipline, but of much less importance on aid matters. Thus, the French Canadian middle-class parents rank as very lenient on both discipline and aid issues while the working-class subgroup ranks among the harshest on discipline, but unlike their English Canadian counterparts, relatively lenient on aid matters. Interestingly, the French Canadian middle-class parents are comparatively harsh only in response to non-social temper outbursts, the same feature that stood out for middle- and working-class English Canadian subgroups. There appears then to be a distinctively Canadian middle-class reaction to a child's threat to break things; both French and English middle-class subgroups react with relative severity in this instance.

On the sex-role issue, the French Canadian parents are also similar to English Canadians since both groups have low expectations of sex-role differentiations, and in both cases, sex-role perceptions are generally in line with expectations.

In French Canadian families, fathers are more prone than mothers to extend comfort to a six-year-old, making them different from both American and English Canadian fathers, and on the child-guest dispute issue, sons are treated more leniently than daughters, making French Canadian parents like both their American and their English Canadian counterparts.

Overall, however, the French Canadian, English Canadian and American parents form a North American set. Although they differ from each other in distinctive ways and in the degrees of harshness or leniency displayed in their approaches to child rearing, they are alike in so many ways that, as a regional set, they contrast with our European samples on issues like autonomy and sex-role differentiations. Furthermore, in each of the three North American settings, there is a sharp difference in approach to matters of discipline, depending upon the social-class background of the family: middle-class North American parents are much more permissive and lenient than working-class parents when the child's behaviour calls for discipline. In fact, North American middle-class parents prefer to divert, distract or at the most scold rather than threaten or actually punish a child who misbehaves. Social class is less important on aid issues for American families. Finally, parents in North America have relatively low sex-role expectations—they tend toward unisexism—and their perceptions of sex-role differences are generally in line with their expectations.

What we come to then is the intriguing conclusion that, if one takes a broad enough perspective, English Canadian and French Canadian parents are not all that distinctive in their approaches to child rearing. They actually end up being pretty much North American and not nearly so "English" Canadian or "French" Canadian as those ethnic suffixes imply. In fact, our results indicate that English Canadian and French Canadian parents of the same social-class background are more similar in their child-rearing values than either group is with same-ethnic parents of a different social class. Furthermore, it appears that English Canadian and French Canadian parents of a particular social-class background are, in terms of these values, more like American, Greek, Portuguese, Italian or Belgian parents of the same social-class background. Thus, we come full circle here, and now begin to seriously wonder how much "distinctiveness" is real and how much is imaginary with adults who, in large measure, get the own-group–other-group contrasts started in the first place.

In conclusion, what I have tried to do here is to show how some of us in social psychology in Canada are exploring the processes by which children develop their identities, as individuals and as members of particular groups. At the same time as we develop various ideas about the general phenomenon of identity formation, we also develop and try out various methodologies in order to evaluate the worth of our hunches. Some of these hunches and methodologies have been sketched out here, and although we are as yet far from having all pieces of the puzzle in place, we are nonetheless excited with the prospect that we have at least some of the parts in hand, and that some of these are beginning to fit.

FOOTNOTES

[1] The parents' responses to each taped episode were coded in terms of the following scales: *Help Withholding, Comfort Withholding, Temper Control, Social Temper Control, Insolence Control, Siding with Baby vs. Child, Attention Denial, Autonomy Control, Guest Restrictions,* and *Siding with Guest vs. Child.* In addition, parents were also asked to complete two questionnaires: a scale of *Perceived Differences in Sex-Roles* which probed parents' perceptions of how similar or different boys and girls are in their typical behaviours or reactions, and a scale of *Expected Differences in Sex-Roles* which measured parents' expectations about sex-role differences in behaviour.

[2] The details of the procedure, the coding and the reliability of coding are given in chapter 1 and the Appendices of Lambert, Hamers and Frasure-Smith (1979).

[3] Data for middle-class Japanese parents are also given in Lambert, Hamers and Frasure-Smith (1979).

REFERENCES

Aboud, F.E., & Taylor, D.M. Ethnic and role stereotypes: Their relative importance in person perception. *Journal of Social Psychology.* 1971, *85*, 17-21.

Allport, G.W. *The Nature of Prejudice.* Boston: Beacon Press, 1954, 307-308.

Allport, G.W. The historical background of modern social psychology. In Lindsey, G. and Aronson E. (eds.), *The Handbook of Social Psychology.* Don Mills: Addison-Wesley, 1968.

Bronfenbrenner, U. *Two Worlds of Childhood: U.S. and U.S.S.R.* New York: Russell Sage Foundation, 1970.

DeKoninck, J., & Sirois-Berliss, M. La motivation au rendement dans les rêves et durant l'éveil chez des étudiants canadiens-français et canadiens-anglais. *Canadian Journal of Behavioural Science,* 1978, *10*, 329-338.

Guterman, S.S. *The Machiavellians.* Lincoln: University of Nebraska Press, 1970.

Isaacs, H.R. *Scratches on Our Minds: American Images of China and India.* New York: John Day, 1958.

Lambert, W.E., Hamers, J.F., & Frasure-Smith, N. *Child-rearing Values: A Cross-national Study.* New York: Praeger Publications, 1979.

Lambert, W.E., & Klineberg, O. *Children's Views of Foreign Peoples: A Cross-national Study.* New York: Appleton-Century-Crofts, 1967.

Lambert, W.E., Yackley, A., & Hein, R. Child-training values of English Canadian and French Canadian parents. *Canadian Journal of Behavioural Science,* 1971, *3*, 217-236.

McClelland, D.C. *The Achieving Society.* New York: Van Nostrand, 1961.

Morse, N.C., & Allport, F.H. The causation of anti-semitism: An investigation of seven hypotheses. *Journal of Psychology,* 1952, *34*, 197-233.

Piaget, J., & Weil, A.M. The development in children of the idea of the homeland and of relations with other countries. *International Social Science Bulletin,* 1951, *3*, 561-578.

Rosen, B.C. Race, ethnicity and the achievement syndrome. *American Sociological Review,* 1959, *24*, 47-60.

Rosen, B.C. Family structure and achievement motivation. *American Sociological Review,* 1961, *26*, 574-585.

Rosen, B.C., & D'Andrade, R.G. The psychosocial origins of achievement motivation. *Sociometry,* 1959, *22*, 185-218.

Rothbart, M.K. & Maccoby, E.E. Parents' differential reactions to sons and daughters. *Journal of Personality and Social Psychology,* 1966, *4*, 237-243.

Section III
The Language Issue

Chapter 5

Social Policy and Second Language Teaching

G. Richard Tucker, Center for Applied Linguistics

During the past decade a great deal of research, theorizing and discussion about various facets of language learning and language teaching have occurred in Canada and in other countries. The continuing dialogue has involved parents, educators, researchers and even policy makers at the highest levels. This really should not seem surprising if you stop to consider that there are many more bilinguals in the world than mono-linguals and that there are many more students who by choice or by necessity attend schools where the medium of instruction is their second or later acquired language rather than their mother tongues. Bilingualism is the rule, rather than the exception, in many heavily populated countries such as China, India, Nigeria and the Philippines and a majority of the children in many countries receive at least some portion of their schooling in a language other than their mother tongue—for example, Afghanistan, Kenya, Morocco, and Paraguay.

In Canada, the necessity exists to develop a citizenry of whatever ethnic origin who are functionally bilingual in English and in French. The policy of the federal government through the Official Languages Act of 1969 explicitly advocates the encouragement of bilingualism. Although drastic steps have been taken within the last five years to upgrade the second language skills of federal civil servants at all levels, the effective development of a bilingual citizenry will probably necessitate major educational reform such as that now occurring within English school boards in many areas of Quebec and Ontario and take several generations. To date, the language-training programs conducted by the Public Service Commission seem to have been singularly unsuccessful. Bibeau (1976) has shown, for example, that a majority of trainees—highly placed federal civil servants—remained disfluent in the second language despite lengthy training and that they resented being taken away from their jobs.

In the United States, many of the recent educational innovations have been prompted by the challenge to provide effective second language teaching within the context of a public school system while simultaneously nurturing the native language development and sociocultural tradition of increasingly large and heterogeneous student populations. According to the most recent survey, approximately twenty-eight million persons (one in eight) in the United States are estimated to have non-English language backgrounds. Contrary to common belief, most of these persons are *not* foreign, but are native born. Some 10.6 million of these people have

Spanish language backgrounds, so that the United States has the fifth largest Hispanic population among the nations of the world.

Of the total, there are an estimated 3.6 million school-age children of varying levels of English ability in the four- to eighteen-year age group. They represent approximately 6 per cent of the school-age population and are concentrated in the southwestern United States. Spanish is by far the most prevalent non-English language spoken among the minority language groups, accounting for some 69 per cent—an estimated 2.1 million children. A review of enrollment patterns in the public school system reveals a very clear trend: while general school enrollment continues to decline, there is a definite projected increase in the numbers of limited English-proficient students. For example, in New York, the population of such students has grown from 28.2 per cent in 1975 to 29.5 per cent in 1978. In Los Angeles, there has been an increase from 56,036 in 1973 to 85,337 in 1977: by the year 1985, it is estimated that the Hispanic population will comprise over 50 per cent of the school-age population. When it is realized that this group of non-English speakers is larger than the population of Canada, the myth of the United States as a linguistic and cultural melting pot is cast into sharp relief. The challenge, in this case, appears to be leading to the implementation of federally or state funded bilingual education programs for non-English speakers in many communities (see, for example, Alatis & Twaddell, 1976; Troike & Modiano, 1975). It is interesting to observe, however, that the recently completed report by the President's Commission on Foreign Language and International Studies (1979) (a President's Commission in the United States is similar to a Royal Commission in Canada) noted widespread concern in the United States about the general apathy toward foreign language study.

In many other countries of the world—particularly those of the so called Third World—a very different situation seems to exist. With the relatively recent advent of universal primary education—that is, the right of *all* children in a particular country to receive government financed primary education—the desire to ensure literacy in the mother tongue, to maximize the relevance of education for those who will likely not complete their schooling and to enhance national pride and unity probably far overshadow the goal of developing the highest possible level of second language proficiency in a select elite. Thus, in many countries, decisions have recently been taken to *decrease* the use of a foreign language as a medium of instruction in that country's schools (e.g., French in Algeria, English in the Philippines, English in the Sudan) or even to *decrease* the amount of time devoted to teaching the foreign language as a subject (e.g., English in Jordan and in the Sudan). Despite such decisions, many individuals have a demonstrated need for greater foreign language proficiency than ever before and, of course, with the advent of universal primary education more individuals are in school than ever before (see, for example, Harrison, Prator & Tucker, 1975; Tucker, 1977).

It is within the context of evolving social realities such as these that diverse investigators have examined the influence of individual, instructional and social factors on second language learning. They have attempted to define more precisely "what it is" that the student or learner acquires and *how* as well as *why* this changes over time as a result of continued instruction or exposure to a community of target language speakers.

National Policy, Educational Planning and Language Teaching

A basic assumption underlying this chapter is that it is essential to examine various aspects of second language learning and teaching within the broad framework of educational planning. The selection of a language to be taught or to be used as a medium of instruction clearly constitutes an important aspect of educational and of national planning (see, for example, Fishman, 1974). Educational or national policy serves to define the parameters within which language-teaching programs can be developed.

The Situation in Other Countries

Consider the Sudan—a linguistically diverse, geographically immense country (the largest in Africa) with the potential, as yet unrealized, to become a major agricultural resource for the entire Arab World. During the time of the Anglo-Egyptian Sudan, English was the medium of instruction in many of the schools throughout the country. More recently, a number of small but incrementally rather dramatic changes have occurred which have eroded the official position of English within the country but not diminished its importance. In the northern provinces of the country, Arabic is the exclusive medium of instruction in the "public" schools through the end of the secondary cycle. The introduction of English as a subject for study was changed from Grade 5 to Grade 7; the number of periods per week devoted to English instruction was reduced by two; the length of individual periods for all subjects was reduced; English was declared to be no longer a required "pass" subject for the secondary school leaving examination; *but* English remains the medium of instruction at the University of Khartoum as well as at the two newly opened universities of Gezira and Juba. It has long been rumoured that the universities will eventually arabicize.

The situation in the north of the Sudan contrasts sharply with that in the six southern provinces. In the south, English continues to be the major link language and, in fact, is used in many different situations to link the north and the south. It has been decided to use one of the (at least nine) local vernaculars as the initial medium of primary education with English and Arabic to be taught as second languages and English to be used as the medium of instruction at the secondary level. This radical difference in policy between north and south represents a major concession by the north—a concession articulated in the Addis Ababa agreement of 1972 which concluded a seventeen-year civil war in which language was one of the precipitating factors. If the country is to survive politically, linguistic diversity must not only be tolerated, it must be encouraged.

The Situation in Canada

Consider the case of Canada—in particular the Province of Quebec. With the passage in 1974 of the Official Language Act, French became the sole official language of the province. A number of associated regulations—most prominent of which was Bill 101, the Charter of the French language—were promulgated to insure that French became the *de facto* as well as the *de jure* language. For example, demonstrable proficiency in French is now a requisite for membership in professional groups such as the corporation of dentists, psychologists or physicians. In addition, companies are required to obtain "francization" certificates to be eligible to compete for government contracts, subsidies, and so forth. To qualify, French must not only be the actual working language of the organization, but Francophones must also be represented at various levels of the company hierarchy including upper managerial positions.

Perhaps the single most important and controversial provision of Bill 101, however, was that which limited future access to English-medium schools to the children of Anglophone parents who had themselves received their primary schooling in English in Quebec. The passage and implementation of Bill 101 has meant that a majority of the Quebec population can no longer receive some portion of their education in English-medium schools, nor can they work at jobs where English is the *de facto* language of wider communication. Even formal programs of French-English bilingual education are specifically prohibited for the children of non-Anglophone parents or the children of Anglophone parents from other Canadian provinces or countries. Despite this government action, the need for English by Quebec residents—Anglophone, Francophone or other immigrant—who wish to pursue business or trading opportunities with representatives from an increasingly large array of industrialized or developing countries has *not* diminished. The burden of responsibility for meeting this need thus falls on the English as a second language (ESL) program within the French educational sector.

Acheson, d'Anglejan, de Bagheera and Tucker (1978) conducted a survey of 112 Quebec provincial ESL teachers participating in a government-sponsored in-service-training program. Despite the fact that the Anglophone population of Quebec numbers at least 400,000, fewer than 2 per cent of the teachers spoke English as their native language. Only 21 per cent had previously completed an ESL training program; a majority reported that they were teaching English because it was essentially the only job available to them; and as a group the teachers' English-language proficiency scores on the Michigan Test of English Language Proficiency were such that they would *not* have qualified for admission to the majority of North American English-medium universities. Furthermore, and perhaps most discouraging, there was no indication that the teachers represented in this sample would be able to contribute to the promotion among their students of a sensitivity to and appreciation for the cultural values of the Anglo-Canadian group.

How different the situations are in the Province of Quebec and in the south of the Sudan and how different the outcomes of the English teaching programs are likely to be in these two disparate settings! Clearly, educational or national policy defines the parameters within which language teaching programs can be developed. Furthermore, it is obvious that social pressures motivated by a diverse array of contributory factors can lead to policy change. The results *per se* of empirical research—even when widely publicized—however, rarely do.

Specifying Language Teaching Objectives

Much more serious attention needs to be given to the task of defining, publicizing and implementing *locally appropriate* language teaching goals. For example, is it realistic to expect all pupils to develop native speaker control in each of the four skills—listening, speaking, reading, writing—of the target language? Should the objective, rather, be for an individual to develop native-like receptive skills together with the communicative ability necessary to express his/her ideas even if the resulting message is not grammatical? How do prospective teachers, employers or other native speakers of the target language react to spoken or written messages that, although comprehensible, are marked by deviant grammar or pronunciations (see, for example, research by Schachter, Tyson & Diffley, 1976; Tucker & Sarofim, 1979)? It may, for example, be perfectly acceptable for an English Canadian member of the Ontario Provincial Parliament who lives in Toronto to understand spoken and written French with ease while producing utterances which are markedly deviant. On the other hand, it would probably be totally unacceptable for an English Canadian member of the Quebec National Assembly to perform similarly. This is an area in which very little systematic research has been conducted to date. The task of defining a set of locally appropriate goals—now frequently referred to as conducting a "needs assessment"—necessitates an understanding of the sociolinguistic context in which the graduates of the language program will live and work. Such research is often conducted by applied linguists working with anthropologists trained in ethnographic field methods.

Within the past decade, sociolinguistic or language policy surveys have been conducted in a number of countries to provide information about the patterns of language use within a particular region or country, the aims for language teaching, the dimensions of the language teaching effort, the various resources available to implement the programs—all within the context of the actual demonstrated needs which people have for the target language(s) in diverse daily activities (see, for example, the work of Bender, Bowen, Cooper & Ferguson, 1976 in Ethiopia; Harrison, Prator & Tucker, 1975 in Jordan; Ladefoged, Glick, & Griper, 1972 in Uganda; Ohannessian & Kashoki, 1978 in Zambia; Royal Commission on Bilingualism and Biculturalism, 1967 in Canada; Whiteley, 1974 in Kenya). Such surveys are based on the assumption that people's needs for a particular target language should be allowed to influence the scope and design of the language teaching program—an assumption which has certainly not characterized the development of programs in many countries. Tucker and d'Anglejan have suggested that the first step in establishing an innovative language teaching program "should involve a small-scale sociolinguistic survey of the local community where the program will be situated" (1971, p. 492). In practice, this is rarely done.

But how are language teaching objectives to be developed? Consider the directive of the Official Language Act, the predecessor of Bill 101 of the Province of Quebec:

> The curricula must ensure that pupils receiving their instruction in English acquire a knowledge of spoken and written French, and the Ministry of Education shall adopt the necessary measures to that effect.

> The Ministry of Education must also take the necessary measures to ensure instruction in English as a second language to pupils whose language of instruction is French. (Bill No. 22, Title III, Chapter V, Article 44)

This directive is certainly not very precise. Although one might argue that the task of a legislature is simply to provide the mandate under which appropriate experts will develop the explicit goals or objectives of the language-teaching program, consider the set of "specific" objectives for Jordanian students which were developed by experts from the national Ministry of Education. By the end of the Compulsory Cycle (i.e., after studying English as a foreign language for five years from Grades 5-9), students are expected to be able to:

1. Understand simple English spoken at a normal speed.
2. Communicate sensibly with an English-speaking person, within certain reasonable areas.
3. Read simple English with ease, fluency and understanding.
4. Write a basic paragraph in English, using the basic structure of the language.

These "specific" aims typify the conventional goals so often cited for language study. They lack precision, and fail to make clear precisely what degree of English or other language proficiency students are expected to achieve. A similar lack of specificity characterizes the goals of second language teaching programs—whether they are English or French—in most of the provinces of Canada. Ultimately, of course, in many parts of Canada the success of a second language program will be measured by the ability of school graduates to perform successfully at jobs in the public or the private sector where they use the second language without having to take remedial or other supplementary language training.

Another major factor which shapes the actual language teaching program is the examination system. In many areas the final second language attainment of each school graduate is evaluated by his/her success or failure on the English (or French) paper of a secondary certificate examination, and often the form and content of this examination affects the manner and substance of second language teaching. Even where there exist relatively explicit objectives for second language teaching, there is often a lack of correspondence between the objectives and the items on the examination. In such cases, teachers often concentrate their attention on "preparing" their students for the required examination. It is not inconceivable that students who pass the English paper of the Egyptian Thannawiyya 'amma or of the Quebec matriculation exam can also communicate accurately and confidently, but the hypothesis remains for the most part untested.

The Implementation of Language Teaching Policies
In recent years, the topic of second language learning and teaching has attracted the attention of an increasing number of researchers drawn from a wide range of academic disciplines (see, for example, chapters 6 and 7 of this volume). In addition to educators concerned with discovering and applying new and better pedagogical techniques, there is now also an active group of anthropologists, linguists, psychologists and sociologists engaged in the systematic study of the complex interplay among affective, cognitive, social and other factors in second language acquisition.

A number of scholars have proposed useful models or frameworks within which questions related to second language learning and teaching can be examined (see, for example, Fox, 1975; Strevens, 1976). In Figure 5.1, this domain is represented graphically by using three concentric circles.

The outermost represents the *sociocultural* context in which the langugae is spoken natively, in which it is to be learned as a second or foreign language and is to be used for diverse purposes. It comprises elements such as: (1) the official position and allocated role(s) of the target language in the community, nation or region; (2) the perceived status of the language and its speakers; (3) the existence of structures which encourage or facilitate the use of the target language; (4) the size and cohesiveness of the groups in contact; and (5) the correspondence between their values, attitudes and traditions (cf. Gardner, 1977).

The middle circle represents the *instructional* or pedagogical setting—the context in which the language is to be transmitted "formally" from a teacher or other resource person to the learner. Salient components at this level are factors such as (1) the goals whether explicit or implicit for second language teaching; (2) the pedagogical techniques to be employed; (3) the design of the syllabus including the choice or development and sequencing of materials and the allocation of time; (4) the training and language proficiency of the teacher as well as the attitudes of teachers and administrators; and (5) the procedures for evaluation. The interface between these two circles is effected by educational planning within the context of national or regional priorities.

Figure 5.1
Context for Language Learning and Teaching

Sociocultural
Context

Instructional
Setting

Individual
Factors

Educational
Planning

Choice of
Instructional Track

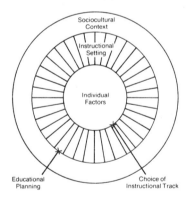

The innermost circle represents *individual* factors. The second language learner brings with him to the learning environment a variety of attitudes, biological predispositions, learned behaviour and societal experiences that affect the course, the duration and the speed of second language learning. Important factors at this level may be elements such as: (1) age; (2) intelligence and language aptitude; (3) learning style or general cognitive processes drawn upon; (4) personality characteristics; and (5) motivation and attitude. The interface between the innermost and the middle circle is effected when the learner by choice or by necessity begins to follow one of a large variety of instructional tracks such as the typical Canadian second language programs or French immersion programs. The components or elements identified at each level are, of course, only illustrative; they are by no means exhaustive.

How has research—specifically that conducted during the last decade or so—helped us to understand better the process of second language learning and teaching?

Types of Research Investigations of Second Language Learning

This section will consider some of the important research trends, research applications and existing lacunae where additional investigations may be warranted. The term "research" should be interpreted very broadly to include, for example, attempts: (1) to describe what it is that the learner acquires during his course of instruction; (2) to posit and verify models to describe the process of second language learning; and (3) to examine the contributions or relationships among the diverse elements described earlier.

During the 1960s the efficacy of language teaching programs based upon notions derived from behaviourist views of learning was seriously questioned. Disenchantment with student achievement was rampant. In Quebec, for example, it seemed to be the case that an English-speaking youngster who had studied French as a second language for eight years was still not able to engage in extended conversation with Francophones in downtown Montreal.

As a result of provocative writing and research by Chomsky (1965, 1972) and his colleagues, the operational definition of language learning underlying most research shifted from one which considered the child's linguistic growth to be the result of reinforcement or shaping by the environment to what Brown (1973) has described as a creative construction process. Child language was no longer viewed as a defective or haphazard form of adult speech but rather as an orderly, rule-governed system which evolves through a series of predictable stages toward eventual adult competence.

The incisive notion that second language learning, even within the classroom context, might reveal patterns and regularities similar to those found in native language learning had, of course, been posited by a number of scholars. Researchers observed that in addition to errors in second language learning attributable to interference from the learner's mother tongue (which seem especially prominent at the elementary stages of instruction) there are other common systematic errors which *cannot* be attributed to interference and which are found in the speech of learners from a variety of language backgrounds studying the same target language. For example, speakers of French, Spanish, Russian, and Tagalog studying English would all show a common set of errors, which probably result from the application of general operating principles, learning strategies or cognitive processes to the task at hand. These errors are in a sense perfectly natural and predictable. An important pedagogical notion which derives from this work is that second language teachers should come to regard "errors" as indicators of progress while at the same time continuing to provide their students with well-formed and varied models.

Research Concerned with what the Learner Acquires

One important direction to this research has been the attempt to define more precisely *what* it is that the student (or the "free" learner) acquires and *how* as well as *why* this changes over time as a result of continued instruction or exposure to a community of target language speakers. Thus, a broad-ranging series of studies (see Hatch, 1978) have been conducted to examine the acquisition of various features of the second language such as grammatical or semantic information—the auxiliary system, negation, *wh* questions, and other perhaps "higher order" syntactic structures such as the use of embedding devices or other connectors, as well as phonology. Researchers have attempted to draw inferences from a variety of cross-sectional or longitudinal studies conducted with learners from different backgrounds about the effects of factors such as age, formality and type of language training and frequency of exposure, on second language acquisition.

The results of the research completed to date indicate that the performance of the learner is *not* random or disorganized. For example, French-speaking as well as Spanish-speaking students pass through the same series of stages on the way to acquiring the rules for English negation. At an early stage students negate by simply saying "No + verb," for example, *I no want, I no study.* Later they use "don't + verb" as in *he don't study, he don't like.* Finally, they analyze and use appropriately the "helping" element as in *he doesn't like.* This type of research which is concerned with defining more precisely what it is that the learner acquires and how and why this product changes over time is of central importance for the development of effective second language teaching programs. A clearer understanding of the discrepancy between well-articulated goals for second language teaching and the typical product should aid diagnostic procedures and facilitate the introduction of corrective action when and where appropriate.

Research has also been conducted which has examined the contributions or relationships among factors or elements of the three concentric circles referred to earlier and used to define the context for second language learning and teaching.

Research Concerned with Sociocultural and Individual Factors

At the outermost or sociocultural level, many researchers such as Fishman (Fishman, *et al.,* 1966; Fishman, Cooper & Ma, 1971), Lambert (1973) and

Lieberson (1970) have provided continuing reminders that language learning occurs within a social context, that research strategies must involve attempts to examine the values, attitudes, traditions, political factors and sociocultural dynamics that underlie language learning and that research must be interdisciplinary.

At the innermost, or *individual* level a plethora of studies have been conducted which seek to examine, to measure or to manipulate a diverse array of individual characteristics. Research involving attitudinal/ motivational variables and language aptitude has been treated in more detail in chapter 6 of this book. For example, researchers have investigated in various permutations the relationship among age, affective factors, "ability" factors, learning stages or style, and second language learning. Two general conclusions can be drawn from these studies: (1) aptitude and attitude/motivation comprise statistically independent and significant predictors of language learning success; and (2) youthful vs. adult learners *may* approach the language learning task differently and hence profit from different teaching approaches. The influences of personality variables and differences in cognitive learning styles remain as yet little understood and research continues in these areas (see, for example, Naiman, Fröhlich & Stern, 1975). The major application of these studies derives from the fact that teachers can affect or manipulate attitude and motivation and can design programs of instruction appropriate to the age, experience, ability and interest of their students. The apparent popularity and success of "English for Special Purposes" programs lend credence to this claim (see, for example, Crandall, 1979; ESPMENA).

During the past two years, a few researchers working at this level have begun to phrase their questions and shape their data gathering techniques slightly differently. They are attempting to define the constellation of individual factors associated with successful second language learning and, furthermore, to determine whether the effects of these factors can be modulated by the language teaching program which a student is following. The results of the few studies conducted to date indicate that the study of individual differences in second language learning and factors associated with them can be pursued usefully.

Research Concerned with the Instructional Setting

Research at the *instructional* level has been profoundly affected by the theoretical insights and empirical research results of the past decade. One of the important pedagogical notions which derives from insights about native language learning is that the major focus of second language classroom activity should be on communication—not just of simulated dialogues—but on genuine communication where the validity of student utterances will be judged on the basis of their content rather than on the appropriateness of their grammatical form (Diller, 1975; Tucker & d'Anglejan, 1975). The apparent acceptance of this notion manifests itself in diverse ways: (1) by the adoption of seemingly radical objectives and techniques on the part of some teachers in which they emphasize the ability to *communicate* effectively rather than the necessity to be grammatically perfect; (2) by the switch from structurally graded syllabi to ones based on the "notions" (such as promising, requesting, denying) that learners must acquire; (3) by the development of English for Special Purposes texts and courses throughout much of the Third World where English occupies the role of an important foreign or second language; (4) and by a widespread move toward the implementation of apparently successful bilingual education programs in many parts of North America and particularly of French immersion programs for Anglophone youngsters in many parts of Canada (Swain, 1978). Such innovations all attempt to capitalize on the observation that a student can acquire effectively a second language when the task of learning the language becomes incidental to the task of communicating with someone about something which is inherently interesting.

Immersion Programs in the Canadian Context
The French immersion programs represent an exciting, locally initiated response to a vexing linguistic and social problem. The original program in the community of St. Lambert, Quebec, was developed in direct response to *parental* pressure for improved French language teaching programs for English youngsters (see Lambert & Tucker, 1972).

In September 1965, the South Shore Protestant Regional School Board began its first experimental French "immersion" classes for a group of kindergarten children. This project, designed to promote functional bilingualism through a policy of home and school language switch, was initiated by the Board on an experimental basis in response to numerous requests from parents living in the community. The program which started out with two kindergarten classes in one school during 1965-66 has expanded throughout the South Shore system, throughout the Protestant school system of Quebec and indeed throughout all of Canada. In fact, there are now immersion programs operating in all ten provinces. They share a number of common features which are described below.

The kindergarten curriculum has been left largely to the discretion of the participating teachers who stress vocabulary development and passive comprehension skills in French along with other traditional kindergarten activities. They use a direct native language approach, in contrast to the second language methods typically used with English-speaking children. By the end of the school year, most children have built up an extensive recognition vocabulary and attempt to use single French vocabulary items as well as occasional short sentences. Productive skills vary considerably from one child to the next, but all are able to comprehend, without difficulty, simple children's stories as well as their teacher's directions.

At Grade 1, reading, writing and arithmetic are introduced exclusively via French. No attempt is made to teach the children to read in English, and parents are specifically urged *not* to do so in the home. In Grade 2 (in some schools, Grade 3), two daily half-hour periods of English Language Arts are introduced. The rest of the curriculum remains essentially the same, with reading, writing, arithmetic and elementary science being taught via French. The amount of instruction via English is increased gradually and by Grade 6 approximately 50 per cent of the curriculum is taught in English by Anglophone teachers and approximately 50 per cent in French by Francophones.

Thus far, the program for secondary school has been less well regulated although attempts are being made to provide appropriate follow-up or maintenance courses in French Language Arts and to offer selected content subjects in French. Typically, this has meant that graduates of early immersion programs have followed an accelerated or native speaker French Language Arts program during Grades 7 to 11 and have had the option of studying one content subject (e.g., geography, economics) per year in French. The options available to students have been relatively limited but they will presumably increase as larger numbers of pupils with immersion training enter the secondary system.

During the past decade, there has been a plethora of research studies conducted with children participating in early immersion programs in the provinces of Quebec, Ontario and New Brunswick which has been summarized in a number of reports published in *The Canadian Modern Language Review*.

In general, the progress of pupils in experimental classes has been compared each year with that of carefully selected control classes of French children instructed via French and English pupils taught via English. Control classes in all settings (Montreal, Ottawa, Toronto, St. Johns) were selected from schools in comparable middle-class neighbourhoods.

Each spring, starting at Grade 1, experimental and control classes in various settings have been given an extensive battery of individual and group tests devised to assess their intellectual and cognitive development: achievement tests in French and English Language Arts; tests in mathematics involving both problem solving and computation given in French and English; tests in science; listening comprehension in both languages; English and French-speaking skills; foreign sound discrimination tests; flexibility and creativity measures; verbal and non-verbal IQ tests as well as attitudinal inventories designed to measure the attitudes of the children in the experimental and control groups toward their own and other selected ethnolinguistic groups such as European French and French Canadians.

On the basis of this comprehensive testing program it can be concluded that this innovative approach to second language teaching has *not* resulted in any native language or subject matter (i.e., arithmetic or science) deficit. Nor does there appear to be any cognitive retardation attributable to participation in this program. In summary, experimental pupils appear to be able to read, write, speak, understand, and use English as well as youngsters instructed via English in the conventional manner. In addition and at no "cost" they can also read, write, speak and understand French in a way that English pupils who follow a traditional French as a Second Language program never do. These children have acquired a mastery of the basic elements of French phonology, morphology and syntax; but they have not developed the inhibition which so often characterizes the performance of the foreign or second language student. With additional experience in the spontaneous use of the French language in diverse, out-of-school settings, while maintaining progress with the more formal skills through a continuing program of bilingual instruction, these children and others with similar opportunities could progress toward balanced bilingualism.

In conclusion, it is important to note that the first two classes of youngsters have now graduated from secondary school and have reported satisfaction with the early immersion experience as a means of developing a high degree of skill in French as well as a feeling of confidence that they could work, study or live in either a French or English environment and a willingness and desire to meet and integrate with French-speaking Canadians.

There is no "scientific" data base or empirical evidence which demonstrates conclusively that we have yet designed the ideal program or programs by which a second language can be *taught*; but we do know, that almost any student (and we see ample evidence) placed in the appropriate milieu, given ample opportunity and the support of his parents, peers and teachers can *acquire* successfully a second language—the paradox may be semantic or illusory but clearly the challenge to provide effective second language training to an increasingly large and heterogeneous group of students remains.

REFERENCES

Acheson, P., d'Anglejan, A., de Bagheera, I., & Tucker, G.R. English as the Second Language of Quebec: A Teacher Profile. *McGill Journal of Education*, 1978, *13*, 189-197.

Alatis, J.E., & Twadell, K. (eds.) *English as a Second Language in Bilingual Education.* Washington, TESOL, 1976.

Bender, M.L., Bowen, J.D., Cooper, R.L., & Ferguson, C.A. (eds.). *Language in Ethiopia.* London: Oxford University Press, 1976.

Bibeau, G. *Report of the independent study on the language training programs of the Public Service of Canada (General Report).* Ottawa, Public Service of Canada, 1976.

Brown, R. *A First Language: The Early Stages*. Cambridge: Harvard University Press, 1973.

Chomsky, N. *Aspects of the Theory of Syntax*. Cambridge: MIT Press, 1965.

Chomsky, N. *Language and Mind*. New York: Harcourt, 1972.

Crandall, J. Adult Vocational ESL. *Language in Education*. Arlington: Center for Applied Linguistics, 1979, 22.

Diller, K.C. Some new trends for applied linguistics and foreign language teaching in the United States. *TESOL Quarterly*, 1975, *9*, 65-73.

ESPMENA, *English for special purposes in the Middle East and North Africa*. English Language Servicing Unit, University of Khartoum, Sudan.

Fishman, J.A. Language modernization and planning in comparison with other types of national modernization and planning. In J.A. Fishman (ed.) *Advances in Language Planning*. The Hague: Mouton, 1974, 79-102.

Fishman, J.A. *et al. Language Loyalty in the United States*. The Hague: Mouton, 1966.

Fishman, J.A., Cooper, R.L., Ma, R., et al. *Bilingualism in the Barrio*. Bloomington: Indiana University Press, 1971.

Fox, M.J. *Language in Education: Problems and Prospects in Research and Training*. New York: The Ford Foundation, 1975.

Gardner, R.C. Social factors in second language acquisition and biliguality. In W.H. Coons, D.M. Taylor & M. Tremblay (eds.). *The Individual Language and Society in Canada*. Ottawa: The Canada Council, 1977.

Harrison, W., Prator, C., & Tucker, G.R. *English-Language Policy Survey of Jordan*. Arlington: Center for Applied Linguistics, 1975.

Hatch, E. (ed.). *Second Language Acquisition*. Rowley: Newbury House, 1978.

Jordan, Ministry of Education, Curricula and Textbooks Divison. *English Curriculum: Compulsory Stage*, second edition. Amman: Cooperative Printing Presses Workers Society, 1969.

Ladefoged, P., Glick, R., & Griper, C. *Language in Uganda*. Nairobi: Oxford University Press, 1972.

Lambert, W.E. Culture and language as factors in learning and education. Paper presented at the Fifth Annual Learning Symposium at Western Washington State College, Bellingham, Washington, November 1973.

Lambert, W.E. & Tucker, G.R. *The Bilingual Education of Children*. Rowley: Newbury House, 1972.

Lieberson, S. *Language and Ethnic Relations in Canada*. New York: Wiley, 1970.

Naiman, N., Fröhlich, M. & Stern, H.H. The good language learner. Modern Language Centre, Ontario Institute for Studies in Education, Multilith, 1975.

Ohannessian, S. & Kashoki, M.E. (eds.). *Language in Zambia*, London: International African Institute, 1978.

President's Commission on Foreign Language and International Studies. Strength through Wisdom: A Critique of U.S. Capability. Washington: Government Printing Office, 1979.

Royal Commission on Bilingualism and Biculturalism. Ottawa: Queen's Printer, 1967.

Schachter, J., Tyson, A.F., & Diffley, F.J. Learner intuitions about grammaticality. *Language Learning*,. 1976, *26*, 67-76.

Strevens, P. A Theoretical model of the language learning/language teaching process. *Working Papers on Bilingualism*, 1976, *11*, 129-152.

Swain, M. Home-school language switching. In J.C. Richards (ed.) *Understanding Second and Foreign Language Learning: Issues & Approaches*. Rowley: Newbury House, 1978, p. 238-250.

Troike, R.C., & Modiano, N. (eds.). *Proceedings of the First Inter-American Conference on Bilingual Education*. Arlington: Center for Applied Linguistics, 1975.

Tucker, G.R. Some observations concerning bilingualism and second-language teaching in developing countries and in North America. In P.A. Hornby (ed.). *Bilingualism: Psychological, Social and Educational Implications*. New York: Academic Press, 1977, 141-146.

Tucker, G.R. & d'Anglejan, A. Some thoughts concerning bilingual education programs. *The Modern Language Journal*, 1971, 55, 491-493.

Tucker, G.R., & d'Anglejan, A. New directions in second language teaching. In R.C. Troike, & N. Modiano (eds.). *Proceedings of the First Inter-American Conference on Bilingual Education*. Arlington: Center for Applied Linguistics, 1975, 63-72.

Tucker, G.R., & Sarofim, M. Investigating linguistic acceptability with Egyptian EFL students. *TESOL Quarterly*, 1979, 13, 23-39.

Whiteley, W.H. (ed.). *Language in Kenya*. Nairobi: Oxford University Press, 1974.

Chapter 6

Second Language Learning

Robert C. Gardner, Department of Psychology, University of Western Ontario

Have you ever studied another language such as French, German or Spanish? If so, did you find it easy or difficult? Did you look forward to your classes as enjoyable experiences, or did you wish they would never come? During classes, did you have fun and actively seek to learn the material and respond whenever you could, or did you find them unpleasant and feel uncomfortable when called upon to contribute? In this chapter, we intend to investigate these questions, and show the type of answers researchers have uncovered for them. In the process, we will also demonstrate that learning another language (referred to as second language acquisition) may be more of a social phenomenon than an educational one in some cultural contexts.

Perhaps you have never considered second language acquisition as a large social problem, or at least not until recently. For many, it wasn't until the passage of Bill 101—the Charter of the French language—in Quebec in 1976 that the learning of another language had any particular meaning. There was a saying that a bilingual Canadian was an individual born into a French Canadian family, but the social implications of this generally were not appreciated among English Canadians. With the passage of Bill 101, however, a greater realization of the social implications of Canada as an officially bilingual country became evident. We can only guess what the future holds, and it is not the intent of the present chapter to engage in such prognostication. Instead, the aim is to consider the process of learning a second language as it has been investigated by researchers and to highlight the major findings. It will be observed that one important factor involves attitudinal reactions toward the other language community, and that consequently second language acquisition is a meaningful topic to consider under "ethnic relations."

The Influence of Culture on Researchers

A survey of the literature on second language learning suggests that the larger sociocultural milieu influences the way researchers view the problem. Initial attempts to predict who would and who would not successfully learn a second language originated in the United States and focussed primarily on the concept of intelligence (Henmon, 1929). Given the nature of the times, the make-up of the language courses, and the interests of psychologists and educators in the United States, this approach seems very meaningful. Intelligence testing was becoming popular, and language programs were highly academic in their outlook. Use of intelligence tests to predict achievement in a second language, however, soon gave way to "special prognosis tests" (Symonds, 1929). In the 1950s, this interest shifted slightly and was reflected in the development of language aptitude batteries, which in addition to providing indices of the relative degree of success, also attempted to measure abilities believed to be important in second language learning. This entire orientation, it should be emphasized, developed in the United States at a time when considerable attention was being directed toward abilities in all aspects of life.

Although ability testing was popular throughout the world at that time, this was not the only orientation adopted in the investigation of the second language acquisition process. In England, in the 1940s, where the social context was less concerned with ability differences, research attention was being directed toward the concept of attitude. Jordan (1941) broke new ground when he demonstrated, among English grammar school students, that attitudes toward learning French generally were related positively to grades in French. Jones (1950a;b), however, was the first to demonstrate the particularly social nature of such attitudes. He was concerned with students learning Welsh as a second language, and showed that attitudes toward learning Welsh were influenced by home language background; students who came from homes where Welsh was spoken evidenced more positive attitudes than students without this background. Attitudinal variables in second language acquisiton were also investigated in Canada, but, probably because of the influence of the United States, most of this research has considered both attitudinal and ability character-istics (Gardner and Lambert, 1959).

Of course, it is always easy after the fact to identify "causes" for any phenomenon; however, it does seem that researchers' interests and approaches often reflect the social contexts in which they live. With Canadian research, for example, it is hardly a chance occurrence that it began in Montreal, and that rather than being concerned with attitudes toward learning French, it emphasizes attitudinal reactions toward the French-speaking community. Similarly, it is understandable that with a growing interest in ethnicity among people in the United States, re-searchers there are now developing an interest in attitudinal variables in second language acquisition (see, for example, Oller, Hudson & Liu, 1977), and that the majority of these studies are concerned with non-English speakers learning English as a second language.

Theories of Second Language Acquisition

From a purely educational point of view, the acquisition of a second language can be viewed simply as the acquisition of an academic skill. The teacher is faced with the task of developing in his/her students reading, writing, speaking and listening skills in the second language. In order to achieve a high level of proficiency, a student must merely acquire elements of vocabulary, grammatical principles, and the ability to produce and comprehend meaningful utterances in the other language. Viewed in this light, learning a second language is not that much different from learning mathematics, history, social studies and the like, and it makes a great deal of sense to adopt the position that achievement is highly dependent upon the necessary abilities. In this context, one might argue whether or not these abilities are acquired or innate (and in fact such questions have been raised by Carroll (1974) and Neufeld (1974)), but the research problem is simply one of identifying those abilities which are involved in learning a second language.

A more socially oriented view argues that the acquisition of a second language involves the incorporation of elements of behaviour which are characteristic of another language community. This position does not deny that the student must develop reading, writing, speaking, and listening skills, but it goes further in that it implies that in developing these skills, the individual is making characteristics of another cultural community part of his/her own behavioural repertoire. Such an orientation places much greater emphasis on the fact that the material being presented actually is a significant representation of the other language community.

An Educational Model

The largely educational view of second language acquisition is represented in a theoretical model presented by Carroll (1962). In this model, Carroll hypothesizes that achievement in a second language is a function of two classes of variables, instructional characteristics and individual differences. Carroll differentiates between two types of instructional variables, the adequacy of presentation of the material, and the opportunity for learning it. These two attributes are under the control of the educational system and the teacher, and in any given classroom situation can be viewed as a constant. Adequacy of presentation of the material refers to how clearly the task is presented and explained and how appropriately it is placed in the sequence of tasks to be learned. Good textbooks and good teachers would reflect a high level of adequacy, and attempts to develop programmed instructional materials would represent efforts to maximize this variable. Other things being equal, the more adequately the material is presented the better the learning. Opportunity to learn refers to the amount of time individuals have for learning the material. If it is presented slowly, with ample opportunity to review, this index similarly would be high.

Carroll identifies three basic classes of individual difference variables which he believes are important for second language acquisition. The first is general intelligence. It plays a role in influencing the extent to which the individual is able to understand the directions and explanations of the teacher. The second is language aptitude. Within Carroll's model, language aptitude is defined as the amount of time needed by the individual to learn a particular task, but it is defined operationally in terms of a subset of verbal abilities. Students with high levels of verbal abilities will learn the language better and faster because of positive transfer of the new verbal skills on the old ones. The third individual difference variable is motivation. It is defined as the amount of time the individual is willing to expend on the learning task. Other characteristics of motivation which are to be discussed below are not considered in Carroll's analysis.

Carroll postulates that the individual's level of achievement in the second language will be influenced by his/her general level of *intelligence,* his/her *language aptitude,* and his/her *motivation,* but that the relative importance of these variables will be influenced by the two instructional characteristics. For example, if students are given a greater opportunity to learn the language, by more free time for study, this would increase the relationship between achievement and motivation, but decrease the relationship between achievement and aptitude. On the other hand, if there were little opportunity to study, the relationship between achievement and motivation would decrease. Motivation, therefore, plays its greatest role where students have the opportunity to review the material, since highly motivated students will capitalize on these opportunities. Language aptitude plays its greatest role where the opportunities for review and rehearsal are relatively rare. Under these conditions a person with the aptitude to profit from the material as it is presented will do well.

Although Carroll's model defines language aptitude in terms of the amount of time required to learn a task, attempts to assess individual differences in language aptitude have focussed on verbal abilities, thus stressing the educational aspects of language learning. Original assessments of language aptitude date back to 1929 when researchers attempted to develop "special prognosis tests" for language students concentrating to a considerable extent on short artificial language learning tasks (Symonds, 1929). A more recent assessment tool, the Modern Language Aptitude Test (MLAT) (Carroll & Sapon, 1959), consists of five subtests designed to measure abilities believed to be important in language learning. According to Carroll (1962; 1974) there are at least four important abilities. Phonetic coding refers to the abiity to code auditory material in memory so that it can be recognized or reproduced at a later time. Grammatical sensitivity is the ability to recognize and use grammatical functions of language material. Rote memory refers to the capacity to form associations between verbal materials. Inductive language learning ability is the ability to infer rules and principles from language material without direct instruction or supervision. Each of these abilities is tapped, to some extent at least, by the subtests of the MLAT. In order to understand how this is done, consider the example of the Words in Sentences subtest which measures grammatical sensitivity. In this test students are presented with a set of key sentences in which a word or phrase is underlined. In a sentence (or sentences) following each key sentence, a number of alternatives are underlined and the students must indicate which one performs the same function in its sentence as the item from the key sentence. For example, you might be given a key sentence like "The dog *bit* the mailman," and a test sentence like, "Many *happy* children *swim* in our *pool* in the *summer* time." Rather than being asked to indicate the verb in the test sentence, you would be asked to identify which of the underlined words in the test sentence performs the same function in its sentence as the word "bit" in the key sentence. This is not one of the items from the MLAT; merely a simple example of the concept.

Predictions based on the Carroll (1962) model are consistent with results obtained with the MLAT (Carroll & Sapon, 1959). Correlations of aptitude with proficiency in the second language are highest for intensive second language programs where considerable material is presented in relatively short periods of time to individuals who are at a high level of motivation. Correlations of the MLAT with achievement tend to decrease for university and high school students, where it would be expected that the opportunities to learn the material are increased and there is a much broader range of language aptitude. The model, therefore, has utility in that it reflects the data available in the literature. It is clearly an educationally based model, however, in that very little attention is directed to the nature of the material to be acquired. In point of fact Carroll (1962, p. 121) states that his model "is stated in general terms so that it is not restricted to the case of foreign language learning."

A Social Psychological Model

The social psychological view of second language learning is represented in the theoretical model of Lambert (1963; 1967). He propoes that the student acquiring a second language must be able and willing to adopt various aspects of the behaviour of the other language community, including their verbal behaviour. He argues that the learner's ethnocentric tendencies and attitude towards the other community will determine how successful the student will be in acquiring that language. He proposes further that the individual's motivation to learn the other language is determined by both his/her attitudes and the nature of his/her orientation towards learning a second language. He contrasts two types of orientations. Students exhibit an instrumental orientation when their major reason for learning the other language is for its utilitarian value. The most common example of an *instrumental* orientation would be learning the language for occupational advancement. Students display an *integrative* orientation when language acquisition reflects a desire to learn more about the other community possibly with a desire of becoming a member of that group. An integrative orientation could reflect a desire to leave one's own community, or simply a desire to join both cultures.

This aspect of the model proposes that attitudinal variables will influence students' achievement in the second language in a way very similar to that proposed with respect to language aptitude. If attitudinal variables are involved in language acquisition, however, there are additional implications which are not applicable to language aptitude. Lambert argues further that in the process of acquiring a second language the individual will discover that his/her position in his/her own membership group is changed somewhat in that the other linguistic community becomes something more than a reference group. That is, in the process of developing proficiency in the second language, the individual may experience feelings of anomie (i.e., dissatisfaction with his/her role in society) as he/she feels drawn simultaneously toward both communities.

Whether or not this occurs depends considerably on the social consequences of bilingualism. Lambert (1974) distinguishes between two types of bilingualism, and in the process highlights the important role of language in one's feelings of self-identity. Subtractive bilingualism occurs when an individual learns a second language because of national policies and pressures to become part of a majority language community. In the process, it is quite possible that the individual could lose at least some proficiency in his/her own language, and over a number of generations that the language would die out altogether as a means of communication within the family. This type of bilingualism confronts many people, and is often characteristic of immigrants to a country. Additive bilingualism, on the other hand, occurs when the acquisition of a second language represents an enriching experience, and in no way involves any loss in the native language. In his article, Lambert suggested that subtractive bilingualism could be characteristic of many French Canadians who learn English, while additive bilingualism would generally typify English Canadians who learn French. The important point is that second language acquisition must be viewed in the cultural context in which it occurs.

A Social-Educational Model

The educational model of Carroll and the social psychological one of Lambert have been incorporated into one model which might best be labelled a social-educational model. This model (see Gardner & Smythe, 1975; Gardner, 1979) focusses on the three major individual difference variables postulated by Carroll—intelligence, aptitude and motiviation, but places considerable emphasis on the social psychological implications of language study as proposed by Lambert. It attempts, furthermore, to identify the major parameters of motivation in second language study so that individual difference measures of important motivational characteristics can be assessed.

A schematic representation of the major elements of this model is presented in Figure 6.1. In this model it is proposed that second language acquisition must be considered in the context of the particular social milieu in which the student resides (see chapter 5 in this book). It is proposed that the cultural milieu will influence the approach taken by the learner in acquiring the second language because of shared cultural beliefs. That is, beliefs about the value of learning the language or about the possibility of attaining a high level of competence in the language will influence the roles played by intelligence, aptitude and motivation. If it were believed in a community that all students would develop proficiency in the language, motivational variables would play a much smaller role than if such expectations did not exist. This rather obvious generalization concerning the role of the community in second language acquisition appears to have been ignored in the other theoretical models.

It is hypothesized that three major individual difference variables, intelligence, language aptitude and motivation are implicated in the acquisition of a second language, and that the role of these three variables will differ depending upon the second language acquisition context. Two contexts are referred to, one a formal language training situation, and the other informal language experiences. Formal language training contexts refer to any type of situation where students receive specific instruction in the second language (as in a language class for example). Informal language experiences on the other hand refer to any situation where second language skills might be acquired, but in the absence of direct instruction. Instances of such experiences might be listening to the radio, reading French magazines or newspapers.

Figure 6.1
Schematic Representation of the Social-Educational Model

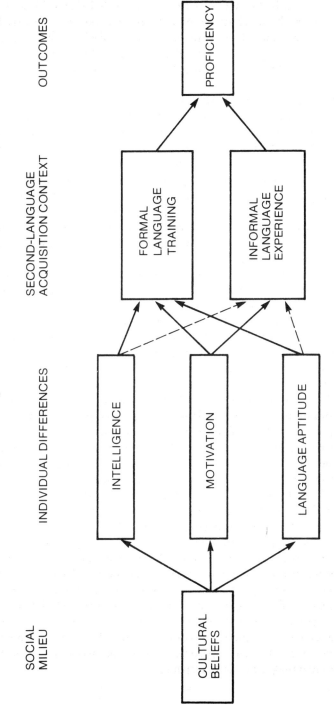

The three individual difference variables, intelligence, language aptitude and motivation would be expected to play direct roles in the acquisition of any language skills developed in the formal context, and this is indicated by the solid lines in Figure 6.1 linking them to the formal context. Intelligence is considered to be important because it would influence the extent to which students would be able to understand the nature of the task to be learned and the process to follow in its learning. Language aptitude would be expected to play a role since individuals with high levels of language aptitude would be able to generalize these abilities to the new language situation. Motivation would be important in the formal language context simply because differences in motivation would result in differing amounts of effort being expended towards learning the material. In informal contexts, only motivation is viewed as playing a direct role (as indicated by the solid lines linking the two), while both intelligence and language aptitude would be involved indirectly (as indicated by the broken lines). That is, motivation affects the extent to which individuals seek out and avail themselves of informal experiences and thus has a primary role. Individual differences in intelligence and language aptitude would be effective only after the individual entered an informal language learning context, and thus are less influential.

Proficiency in the second language would obviously develop from both language learning experiences. As a consequence, we would hypothesize that measures of intelligence, language aptitude and motivation would tend to be equally related to those language skills which are developed in formal contexts, but that indices of motivation would tend to be somewhat more related to skills developed in informal contexts. Direct tests of such a hypothesis are not possible with language students since it is not an easy matter to determine the contents in which any particular skill is acquired. Indirect tests of this generalization are, however, possible by identifying which classes of variables relate most highly to the willingness to continue second language study. This area of research will be discussed in a subsequent section.

Much of the research associated with this theoretical model has been concerned with identifying parameters of the motivational component. Because of the social implications of language study, most attention has been devoted to investigating attitudinal variables. It has been assumed (Lambert, 1967; Gardner, 1979) that attitudes influence an individual's level of motivation and that the level of motivation influences how successfully an individual learns the language. It seems necessary to include a concept of attitude in the general motivational configuration because the acquisition of a second language requires considerable time and effort and that, as a result, a stable attitudinal base is needed to maintain motivation over these long periods of time. Because of the long time periods involved, it is reasonable to assume that the ultimate goal is something other than the acquisition of the other language. This entire motivational construct has been labelled an integrative motive to emphasize the cultural implications of language study. This integrative motive is described as a high level of drive on the part of the individual to acquire the language of a valued second language community in order to facilitate communication with that group (Gardner, Smythe, Clément & Gliksman, 1976).

Considerable research has been concerned with assessing those attitudinal and motivational variables which reflect this motivational complex, and in constrasting their relations to second language achievement with those of measures of language aptitude. The following sections examine in some detail the relationships of measures of attitudes and motivation to achievement in the second language, perseverance in language study, and behaviour in the French classroom. Each of these are presented in the context of second language acquisition but it will be recognized that the issues raised are central problems in social psychology. A final section of this chapter focusses on this broader perspective.

Social Factors in Second Language Achievement

Attitudes Toward the Language

The earliest investigations of the relationships of attitudes to achievement in the second language were conducted in England. In the first investigation, Jordan (1941) measured attitudes toward learning a number of school subjects and determined the correlations between these attitudes and achievement in that subject. Although the correlations were not high (ranging from .21 to .33) those involving attitudes towards learning French were consistently among the highest, and were significant, indicating that attitudes toward learning French were related to achievement in French. Very similar results were obtained by Duckworth and Entwistle (1974), also in England. These findings suggest that perhaps attitudes toward language courses are more related to proficiency in that course than are attitudes toward other subjects related to proficiency in those subjects. This generalization is in fact supported by results obtained by Neidt and Hedlund (1967). They assessed attitudes of university students towards English, German and Anatomy five times throughout the academic year. None of the five correlations between attitudes toward learning Anatomy and final grades in Anatomy were significant, while all five correlations were significant for French and two were significant for English. Neidt and Hedlund (1967) were also able to remove the effects of ability by making use of a technique known as partial correlation. Once the effects of ability were removed, the correlations between attitudes towards German and achievement in German remained significant. In short, proficiency in the second language was related to attitudes towards that language, regardless of ability.

Two studies conducted by Jones (1950a, 1950b) indicate initial concerns about learning the language of another group because of the possible social implications involved. Both of these studies were conducted in Wales, and the second language in question was Welsh. In the first investigation, Jones (1950a) found that the attitudes of children of non-Welsh-speaking parents were significantly less favourable than attitudes of children with parents who had at least some knowledge of Welsh. He concluded (p. 124) that "amongst social conditions the verbal and general cultural background of the home and parental attitude and interests would undoubtedly be factors of primary importance." In the other study, Jones (1950b) studied the correlation between attitudes towards learning Welsh as a second language and achievement in Welsh for four groups of students varying in age. He found positive correlations between attitude and achievement for each of the four grade levels, though the correlations were significant only for the two groups of older students. Much more consistent relationships were obtained by Burstall, Jamieson, Cohen and Hargreaves (1974) in their ten-year evaluation of the elementary French program in Great Britain.

The complexities and challenges involved in this area of research are demonstrated in a study conducted by Randhawa and Korpan (1973) in Saskatchewan. They set out to construct a scale to measure what would seem to be a relatively simple construct like attitudes toward learning French. They found, however, that this assessment involved four factors. That is, a factor analysis of the items making up their scale to measure attitudes toward learning French revealed four clusters of items. They identified three of these factors as tolerance (an acceptance of the language), aestheticism (an appreciation of the language) and a utilitarian predisposition (a recognition of the usefulness of learning the language). These tended to correlate quite highly with teacher ratings of French proficiency, but maximum prediction of proficiency was obtained with a combination of the tolerance score and scores on a test of motivational intensity based on that used by Gardner and Lambert (1959), and indexing the amount of effort expended in learning French.

Attitudes Toward the Language Community

Many other studies have investigated the relationship between measures of attitudes toward the other language community and achievement in the language, sometimes yielding conflicting results. Anisfeld and Lambert (1961), for example, obtained negative relationships between a measure of anti-semitism and achievement in Hebrew as a second language among six classes of senior elementary school children, but pointed out that the relationships were influenced by a number of social factors. Similarly, Lambert, Gardner, Barik and Tunstall (1963) found a positive relationship between attitudes toward French-speaking people and French achievement for adults studying French at a beginning level, but a negative relationship for more advanced students. Negative relationships between second language achievement and attitudes toward the other language community, furthermore, have been reported for Mexican-American women studying English (Oller, Baca, and Vigil, 1977), and Japanese students learning English (Chihara and Oller, 1978). On the other hand, positive relationships between second language achievement and attitudes toward the other language have been reported for university students studying French as a second language (Mueller, 1971), and for missionaries studying Japanese (Jacobsen and Imhoof, 1974). All of these results indicate that a number of factors influence the relation between attitudes and achievement and that the problem is indeed complex.

Attitudes, Motivation and Language Aptitude
A number of studies have attempted to take into account the complex nature of the language learning process by investigating the relationship among a number of measures of attitudes, motivation, language aptitude and second language achievement. In the first of these studies, Gardner and Lambert (1959) made use of the technique known as factor analysis to investigate these variables with English-speaking students in Montreal. It is beyond the scope of this chapter to explain the technique of factor analysis. Suffice it to say that it is a procedure that isolates clusters of variables which are related to each other. These clusters are referred to as factors. In the Gardner and Lambert investigation, two independent factors were obtained and both of these were shown to be related to achievement in French. The first factor was identified as a language aptitude dimension in that the variables defining it were the subtests of the MLAT and other measures of verbal ability. The second factor was referred to as a motivation factor, and the nature of the variables defining it indicated that it denoted a motivation characterized by a willingness to be like valued members of the language community. This particular motivational complex was subsequently referred to as an integrative motive.

The results of this investigation were important for two reasons. First, they demonstrated rather clearly that ability characteristics were relatively independent of motivational ones. That is, it wasn't simply the case that students who had a high level of language aptitude were more motivated to learn a second language. Secondly, the results indicated a rather substantial relationship between motivation to learn a second language and attitudinal reactions involving the second language community. That is, those students who expended a considerable amount of energy in learning French as a second language were those who had favourable attitudes towards French-speaking people and who expressed an interest in learning French in order to get to know them better.

A number of studies have used this type of approach in different communities, with students of different ages, with different numbers and types of attitudinal and motivational characteristics and with various measures of second language achievement ranging from grades to objective measures to speech samples. English-speaking teenagers learning French have been investigated in Montreal (Gardner and Lambert, 1972), London, Ontario (Smythe, Stennett & Feenstra, 1972) in Maine, Louisiana and Connecticut (Gardner & Lambert, 1972) and in California (Cavanaugh, 1977). Franco-American students studying *French* have been studied in Maine and Louisiana (Gardner & Lambert, 1972), French Canadian students studying *English* have been investigated in the provinces of Quebec (Clément, Gardner & Smythe, 1977) and Ontario (Clément, Major, Gardner & Smythe, 1977) and Filipinos learning English as a second language have been studied in Manila, Republic of the Philippines (Gardner and Lambert, 1972).

It would be an unwarranted simplification to claim that each of these studies produced results which were directly comparable to those obtained by Gardner and Lambert (1959). It is reasonable, however, to make the generalization that all of the studies demonstrated relationships between proficiency in the second language and at least two independent factors—language aptitude, and an attitudinally based motivation to learn the second language. It must be emphasized that all of these data are correlational in nature, and that as a result inferences about the possible causal factors are open to alternative interpretations. That is, with respect to the relationship between the attitudinal-motivational factor and achievement in the second language it might be argued that (a) attitudinal-motivational variables influence the level of achievement, or that (b) the level of achievement results in particular attitudinal-motivational characteristics, or that (c) their relation is due to some common third factor. Interpretation (a) is the one favoured by many of the researchers who conducted these studies, but interpretation (b) is favoured by Burstall, Jamieson, Cohen and Hargreaves (1974), and interpretation (c) is proposed by Oller and Perkins (1979). It isn't an easy task to design research to determine which if any is the correct interpretation, but as you might well imagine investigations are proceeding along these lines.

Researchers who develop aptitude batteries often provide ways by which the individual's aptitude can be described by one score so that direct predictions can be made of the behaviour of interest. Gardner, Clément, Smythe and Smythe (1978) have developed a similar approach with respect to attitudes and motivation. Basing their decisions on the factor analytic studies discussed earlier, they have identified three composite indices reflecting different attitudinal-motivational components and one major index to be used for prediction and have developed a test battery to assess these characteristics. The three composite indices are referred to as integrativeness, motivation, and attitudes towards the learning situation.

Integrativeness assesses attitudinal reactions toward the second language community and outgroups in general, and summarizes in one index the group-related interest in language learning. Integrativeness is reflected in attitudes toward communities that speak the language, interest in other languages, and an interest in learning the language in order to facilitate communication with members of the other language community. Motivation refers to goal-directed behaviour, and is seen to consist of three components; the effort involved in achieving the goal of "learning the language," the wants and desires to achieve this end, and favourable attitudes toward the activity of learning the language. Attitudes toward the learning situation reflect evaluative reactions developed in the actual situation where the language is acquired, primarily toward the course and the teacher.

One composite score, the attitudinal-motivational index (AMI) has been developed in order to permit direct prediction of second language achievement on the basis of all attitudinal/motivational variables. This index involves the sum of the subtests which make up the three indices referred to above plus two additional measures, ratings of an instrumental orientation, and French classroom anxiety. This last measure is negatively weighted in the sum so that an absence of anxiety contributes positively to AMI. The AMI index provides a direct measure of the important attitudinal-motivational attributes for second language acquisition, permitting direct comparisons with a comparable index for aptitude of its relation to achievement.

Correlations of the AMI and MLAT with grades in French have been reported for 28 samples (varying in size from 62 to 239 with a median of 180) of students from Grades 7 to 11 across Canada (see Gardner, Clément, Smythe and Smythe, 1978). These results indicate that aptitude is only a slightly better predictor than attitudinal-motivational characteristics. Correlations of the MLAT with grades in French vary from .19 to .59 with a median of .42. The correlation of the AMI with grades varies from .15 to .50, with a median of .37. Of even greater importance, however, is the fact that the AMI and MLAT are virtually unrelated to each other. The correlations between the AMI and MLAT vary from –.06 to .33 with a median of .12. These results agree with those described earlier in the discussion of the factor analytic investigations which also indicated the relative independence of the attitudinal/motivational and the aptitude characteristics. Furthermore, this independence helps to provide for maximum prediction of achievement by considering both factors. When both factors are combined, the multiple correlations with French grades vary from .35 to .69 with a median of .52. Such correlations are substantial for the purposes of psychological prediction, and indicate the very definite advantage of considering both facets in the second language learning process.

Results such as these, as well as the factor analytic studies described earlier, indicate a considerable degree of construct validity (see Crano and Brewer, 1973) for both the attitudinal-motivational and language aptitude indices. In this regard we can distinguish between two aspects of validity. Convergent validity is demonstrated when an index correlates with other measures with which it should correlate if the index assesses what it is believed to measure, and the theory is correct. Discriminant validity, on the other hand, is demonstrated if the test does *not* correlate with measures with which it should not correlate. In the present case, AMI and MLAT demonstrate convergent validity in that they correlate with French grades. We would expect, however, that if they measure attributes which are related primarily to learning a second language, they should also not correlate with measures not involving second language learning, as for example, academic average (minus French grades, of course).

Gardner, Clément, Smythe and Smythe (1978) present data from two samples from different regions in Canada at each of five grade levels relevant to the discriminant validity of both the AMI and MLAT, that is, their correlations with Academic Average. The ten correlations involving AMI range from –.03 to .32 with a median of .12, and only two of them are statistically significant. These results demonstrate good discriminant validity for the AMI. The ten correlations of the MLAT with Academic Average range from .22 to .54, and nine are significant. Obviously, the MLAT does not evidence discriminant validity if one were to argue that the abilities measured by it are important only for second language learning. It seems reasonable, however, that the abilities measured by the MLAT would be related to academic performance, hence this lack of discriminant validity is not that critical for the MLAT. The good discriminant validity for the AMI is reassuring, however, since it suggests that the attitudinal-motivational variables measured by it are not simply related to good school performance. They are specifically related to achievement in a second language as suggested by the underlying theoretical formulation.

Attitudes, Motivation, and Persistence in Language Study

Given that attitudes and motivation are related to achievement in the second language, we can ask what other aspects of language learning are influenced by such variables. One aspect which has been investigated and which is important in the acquisition of a second language is the willingness to continue language study, since in many settings the language classroom represents one of the few ways in which the second language can be learned. Where the second language is optional, therefore, registration in a language class can be viewed as comparable to availing oneself of the opportunity to enter into a language learning context. The available research literature suggests that attitudinal-motivational variables are better predictors of persistence in language study than are either measures of language aptitude or second language proficiency.

The original investigations of persistence in language study were conducted in California by Bartley (1969; 1970). Bartley (1970) administered a language attitude test to senior elementary students on two occasions, once at the beginning of their language course and again at the end of the year, at which time they also decided whether they were going to continue language study the next year or drop languages altogether. On both assessments, those continuing language study had much more positive attitudes than those dropping out. Furthermore, those who dropped out showed a decrease in attitudes from the first to the second testing, while those continuing language study maintained relatively stable attitudes. Bartley (1969) also assessed students' language aptitude, and in addition to demonstrating that students who continued language study initially had more favourable attitudes, she also found that they were higher on language aptitude.

Gardner and Smythe (1975) extended this line of research but included measures of language aptitude, a series of attitudinal-motivational indices, and objective assessments of achievement in French. The subjects for this investigation were registered in Grades 9, 10 and 11 at the time they were tested and were classified as "drop-outs" or "stay-ins" the following year on the basis of whether or not they were studying French. When these two groups were compared at each grade level it was found that the "stay-ins" had, the previous year, demonstrated significantly more favourable attitudes towards French Canadians, the French class, and toward learning French, were more interested in foreign languages, expressed more of an integrative and instrumental orientation, reported more motivation and desire to learn French, felt more parental encouragement to learn French and were less anxious in the French class. The groups tended not to differ on other characteristics such as attitudes toward the English class, or European French people, school anxiety, need achievement, Machiavellianism, anomie, authoritarianism or ethnocentrism. At each grade level also, the two groups tended to differ predictably on language aptitude, intelligence and the objective measures of French proficiency (vocabulary, grammar, comprehension and pronunciation), though particularly for the Grades 9 and 10 students the differences were not as pronounced as they were for the attitude and motivation variables. That language aptitude is not a major determinant of perseverance in language study is also suggested by a study conducted by Mueller and Harris (1966) who found no differences in aptitude between "stay-ins" and "drop-outs" in a university level French program.

Gardner, Smythe, Clément and Gliksman (1976) report the relationships between measures of attitudes, motivation, language aptitude, and French grades and the stated intention to withdraw from, or continue, French study for approximately 1000 students in each of five grade levels (7 to 11) in six provinces across Canada. Measures of attitudes and motivation tend to be high correlates while the measure of language aptitude was consistently a low correlate. French grades correlated more highly with the behavioural intention to continue language study than did language aptitude, but not as highly as the motivational indices.

These results suggest that attitudinal-motivational variables are related to perseverance in language study, and give support to the theoretical proposition made earlier that motivational attributes will influence the extent to which students avail themselves of the opportunity to practice the second language. That proposal was made in the context of participation in informal language learning situations but to the extent that re-enrolling in a language program is voluntary, the implications are the same.

Attitudes, Motivation and Behaviour in the Classroom

There is some evidence to suggest that attitudinal and motivational variables are implicated in other aspects of second language acquisition, the most notable being behaviour in the language classroom. Although you might tend to think that your activity in the classroom is dependent upon a number of factors such as the amount of sleep you had the previous night, impending examinations and other momentary extraneous factors, the available evidence suggests that there are attitudinal-motivational characteristics of the individual which relate to behaviour, at least in the French classroom. Furthermore, these relations are consistent with what one would expect adopting the social-educational model described earlier.

The first research concerned with this set of relationships was conducted by Gliksman (1976) in two studies. In each study, students were administered a battery of attitudinal and motivational tests during the first week of classes and in subsequent classes trained observers visited the French classroom and observed a series of behaviours of each student. Three behaviours considered in the first investigation, which involved 90 grade 9 students, were the number of times a student raised his hand to volunteer an answer, the number of correct answers each student gave, and the number of positive reinforcements the student received from the teacher. Students were classified as Integratively Motivated vs. Non-integratively Motivated on the basis of their scores on the attitudinal-motivational tests, and these two groups were compared in terms of their classroom behaviour. The results showed that, for each class session, integratively motivated students volunteered more frequently, gave more correct answers, and received more positive reinforcements from the teacher than non-integratively motivated students.

The second investigation was similar but involved a total of 150 students from Grades 9, 10 and 11 and instead of assessing positive reinforcement obtained from the teacher, the observers rated, at the end of the class, the degree of positive affect exhibited by each student (i.e., how satisfied they seemed to be with the class). As before, the observers also recorded the number of volunteering responses and the number of correct answers. When the integratively motivated students were compared with those who were not integratively motivated the results were comparable to the previous study. In each session, integratively motivated students volunteered more frequently, and gave more correct answers than nonintegratively motivated students. They also were rated as being more pleased with the class.

These results have generally been supported by another investigation conducted by Naiman, Fröhlich, Stern and Todesco (1978). They selected six students from each of four classes in each of three Grades (8, 10 and 12) and observed each student for a total of 250 minutes of class time (over a number of weeks). Their results demonstrated that attitudinal and motivational variables were related to volunteering in the classroom, but not to other types of activity such as asking the teacher questions, demonstrating their knowledge beyond that solicited, or indications of anxiety in their speech.

Neither of these studies investigated the relation of language aptitude to classroom behaviour. It would seem reasonable to predict, however, that language aptitude would be related to indices of competence in the language (such as the number of correct answers given), but not necessarily to volunteering behaviour. You will recall that language aptitude has been shown to be relatively independent of attitudinal-motivational variables, and not highly or consistently related to perseverance in language study. For these reasons, it seems unlikely that language aptitude would be related to volunteering in the classroom, though, of course, the research should be conducted before this is considered a valid conclusion. If a relationship were obtained, it would not, in any event, detract from the relationship found between attitudinal-motivational characteristics and aspects of classroom behaviour.

The Problem in Perspective

The preceding discussion has been concerned primarily with the relation of two classes of variables, language aptitude and attitudinal-motivational attributes, to behaviours associated with second language acquisition, proficiency in the language, perseverance in language study, and classroom behaviour. A theoretical model was presented which indicated how attitudinal-motivational variables, language aptitude and intelligence could influence second language acquisition. Data were then presented indicating that the first two classes of variables were associated with proficiency in the second language and that attitudinal-motivational variables were also related to other aspects of second language acquisition. If attention is directed to the role played by attitudinal variables in second language acquisition, much of the research is relevant to a controversy in social psychology. This is often referred to as the attitude-behaviour problem.

The major issue involved in this problem is whether or not behaviour is related to attitudes. Ever since the classic study by La Piere (1934) in which he failed to demonstrate a relationship between expressed attitude toward the Chinese by hotel keepers and the willingness to accept them as guests, there have been periodic questions concerning the relevance of the attitude concept. The complexity of the problems associated with this area can be appreciated by reading review articles by Ajzen and Fishbein (1977), Schuman and Johnson (1976), and Wicker (1969). Wicker initiated the most recent controversy by reviewing a number of studies concerned with the correlation between attitudes and behaviour, and concluding that the relationships were generally so low that it seemed best to conclude that, in fact, attitudes were not involved to any great extent in determining behaviour.

In reacting to what amounted to many as a challenge, a number of investigators, including Ajzen and Fishbein (1977) and Schuman and Johnson (1976), have attempted to account for these low correlations, or to develop procedures to increase the magnitude of the correlations. Whereas some argue that the attitudes to be assessed should be much more specific and more directly related to the behaviour in question, others have argued that more general attitudes are related to more general assessments of behaviour. For example, Fishbein and Ajzen (1974) demonstrated rather substantial correlations between scales measuring general attitudes toward religion and a scale summarizing one hundred different religious behaviours.

A theoretical model proposed by Fishbein and Ajzen (1975) has had a considerable impact in this area. They argue that behaviour is a direct function of behavioural intention, and that an individual's intention to perform any particular behaviour is an additive function of his attitude toward the behaviour and the influence of the social environment on the behaviour. An individual's attitude towards a behaviour is postulated to be a multiplicative function of the person's belief that the behaviour will lead to a specific outcome and the evaluation of the outcome summed over all the outcomes the individual believes can occur. In short, this model proposes that if one is concerned with predicting a specific activity on the part of the individual, the best prediction will be obtained with a measure designed to assess the individual's attitude towards performing that activity. In a subsequent presentation, Ajzen and Fishbein (1977) argue that both attitudes and behaviours are composed of elements involving target, action, context, and time, and that the greatest association between attitudes and behaviour will occur when there is correspondence between the elements associated with both attitudes and behaviour. This model, consequently, places considerable emphasis on contemporaneous prediction, that is, predictions of behaviour based on attitudes toward that behaviour at that particular time.

In the present instance such a model would imply that we assess attitudes toward obtaining a good grade in French if we were interested in predicting proficiency (as assessed by grades), or attitudes toward continuing language study if we were interested in perseverance and so forth. Under such conditions, correlations between attitudes and behaviour would probably be relatively high, but they would not tell us much about the process of learning a second language. An alternative strategy which has been stressed in this chapter is to focus on those characteristics of the individual which appear to influence his/her motivation to learn a second language, and to investigate their relation to different behaviours involved in learning a second language. This approach has resulted in the identification of a series of attitudinal-motivational attributes which seem to play important roles, but should not be viewed as being in disagreement with the general orientation proposed by Ajzen and Fishbein (1977). Even within this framework, Gardner, Gliksman and Smythe (1978) have demonstrated that while some attitudes are more related to some behaviours involved in second language learning, other attitudes are more related to other such aspects of behaviour, thus emphasizing the importance of Ajzen and Fishbein's (1977) concept of correspondence.

The magnitude of many of the relationships presented in this chapter are often comparable to those presented by Wicker (1969) which led to his questioning the utility of the attitude concept. With respect to second language acquisition, however, research has gone beyond considering simply the attitudinal concept, and instead has demonstrated that a series of attitudinal variables are related to each other and to aspects of behaviour which are involved in second language acquisition or which reflect proficiency in the language. The theoretical model which was highlighted focussed on the process of second language acquisition and suggests ways in which attitudes influence motivational characteristics, which in turn can influence behaviour. The present model is explicit in indicating how, in the context of second language acquisition, attitudes do influence behaviour. Moreover, the attitudes involved include a number of social attitudes which help to indicate the role played by social factors in what, on the surface, might appear to be largely an educational problem. Although prediction may not be as good as it is for those models which seek to relate attitudes toward the act with actually performing the act, the broader social implications of the relationships and the non-contemporaneous nature of the predictions seem worth any loss in prediction.

REFERENCES

Ajzen, I. and Fishbein, M. Attitude-behaviour relations: A theoretical analysis and review of empirical research.*Psychological Bulletin*, 1977, *84*, 889-918.

Anisfeld, M., and Lambert, W.E. Social and psychological variables in learning Hebrew. *Journal of Abnormal and Social Psychology*, 1961, *63*, 524-529.

Bartley, D.E. A pilot study of aptitude and attitude factors in language dropout. *California Journal of Educational Research*, 1969, *20*, 48-55.

Bartley, D.E. The importance of the attitude factor in language dropout. A preliminary investigation of group and sex differences. *Foreign Language Annals*, 1970, *3*, 383-393.

Burstall, C., Jamieson, M., Cohen, S. and Hargreaves, M. *Primary French in the Balance*. Berks.: NFER Publishing, 1974.

Carroll, J.B. The prediction of success in intensive language training. In R. Glaser (ed.), *Training Research and Education*. Pittsburgh Press, 1962.

Carroll, J.B. Aptitude in second language learning. *Proceedings of the Fifth Symposium of the Canadian Association of Applied Linguistics*, 1974, 8-23.

Carroll, J.B. and Sapon, S.M. *Modern Language Aptitude Test (MLAT) Manual*. New York: Psychological Corporation, 1959.

Cavanaugh, N.F. The roles of attitude and motivation in second language acquisition. *Dissertation Abstracts International*, 1977, *38*, 674-A.

Chihara, T., and Oller, J.W. Attitudes and attained proficiency in EFL: A sociolinguistic study of adult Japanese speakers. *Language Learning*, 1978, *28*, 55-68.

Clément, R., Gardner, R.C. and Smythe, P.C. Motivational variables in second language acquisition: A study of francophones learning English. *Canadian Journal of Behavioural Science*, 1977, *9*, 123-133.

Clément, R., Major, L., Gardner, R.C. and Smythe, P.C. Attitudes and motivation in second language acquisition: An investigation of Ontario francophones. *Working Papers on Bilingualism*, 1977, *12*, 1-20.

Crano, W.D. and Brewer, M.B. *Principles of Research in Social Psychology*. New York: McGraw-Hill, 1973.

Duckworth, D. and Entwistle, N.J. Attitudes to school subjects: A repertory grid technique. *British Journal of Educational Psychology*, 1974, *44*, 76-83.

Fishbein, M., and Ajzen, I. Attitudes toward objects as predictors of single and multiple behavioural criteria. *Psychological Review*, 1974, *81*, 59-74.

Fishbein, M., and Ajzen, I. *Belief, Attitude, Intention and Behaviour: An Introduction to Theory and Research*. Reading: Addison-Wesley, 1975.

Gardner, R.C. Social psychological aspects of second language acquisition. In H. Giles and R. St. Clair (eds.), *Language and Social Psychology*. Oxford: Basil Blackwell, 1979.

Gardner, R.C., Clément, R., Smythe, P.C. and Smythe, C.L. Attitudes and Motivation Test Battery, Manual, Research Bulletin No. 468, Department of Psychology, University of Western Ontario, 1978.

Gardner, R.C., Gliksman, L. and Smythe, P.C. Attitudes and behaviour in second language acquisition: A social psychological interpretation. *Canadian Psychological Review*, 1978, *19*, 173-186.

Gardner, R.C. and Lambert, W.E. Motivational variables in second language acquisition. *Canadian Journal of Psychology*, 1959, *13*, 266-272.

Gardner, R.C. and Lambert, W.E. *Attitudes and Motivation in Second Language Learning*. Rowley: Newbury House, 1972.

Gardner, R.C. and Smythe, P.C. Second language acquisition: A social psychological approach. Research Bulletin No. 332, Department of Psychology, University of Western Ontario, 1975.

Gardner, R.C., Smythe, P.C., Clément, R. and Gliksman, L. Second language acquisition: A social psychological perspective. *Canadian Modern Language Review,* 1976, *32,* 198-213.

Gliksman, L. Second language acquisition: The effects of student attitudes on classroom behaviour. Unpublished Master's Thesis, University of Western Ontario, 1976.

Henmon, C.A.C. Prognosis tests in the modern foreign languages. *Publications of the American and Canadian Committees on Modern Foreign Languages,* 1929, *14,* 3-31.

Jacobsen, M. and Imhoof, M. Predicting success in learning a second language. *Modern Language Journal,* 1974, *58,* 329-336.

Jones, W.R. Attitude towards Welsh as a second language, a preliminary investigation. *British Journal of Educational Psychology,* 1950a, *19,* 44-52.

Jones, W.R. Attitude towards Welsh as a second language: A further investigation. *British Journal of Educational Psychology,* 1950b, *20,* 117-132.

Jordan, D. The attitudes of central school pupils to certain school subjects and the correlation between attitude and attainment. *British Journal of Educational Psychology,* 1941, *11,* 28-44.

Lambert, W.E. Psychological approaches to the study of language (Part II): On second language learning and bilingualism. *Modern Language Journal,* 1963, *14,* 114-121.

Lambert, W.E. A social psychology of bilingualism. *Journal of Social Issues,* 1967, *23,* 91-109.

Lambert, W.E. Culture and language as factors in learning and education. In Aboud, F.E., and Meade, R.D. (eds.), *The Fifth Western Symposium on Learning: Cultural Factors in Learning and Education.* Washington: Bellingham, 1974.

Lambert, W.E., Gardner, R.C., Barik, H.C., and Tunstall, K. Attitudinal and cognitive aspects of intensive study of a second language. *Journal of Abnormal and Social Psychology,* 1963, *66,* 358-368.

La Piere, R.T. Attitudes vs. actions. *Social Forces,* 1934, *13,* 230-237.

Mueller, T.H. Student attitudes in the basic French courses at the University of Kentucky. *Modern Language Journal,* 1971, *55,* 290-298.

Mueller, T.H. and Harris, R. The effect of an audio-lingual program on drop-out rate. *Modern Language Journal,* 1966, *50,* 133-137.

Naiman, N., Fröhlich, M., Stern, H.H. and Todesco, A. The good language learner. Research in Education Series No. 7, Ontario Institute for Studies in Education, Toronto, 1978.

Neidt, C.O. and Hedlund, D.E. The relationship between changes in attitudes toward a course and final achievement. *Journal of Educational Research,* 1967, *61,* 56-58.

Neufeld, G. A theoretical perspective on the nature of linguistic aptitude. *Proceedings of the Fifth Symposium of the Canadian Association of Applied Linguistics,* 1974.

Oller, J.W., Baca, L., and Vigil, F. Attitudes and attained proficiency in ESL: A sociolinguistic study of Mexican-Americans in the Southwest. *TESOL Quarterly,* 1977, *11,* 173-182.

Oller, J.W., Hudson, A. and Liu, P. Attitudes and attained proficiency in ESL: A sociolinguistic study of native speakers of Chinese in the United States. *Language Learning,* 1977, *27,* 1-27.

Oller, J.W. and Perkins, K. Intelligence and language proficiency as sources of variance in self-reported affective variables. *Language Learning,* 1979, *28,* 85-97.

Randhawa, B.S., and Korpan, S.M. Assessment of some significant affective variables and the prediction of achievement in French. *Canadian Journal of Behavioural Science,* 1973, *5,* 24-33.

Schuman, H., and Johnson, M.P. Attitudes and behaviour. *Annual Review of Sociology*, 1976, 2, 161-207.

Smythe, P.C., Stennett, R.G. and Feenstra, H.J. Attitude, aptitude and type of instructional programme in second language acquisition. *Canadian Journal of Behavioural Science*, 1972, 4, 307-321.

Symonds, P.M. A modern language prognosis test. *Publication of the American and Canadian Committees on Modern Foreign Languages*, 1929, 41, 91-126.

Wicker, A.W. Attitudes vs. actions: The relationship of verbal and overt responses to attitude objects. *Journal of Social Issues*, 1969, 25, 41-78.

Chapter 7

Cognitive and Social Consequences of Bilingualism

Fred Genesee, Department of Psychology, McGill University

It is probably not unreasonable to speculate that there are as many bilingual as monolingual individuals in the world. Even in Canada, the incidence of bilingualism is high. For example, a survey conducted in the Vancouver public schools during 1974 indicated that approximately 34 per cent of the elementary school students and 21 per cent of the secondary school students did not speak English as a first language (Ellis, 1975). This means that at some point during their educational careers these children will probably become bilingual in English and their respective native languages; many of these individuals may well retain bilingual competence throughout adulthood as well. A similar picture probably characterizes other parts of Canada where recent immigration is high. The growing popularity of immersion-type school programs, where school children are educated in a second, non-native language, suggests that the incidence of bilingualism is on the increase among native-born Canadians as they attempt to learn the other official language, through French immersion programs for example (Genesee, 1978), or to relearn original ethnic languages (Lupul, 1976). In short, bilingualism is a salient aspect of Canadian, as well as world, society.

Classification and Measurement of Bilingualism

Classification
While most people would accept the minimal definition of bilingualism as knowledge of more than one language, there is not unanimous agreement as to what this really means. For example, Bloomfield (1933) maintains that

only individuals who have complete or native-like competence in both their languages should be labelled bilingual. This type of bilingual is sometimes referred to as balanced bilingual. On the other hand, Haugen (1956) and Macnamara (1967a) extend the label to include individuals who have even minimal competence in a second language. But competence in what aspect of the language? Macnamara points out that bilingualism is not a single skill but a combination of numerous skills, including speaking, listening comprehension, reading and writing. Bilinguals differ in the number of language skills they possess, and in terms of their level of competence in each. For example, bilingual A may speak and understand French as a second language very well but read and write it very poorly. Macnamara has suggested that measurement of bilingual competence be extended even further so that each of the four major skills be assessed in terms of the following sub-skills: phonological (or accent), lexical (or vocabulary), syntactic (or grammar) and semantic (or meaning).

Bilinguals can be characterized in other ways as well. Distinctions have been made according to the contexts in which a bilingual uses each language. Weinreich (1953), a pioneer in the field of bilingualism, distinguishes between what he called compound bilinguals who use their languages interchangeably in all contexts (e.g., languages X and Y are both used at home, work, and school), and coordinate bilinguals who use each language in certain circumscribed contexts (e.g., language X at home and work, but language Y at school).

Still other bases of classification are related to language acquisition history, and can include the age and circumstances under which the two languages were learned. It has been suggested that individuals who learn both languages simultaneously (infant bilinguals) and/or in the same contexts (compound bilinguals) are different from bilinguals who learn the second language after the first one has been mastered (childhood or adolescent bilinguals).

Measurement

A variety of measuring instruments and devices have been used to assess the language competence of bilinguals or to determine their classification according to one or more of the criteria discussed earlier. These measurement techniques can be subsumed under three general types: (1) language achievement tests, (2) psycholinguistic tests, and (3) report procedures and questionnaires.

Language Achievement Tests
These tests assess an individual's acquired competence in language by testing performance in different aspects, such as reading, writing, speaking and listening. If the tests are standardized, then it is possible to compare an individual bilingual's achievement in one skill, such as reading, with his/her achievement in another skill, such as writing. Or, one can assess a

bilingual's language achievement by comparing his/her performance on one such test to that of a monolingual on the same test. Thus, achievement tests can satisfy the measurement needs of a competence-based classification.

Psycholinguistic Tests
In contrast with language achievement measures, psycholinguistic tests assess performance using a variety of tasks and situations which are not generally regarded as typical or common language functions. Macnamara (1967b) has subdivided this category of tests into three types: fluency, flexibility and dominance. Tests of language fluency generally measure the speaker's speed of verbal response on the assumption that languages which are poorly mastered will result in slower reaction times. Fluency has been assessed in many ways: by measuring speed of response to simple directions given in two different languages; by counting the number of words beginning with a certain letter than can be given in two languages during a fixed time span; and by measuring the speed with which pictures can be identified in two languages, to mention three examples. Tests of language flexibility assess the speaker's ability to manipulate or analyze language. In Macnamara's (1967a) richness of vocabulary test, for example, the respondent is required to provide as many synonymous words or expressions he/she can to describe a target phrase, such as "he is drunk," while in Lambert, Havelka and Gardner's (1958) word detection test, the subject is required to identify from a long nonsense word as many words possible in either of two languages, e.g., French or English words in the string DANSONODENT.

Tests of language dominance are concerned with determining which of the bilingual's two languages is stronger. Of all the psycholinguistic tests, these are indeed the most clever and amusing. For example, Lambert modified the Stroop colour-word test to assess language balance in bilinguals. In the regular version of this test, the subject is given a list of colour names (blue, red, green and yellow) printed in coloured ink which does not correspond to the colours named by the words. The subject's task is to identify the colours of the ink while ignoring the colour names, a difficult task since subjects cannot usually completely ignore the colour words. To test bilingual language balance, the subject is given lists of colour words in each language on separate occasions and is required to identify the ink colours ignoring the colour names; on some trials the subject responds in one language and on other trials in the other language. By comparing the bilingual's speed of colour identification when the words are printed in each language it is possible to determine whether one language is more dominant than the other, since presumably the words presented in the dominant language will be more difficult to ignore and, therefore, produce more interference in colour naming. If the two languages are equally strong, then there should be equivalent performance in both language conditions.

Report Procedures and Questionnaires

These techniques fall into two types—self reports and other's reports of language competence. These types of techniques have considerable face validity in that they appear to tap language competence as most people perceive it. Research by Macnamara (1967a) provides evidence that such techniques may also possess concurrent validity in that they correlate significantly with language achievement tests.

Questionnaires are also used to gather information about language acquisition history and usage; for example, as part of an empirical test of Weinreich's distinction between coordinate and compound bilingualism, Lambert, Havelka and Crosby (1958) used detailed questionnaires to classify bilingual subjects according to when each language was learned, with whom and under what circumstances. Similarly, current patterns and preferences of language use can be established through direct questioning of the subject. These types of information are difficult to obtain using other techniques.

Cognitive Consequences

Theories about Language and Cognition

There are a number of prominent theories relating language to cognition which would lead one to expect that bilingualism influences cognitive functioning. They are Whorf's theory of linguistic relativity, Vygotsky's theory of language and thought, and Piaget's theory of epistemology.

The linguistic relativity theory of Benjamin Whorf (1956) proposes that a people's perception of the environment is influenced by the language they speak. The classic example is that of the Inuit who has many words to differentiate a wide variety of types of snow. According to a strong version of the Whorfian hypothesis, speakers of languages that lack these linguistic distinctions are unable to make similar perceptual differentiations among these snow types. Few theorists today would accept such a rigid deterministic version of the theory. A weaker version of the theory which maintains that each language encodes cognitive, perceptual or social distinctions that are important to speakers of the language is much more acceptable. Accordingly, to know a specific language is to know and make a specific set of distinctions. The theory, in both its weak and strong form, has fairly evident implications for cognition and bilingualism since it predicts that the perceptual-cognitive system of the bilingual will be influenced by two languages in contrast to the monolingual's one.

Vygotsky (1962) also claims that language has an important role to play in cognitive development. According to Vygotsky, child language is initially vocalized speech and serves interpersonal communicative functions, in much the way that adult language does. In addition, the child uses language to orient and organize his/her activities. Vygotsky refers to the former type of speech as social speech and to the latter as egocentric speech.

While social speech becomes more and more evident with age, egocentric speech becomes more and more abbreviated and idiosyncratic, finally disappearing as overt speech and gradually becoming internalized. As egocentric speech was once used to orient the child's behaviour and activities, internalized or inner speech is used to orient and organize the child's thoughts. Language, as inner speech, influences the course of cognitive development since it provides an abstract symbolic system to represent and organize the child's thoughts. Segalowitz (1977) likens the impact of internalization of language to the development of a "mental calculus" that can be used to manipulate mental symbols or thought. Bilingualism and its resultant internalization of two languages might be likened to advanced mental calculus with alternative rules for symbol manipulation.

Piaget (1959) does not regard language as such an important causal element in cognitive development; for Piaget cognition gives rise to language and, relatively speaking, is uninfluenced by language development. Piaget, nevertheless, believes that language provides a tool by means of which the individual can interact with his environment and by means of which he/she can express abstract cognitive abilities. It is a particularly valuable tool for the developing child since it can supply feedback on operational structures to bring them into conformity with cultural-social-linguistic norms. According to this theoretical perspective bilingualism can influence cognitive development since special cognitive processes may be called into play in order to cope with the potential interference involved in acquiring and coordinating two language systems.

Comparisons of Bilinguals and Monolinguals

Much of the early research on bilingualism and cognition focussed on the intelligence of monolingual and bilingual school-aged children. In reviewing the early studies, Arsenian (1945) and Darcy (1953) have concluded that bilingual children scored lower than monolingual children on tests of verbal intelligence but at the same level on tests of non-verbal intelligence. Macnamara (1966) suggested that the decrement in verbal ability among bilingual children which was often noted in these studies was due to a "balance effect." That is to say, proficiency in the native language was retarded to the extent that proficiency in the second language increased, much in the same way that adding weights to an old-fashioned balance causes one side of the beam to fall as the other side rises.

There were serious methodological flaws in many of these studies, two of which deserve mention. First, the bilingual and monolingual children in many of the studies were often not comparable because socio-economic factors were not controlled. Second, the children's level of proficiency in the language of the IQ test was seldom controlled so that they were often evaluated by their performance in their weaker language.

More recent studies have tried to correct these methodological short-comings and, as well, have used more diversified measures of intelligence or cognitive development.

A study carried out by Peal and Lambert (1962) with ten-year old French-English bilinguals in Montreal marks a turning point in the history of research on this topic. They found that their bilingual subjects were superior to carefully matched monolingual control subjects on a number of verbal and non-verbal cognitive tests. When Peal and Lambert analyzed their test results further, they found evidence of a greater number of statistically independent factors or abilities for the bilinguals than for the monolinguals. This led them to conclude that the bilinguals had performed better because they had access to a greater number of separate cognitive skills. Peal and Lambert argued that this greater cognitive flexibility was a result of switching from one language to the other or, more generally, from one symbol system to another.

Peal and Lambert have suggested also that since bilinguals have two linguistic symbols for the same referents they attend to the underlying semantic features of words more than do monolinguals. This possibility has received some empirical support. Ianco-Worrall (1972), working in South Africa, and Ben-Zeev (1977a) working in Israel and the United States, both report that bilingual children were more willing than monolingual children to accept at an early age that the linguistic labels used to name objects or concepts are interchangeable, that is to say arbitrary. Thus, for example, the animal *dog* could be called a "pencil." A similar observation had been reported by Leopold (1939) in the famous case study of his bilingual daughter, Hildegaard.

The enhanced ability that bilinguals demonstrate in dissociating words from their meanings may be part of a general tendency to attend to the underlying, conceptual aspects of all types of information, verbal or non-verbal. In the case of verbal information, Balkan (1970) found that Swiss bilingual subjects had less difficulty than monolingual subjects identifying words which served different grammatical functions although they had the same graphic representation (e.g., the noun "pitch" as in tar, and the verb "pitch" as in throw). In the non-verbal domain, both Balkan (1970) and Ben-Zeev (1977a) found that bilinguals were better able than mono-linguals to isolate critical components in large, complex visual arrays, such as hidden figures.

Ben-Zeev (1977b) maintains that it is the potential interference inherent in knowing and learning two languages which mediates the cognitive effects of bilingualism. She postulates four strategies by which the bilingual tries to resolve such potential interlingual interference: (1) language analysis; (2) sensitivity to feedback cues; (3) maximization of structural differences between the two languages; and (4) neutralization of structures within a language. Although these strategies are initially developed in order to deal with linguistic interference, they come to be used as general cognitive strategies and are used in non-linguistic domains. For example, the strategy of language analysis which initially emerges to resolve interlingual interference by means of awareness of the alternative linguistic structures that can be used to express meanings develops into a general tendency to attend to underlying, conceptual features as reported by Balkan (1970) and Ben-Zeev (1977a).

Cummins (1978) has hypothesized that certain minimal levels of competence in the two languages may be necessary to benefit cognitively from bilingualism or at least to avoid possible negative cognitive effects resulting from poor mastery of one or both languages. This hypothesis helps explain the apparently contradictory findings reported by the researchers before and after Peal and Lambert. Examination of the bilingual samples that participated in these two generations of research supports Cummins' claim insofar as the early studies tended to use non-balanced bilinguals whereas studies since the 1960s have used balanced or at least highly proficient bilinguals.

Some Social Psychological Consequences
The theoretical models of Whorf, Vygotsky and Piaget would suggest that acquisition of a second language may serve to acculturate the individual to the second language culture, since language embodies socially and culturally relevant distinctions. At the same time, and perhaps more significantly, competence in a second language may give the speaker access to the cultural values or norms of the second language group directly through face-to-face communication with members of the target language group or indirectly through use of the group's literature or media. Lambert (1967) maintains that to acquire competence in a second language is to adopt the habits, perspectives and values of that group, to become almost a member of that group. (See also Chapter 6.)

Language is also relevant to social psychology since it has been identified as an important symbol of ethnic group membership and distinctiveness (Taylor, Bassili & Aboud, 1973). In addition to its significance as an explicit social marker, language may also serve to represent important underlying sociocultural differences that might be difficult to represent otherwise. Acquisition of a second language may similarly provide a basis for perceived group distinctiveness and identity, or may alter the individual's perceptions of himself/herself in other ethnically relevant ways through processes analogous to socialization.

Bilinguals' Perceptions of Themselves
In a review of early work relating bilingualism to personality formation, Diebold (1968) concluded that bilingualism leads to emotional maladjustment. Diebold noted that some early researchers in the field suspected that

bilingualism might give rise to two distinct personality structures, reflecting cultural norms associated with each language, which in turn implied psychodynamic conflict, such as schizophrenia in the extreme case.

In fact, there was virtually no convincing empirical evidence to support such a working model; evidence which was available was often anecdotal and, therefore, ambiguous. Moreover, even as a theoretical position, there are a number of questionable assumptions implied in this causal chain— one, that there are necessarily profound differences of psychological relevance between most cultural groups; two, that any differences between cultural groups are irreconcilable; and three, that cultural differences are necessarily reflected in personality.

Furthermore, to talk about bilingualism or biculturalism as if it had unconditionally negative or positive consequences would be a gross oversimplification. Even among monolinguals where language may be an important aspect of ethnic identity (Taylor et al., 1973), this is not always the case. Adiv (1977) found that native French-speaking Jewish Canadian children were more likely to view themselves as similar to English-speaking Jewish Canadians than to other French speakers who were not Jewish. Gardner and Lambert (1972) found that Franco-Americans in New England and Louisiana had quite different reactions to their dual ethnolinguistic backgrounds. Some individuals appeared to orient themselves exclusively toward one of their ethnolinguistic reference groups and ignored the other; others seemed not to think of themselves in ethnolinguistic terms at all; and, interestingly, some identified positively with both of their ethnolinguistic reference groups.

Lamy (1974) has suggested that bilinguals in communities where intergroup hostilities and competitions are high, where the cultures of both linguistic groups are dissimilar, and where one group is dominant, will lack a strong sense of group identity, will be less ethnocentric and will feel less group loyalty than their monolingual counterparts. Lambert (1977) differentiates between additive and subtractive forms of bilingualism. Additive bilingualism is characterized by the acquisition of two socially useful and prestigious languages which are mutually viable. This type of bilingualism is most likely to occur if the individual is a member of the majority group so that acquisition of a second language is not likely to replace his/her native language or to threaten his/her cultural identity. Subtractive bilingualism, on the other hand, occurs when the acquisition of one language and its associated culture threatens to replace or dominate the other language and culture. This latter type of situation is most likely to happen with members of minority groups whose language and culture are not shared by the majority of the population.

A number of studies suggest that knowledge of a second language by members of a minority ethnolinguistic group may indeed engender some loss of identity with the home group and/or a greater sense of identity with or similarity to the second language group. Lamy (1974) found that bilingual French Canadians in Montreal were less likely than monolingual French Canadians to identify exclusively with the concept "French Canadian." This response was less than universal, however, accounting for 19 per cent of the respondents who spoke French and English equally well and only 5 per cent of the respondents who spoke English less well than French. In a similar vein, Meisel (1978) reports that French Canadians who had some, although not perfect, knowledge of English expressed opinions concerning private values (law and order), general public policy (size and formation of the Canadian armed forces) and policy relevant to ethnic relations (special status for Quebec as a Canadian province) that resembled those of English-speaking majority Canadians. Again, this was not universally true. Pitts (1978) found that adult French Canadians who had attended exclusively French schools as children and adolescents expressed higher levels of self-esteem than did other adult French Canadians who had attended exclusively English schools. She reasoned that French Canadians who had attended all French schools were less likely to have experienced personal discrimination and, therefore, were more likely to have learned to value their own ethnic group than French Canadians who had attended English schools. In contrast, Aellen and Lambert (1969) found no loss of ethnic identity among a group of bilingual French Canadian subjects from Montreal. At the same time, however, their bilingual respondents did express a greater sense of identity with English Canadians than did monolingual French Canadian respondents—a type of dual ethnic identity perhaps. More detailed investigations are needed to delineate and explain the circumstances under which different sociocultural reactions to bilingualism occur among minority group members.

On the other hand, acquisition of a minority group language by members of a majority group does not seem to lead to appreciable change in ethnic identity. Genesee, Tucker and Lambert (1978) found that while English Canadian children in Grades 1 and 2 of all French schools reported significantly greater identity with French Canadians than did control children in all English schools, no such differences were apparent in higher grades. There were no differences between the groups at any grade level when their identity with English Canadians was examined. This finding has been corroborated by Cziko, Lambert and Gutter (1979) using Grade 6 children. Genesee speculated that the ethnic identity of the English children in the French schools was influenced primarily by the sociocultural orientation of their families and community so that the ethnic influence that the school milieu might have been expected to exert was neutralized or offset.

Meisel's (1978) survey of adult Canadians' sociopolitical beliefs is also relevant here. In contrast to the beliefs of bilingual French Canadians which tended to resemble those of English Canadians, the beliefs of bilingual English Canadians did not resemble those of French Canadians. There was little or no evidence of socialization toward minority group beliefs among majority group members who were bilingual.

In a related vein, it is interesting to ask how members of a minority ethnolinguistic group who speak the majority group language as a first language (i.e., they demonstrate linguistic, and therefore possibly cultural, asssimilation) will perceive themselves if they subsequently learn their ancestral language. There is some, although minimal, research on this issue. In a study carried out in a French American community in the state of Maine, Lambert, Giles and Picard (1975) found that ten-year-old French American students attending special French language schools in their communities were much more favourably disposed toward French than were comparable students attending the regular English language schools. Lupul (1976) reports that native English-speaking children of Ukrainian background who attended a bilingual school program where Ukrainian and English were used as media of instruction did not manifest feelings of inferiority. On the contrary, they used Ukrainian spontaneously in and outside the classroom, much to the surprise of their unilingual or barely bilingual parents. Furthermore, the students expressed no antipathy towards English.

Clearly, the sociocultural impact of bilingualism on the individual is more complex than Diebold's early summary suggests. Subgroups of bilinguals which differ with respect to social status appear to have characteristic patterns of reactions to their dual ethnolinguistic background. Although general patterns are discernible, not all individuals within a particular subgroup express the same reaction. Much more research needs to be done to explicate the individual variance.

Others' Perceptions of Bilinguals

Bilinguals may be perceived quite differently depending upon the language they are heard to speak. Lambert, Hodgson, Gardner and Fillenbaum (1960) found that English-French bilinguals from Montreal were perceived significantly more favourably when speaking English than when speaking French. This was true whether the subjects themselves were English or French Canadian. Since the subjects formed impressions of the stimulus persons on the basis of only speech samples that were presented by means of a tape recorder, they were not aware that the persons they were listening to were bilingual and had actually been presented to them twice, once in a French guise and once in an English guise. This procedure has thus come to be called the *matched guise technique*. Lambert and his colleagues interpreted their results as reflecting unfavourable stereotypes of English Canadians toward French Canadians and the internalization of these negative stereotypes by French Canadians as self-denigrating perceptions.

A subsequent study was undertaken by Anisfeld and Lambert (1964) to investigate the development of such perceptions by French Canadian children. In contrast to the adult response pattern reported in the 1960 study, ten-year old French Canadian children did not downgrade French speakers relative to English ones. In fact, monolingual French-speaking subjects expressed preferences for French guises; bilingual subjects, on the other hand, expressed relatively few preferential reactions to the speech samples. Anisfeld and Lambert suggested that the preferences expressed by the monolingual French-speaking children for the French guises was offset in the case of the bilingual children by their enhanced sense of identity with English people which had been engendered by their knowledge of English. This possibility was supported by questionnaire information indicating that the bilingual subjects did indeed identify more with English Canadians than did the monolingual subjects.

Lambert, Frankel and Tucker (1966) have reported that children's impressions of others, as measured by the matched guise technique, may also depend upon socio-economic factors. In particular, they found that relatively affluent French Canadian adolescent girls who were attending private schools showed a marked preference for outgroup English-speaking stimulus persons over ingroup French-speaking stimulus persons. French Canadian girls attending public schools showed little differential preference for either group, but, when they did, they tended to prefer speakers from their own group. The English-speaking stimulus persons may have been highly valued models for the private school girls because of their own socio-economic aspirations; English often being a symbol of economic and social advancement. On the other hand, ingroup allegiance, and thus ethnicity, may have been valued more by the public school girls.

Attributions along socio-economic and personal ethnic dimensions may be differentially related to speech style. It has been found that while stimulus speakers of standard dialects may be upgraded on traits related to intellectual competence and social status relative to speakers of non-standard dialects, the latter may be upgraded on traits related to personal integrity (honesty, reliability) and social attractiveness (friendliness, considerateness) especially by other non-standard dialect speakers (Giles & Powesland, 1975).

The matched guise technique has proven to be a very powerful research tool in Canada and elsewhere where bilingualism is prevalent. It is limited, however, to the case of balanced bilinguals, when, in fact, the incidence of balanced bilingualism may well be much lower than that of non-balanced bilingualism. Research by Gatbonton (in Segalowitz & Gatbonton, 1977) has studied others' perceptions of bilinguals who differed in their level of second language competence, some having a native-like second language accent, some with heavily accented second language speech, and others having intermediate skill. In addition to personal and social traits that were attributed to the speakers, Gatbonton examined the sociopolitical attitudes that were attributed to them, and the subjects' willingness to affiliate with them as a function of their degree of second language competence. In contrast to the matched guise procedure where the subjects are not aware of the speakers' true group membership, Gatbonton's subjects, who were all French Canadians, knew that the stimulus speakers were all French Canadian. She found that speakers with heavily accented English were judged to hold attitudes that were highly pro-Francophone and not at all pro-Anglophone, whereas speakers with native-like pronunciation in English were attributed with very pro-Anglophone but not pro-Francophone attitudes. This was true regardless of the subjects' own English language competence and regardless of their own feelings regarding Quebec nationalism, suggesting that there may be social norms in bilingual communities regarding the relationship of second language competence and ingroup/outgroup allegiance.

On the other hand, the subjects' own feelings did influence their reported willingness to affiliate with the different types of speakers. In particular, subjects who were not very nationalistic reported that they were quite willing to interact with the native-like speakers under most circumstances whereas subjects who were nationalistic were unwilling to interact with the native-like speakers under most circumstances, even though they were always French Canadian. The ingroup speakers who were very competent in the second language may have been deemed undesirable participants in social situations because they were perceived to lack ingroup allegiance, which is valued highly by nationalistic group members.

Genesee and Holobow (1978) have studied the developmental aspects of these findings by examining the reactions of eleven-year old Anglophone children toward other Anglophone children who differed in their level of competence in French. They also investigated the children's reactions to second language speakers from the ougroup—French Canadian. They found that very competent second language speakers, regardless of whether they were members of the ingroup or outgroup, were perceived more positively along a number of personal dimensions; they were judged more desirable as interactants in different types of situations; and they were perceived to hold more favourable attitudes toward the second language group than were the less competent second language speakers. All subjects, regardless of their own second language competence, reacted more favourably to the more competent second language speakers. Moreover, the subjects' reactions to the French Canadian speakers were not influenced by the subjects' attitudes toward French Canadians in general. This latter finding is particularly noteworthy since it contrasts with English Canadians' negative ratings of French Canadians who are heard speaking only French, as reported in Lambert's matched guise studies (Lambert, Hodgson, Gardner & Fillenbaum, 1960).

Differences between the Gatbonton and Genesee and Holobow

findings may be due to a number of factors. English Canadians' reactions to second language competence may differ from those of French Canadians because, as was pointed out earlier, acquisition of a second language may have less serious sociocultural consequences for members of a majority group than for members of a minority one. These results may also reflect the fact that the students in the Genesee and Holobow study were young and immature so that it was difficult for them to integrate and react to diverse pieces of related social information. In other words, young children may be more likely to react to others in terms of immediate superficial characteristics without the mitigating influences of their own social values and experiences. In any event, these children's positive reactions to second language competence could be used to develop and promote favourable attitudes toward members of other language groups.

The significance of language as a social marker is not peculiar to bilinguals. Voice and speech quality have been shown to be generally important factors affecting the way people view others. For example, Seligman, Tucker and Lambert (1972) found that the quality of pupils' speech was as important a determinant of their perceived ability among teachers as were other types of information, such as work samples. The important feature about being bilingual is that in the absence of other information a balanced bilingual may be perceived quite differently depending on the language he/she is speaking. In fact, language may be manipulated consciously by bilinguals to systematically influence others' perceptions of them.

Howard Giles of Bristol University, England, and his associates have studied the social psychological consequences of changing languages or language styles during interpersonal communication. They have investigated three types of language strategies: convergence, divergence and maintenance (Giles & Powesland, 1975). Language convergence occurs when a speaker adopts the language or language style of the interlocutor during interpersonal communication. The social psychological significance of this speech strategy is demonstrated in a study carried out in Montreal by Giles, Taylor and Bourhis (1973) in which they found that French Canadian bilinguals who used English to perform a task with English Canadian subjects were perceived in a more favourable light by the subjects than similar bilinguals who used French to perform the task. Furthermore, when the subjects were asked to return a message, they were more likely to exhibit reciprocal convergence (i.e., use French) when their interlocutor had previously demonstrated convergence toward them than when he had not. Results also showed that the more effort speakers were thought to have expended in order to converge and the more convergence was perceived to reflect voluntary effort rather than external pressure, the more favourable was the reaction (Simard, Taylor & Giles, 1977). Giles and Powesland (1975) have suggested that language convergence results in positive impression formation because it reduces dissimilarities between the speaker and his interlocutor and/or because it facilitates communication.

However, use of an outgroup language or dialect may be viewed negatively by members of one's own group since it may connote a shift in group allegiance. Thus, maintenance of one's speech style or language variety may be favoured under certain circumstances. Adolescent French Canadians in Montreal claimed that they would not shift from Quebec-style French to European-style French to accommodate a European French-speaking person, but rather would maintain their Canadian style of French (Bourhis, Giles & Lambert, 1975). European French is generally regarded as relatively more prestigious than Canadian French and often has more positive personal characteristics associated with it (d'Anglejan & Tucker, 1973). Interestingly, however, in another part of the experiment where these same subjects listened to a simulated radio interview, they did not rate a French Canadian whom they heard switch to European French less favourably than one who maintained Canadian French. Thus, we have evidence of the significance of language as a symbol both of group loyalty and of highly valued personal characteristics. These subjects were evidently caught between the two.

In contrast to situations in which language convergence occurs, other situations favour the deliberate use of a language or dialect that diverges from that of one's interlocutor. Bourhis and Giles (1977) report that Welsh subjects broadened their Welsh accents in English when a member of an English outgroup, who was really working in collusion with the experimenter, threatened them by challenging their reasons for maintaining "a dying language which had a dismal future." Similarly, Flemish-speaking subjects in Belgium diverged from English, a neutral language, to Flemish in response to the perception of ethnic threat from an outgroup French speaker (Bourhis, Giles, Leyens & Tajfel, 1979). Language divergence achieves its impact by dissociating the speaker from his/her interlocutor.

The distinction between divergence and maintenance is not always straightforward since both strategies may be manifested by speakers using their native language. Divergence, as is also true of convergence, presupposes that the speaker has some level of competence in the other language; maintenance, on the other hand, does not. Moreover, divergence entails motivational patterns, such as an explicit desire to assert one's ethnicity, which may not characterize the speaker who is simply exhibiting language maintenance.

It is quite evident from this line of research that a bilingual's decision to use one language or another will have important social consequences in terms of both others' impressions of him/her and their behaviour toward him/her. The precise social circumstances under which language convergence or divergence occurs and whether positive or negative perceptions result remains to be described since most research on this topic has examined the social psychological consequences of interpersonal language accommodation in situations which lack well-defined social or cultural norms. Bourhis and Genesee (1979) have begun to examine the relative importance of social, cultural and discourse variables in judging the appropriateness of bilingual code switching. Their subjects listened to a simulated dialogue, consisting of several speech acts, between a French-speaking salesman and an English-speaking customer in a Montreal store. The results indicated that the subjects evaluated the appropriateness of the language used by the salesman primarily in terms of the social norm that "the customer is always right" and, therefore, should be served in his native language, rather than in terms of emerging cultural norms in Quebec which maintain that French, the language of the majority of the population, be used. Thus, the use of English was generally favoured by all subjects over the use of French. The significance of cultural norms was evident in the responses of French Canadian subjects who favoured greater use of French, even though overall they endorsed the use of English in this situation. While use of French by the salesman was generally regarded as inappropriate, it was more likely to be viewed favourably, if the customer himself had used French earlier in the conversation. Thus, the social psychological consequences of language switching during extended discourse may depend upon subtle and complex interactions among a variety of factors. As research methods to study bilingual language use become more sophisticated and dynamic, our understanding of the social psychology of language switching will also become more sophisticated and dynamic. There has already been considerable progress in the development of methods to study this topic, progressing from the original matched guise procedure, developed by Lambert, to the naturalistic language accommodation techniques of Giles and associates, and now the use of extended discourse paradigms.

REFERENCES

Adiv, E. *The significance of language in cultural identity.* Instructional Services, Protestant School Board of Greater Montreal, Montreal, Quebec, 1977.

Aellen, C. & Lambert, W.E. Ethnic identification and personality adjustments of Canadian adolescents of mixed English-French parentage. *Canadian Journal of Behavioural Science,* 1969, *1,* 69-86.

d'Anglejan, A., & Tucker, G.R. Sociolinguistic correlates of speech style in Quebec. In R.W. Shuy and R.W. Fasold (eds.), *Language Attitudes: Current Trends and Prospects.* Washington: Georgetown University Press, 1973, 1-27.

Anisfeld, E., & Lambert, W.E. Evaluational reactions of bilingual and monolingual children to spoken languages. *Journal of Abnormal and Social Psychology,* 1964, *69,* 89-97.

Arsenian, S. Bilingualism in the post-war world. *Psychological Bulletin,* 1945, *42,* 65-85.

Balkan, L. *Les effets du bilinguisme français-anglais sur les aptitudes intellectuelles.* Bruxelles: Aimav, 1970.

Ben-Zeev, S. The influence of bilingualism on cognitive development and cognitive strategy. *Child Development,* 1977a, 1009-1018.

Ben-Zeev, S. Mechanisms by which childhood bilingualism affects understanding of language and cognitive structures. In P. Hornby (ed.), *Bilingualism: Psychological, Social and Educational Implications*. New York: Academic Press, 1977b, 29-56.

Bloomfield, L. *Language*, New York: Holt, Rinehart & Winston, 1933.

Bourhis, R.Y., & Genesee, F. *Evaluative reactions to code switching strategies in Montreal*. Psychology Department, McMaster University, Hamilton, Ontario, 1979.

Bourhis, R.Y., & Giles, H. The language of intergroup distinctiveness. In H. Giles (ed.), *Language, Ethnicity and Intergroup Relations*. London: Academic Press, 1977.

Bourhis, R.Y., Giles H., & Lambert, W.E. Social consequences of accommodating one's style of speech: A cross-national investigation. *International Journal of the Sociology of Language*, 1975, *6*, 53-71.

Bourhis, R.Y., Giles, H., Leyens, J., & Tajfel, H. Psycholinguistic distinctiveness: Language divergence in Belgium. In H. Giles & R. St. Clair (eds.), *Language and Social Psychology*, Oxford: Basil Blackwell, 1979, 158-185.

Cummins, J. Educational implications of mother tongue maintenance in minority-language groups. *The Canadian Modern Language Review*, 1978, *34*, 395-416.

Cziko, G.A., Lambert, W.E., & Gutter, J. French immersion programs and students' social attitudes: A multidimensional investigation. *Working Papers on Bilingualism*, 1979, *19*, 13-28.

Darcy, N.T. A review of the literature on the effects of bilingualism upon the measurement of intelligence. *Journal of Genetic Psychology*, 1953, *82*, 21-57.

Diebold, A.R. The consequences of early bilingualism in cognitive development and personality formation. In E. Norbeck, D. Price-Williams & W.M. McCord (eds.), *The Study of Personality: An Inter-Disciplinary Appraisal*. New York: Holt, Rinehart & Winston, 1968, 218-245.

Ellis, E.N. *Survey of pupils in Vancouver schools for whom English is a second language*. Research Report 75-23, Department of Evaluation and Research, Board of Trustees, Vancouver, January 1975.

Gardner, R.C., & Lambert, W.E. *Attitudes and Motivation in Second Language Learning*. Rowley: Newbury House, 1972.

Genesee, F. A longitudinal evaluation of an early immersion school program. *Canadian Journal of Education*, 1978, *3*, 31-50.

Genesee, F., & Holobow, N. Children's reactions to variations in second language competence. In M. Paradis (ed.), *Aspects of Bilingualism*. Columbia, S.C.: Hornbeam Press, 1978, 185-201.

Genesee, F., Tucker, G.R., & Lambert, W.E. The development of ethnic identity and ethnic role taking skills in children from different school settings. *International Journal of Psychology*, 1978, *13*, 39-57.

Giles, H., & Powesland, P.F. *Speech style and social evaluation*. New York: Academic Press, 1975.

Giles, H., Taylor, D.M., & Bourhis, R.Y. Towards a theory of interpersonal accommodation through languages: Some Canadian data. *Language in Society*, 1973, *2*, 177-192.

Haugen, E. *Bilingualism in the Americas: A Bibliography and a Research Guide*. Montgomery: University of Alabama Press, 1956.

Ianco-Worrall, A.D. Bilingualism and cognitive development. *Child Development*, 1972, *43*, 1,390-1,400.

Lambert, W.E. The social psychology of bilingualism. *Journal of Social Issues*, 1967, *23*, 91-109.

Lambert, W.E. The effects of bilingualism on the individual: Cognitive and sociocultural consequences. In P. Hornby (ed.), *Bilingualism: Psychological, Social and Educational Implications*. New York: Academic Press, 1977, 15-28.

Lambert, W.E., Frankel, H., & Tucker, G.R. Judging personality through speech: A French Canadian example. *Journal of Communication*, 1966, *16*, 305-321.

Lambert, W.E., Giles, H., & Picard, O. Language attitudes in a French-American community. *International Journal of the Sociology of Language*, 1975, *4*, 127-152.

Lambert, W.E., Havelka, J., & Crosby, C. The influence of language acquisition contexts on bilingualism. *Journal of Abnormal and Social Psychology*, 1958, *56*, 239-244.

Lambert, W.E., Havelka, J., & Gardner, R.C. Linguistic manifestations of bilingualism. *The American Journal of Psychology*, 1958, *72*, 77-82.

Lambert, W.E., Hodgson, R.C., Gardner, R.C., & Fillenbaum, S. Evaluational reactions to spoken languages. *Journal of Abnormal and Social Psychology*, 1960, *60*, 44-51.

Lamy, P. *The impact of bilingualism upon ethnolinguistic identity*. Department of Sociology, University of Ottawa, 1974.

Leopold, W.F. *Speech development of a bilingual child: A linguistic record*. Evanston, Ill.: Northwestern University Press, 1939-1949.

Lupul, M. Bilingual education and the Ukrainians in Western Canada: Possibilities and problems. In M. Swain (ed.), *Bilingualism in Canadian Education: Issues and Research*. Canadian Society for the Study of Education Yearbook, Vol. 3, 1976, 86-106.

Macnamara, J. *Bilingualism and Primary Education*. Edinburgh: University Press, 1966.

Macnamara, J. How can one measure the extent of a person's bilingual proficiency? In L.G. Kelly (ed.), *Description and Measurement of Bilingualism*. Toronto: University of Toronto Press, 1967a, 80-97.

Macnamara, J. The bilingual's linguistic performance: A psychological overview. *Journal of Social Issues*, 1967b, *23*, 58-77.

Meisel, J. Values, language, and politics in Canada. In J. Fishman (ed.), *Advances in the Study of Societal Multilingualism*. New York: Mouton, 1978, 665-718.

Peal, E., & Lambert, W.E. The relation of bilingualism to intelligence. *Psychological Monographs*, *76*, 1962.

Pitts, R.A. The effects of exclusively French language schooling on self-esteem in Quebec. *Canadian Modern Language Review*, 1978, *34*, 372-380.

Piaget, J. *The Language and Thought of the Child*. 3rd Edition. London: Routledge and Kegan Paul, 1959.

Segalowitz, N. Psychological perspectives on bilingual education. In B. Spolsky & R. Cooper (eds.), *Frontiers of Bilingual Education*. Rowley: Newbury House, 1977, 119-158.

Segalowitz, N., & Gatbonton, E. Studies of the nonfluent bilingual. In P. Hornby (ed.), *Bilingualism: Psychological, Social and Educational Implications*. New York: Academic Press, 1977, 77-90.

Seligman, C.R., Tucker, G.R., & Lambert, W.E. The effects of speech style and other attributes on teachers' attitudes toward pupils. *Language and Society*, 1972, *1*, 131-142.

Simard, L., Taylor, D.M., & Giles H. Attribution processes and interpersonal accommodation in a bilingual setting. *Language and Speech*, 1977, *19*, 374-387.

Taylor, D.M., Bassili, J., & Aboud, F. Dimensions of ethnic identity: An example from Quebec. *Journal of Social Psychology*, 1973, *89*, 185-192.

Vygotsky, L.S. *Thought and Language*. Cambridge: M.I.T. Press, 1962.

Weinreich, U. *Languages in Contact*. New York: Linguistic Circle of New York, 1953.

Whorf, B. *Language, Thought and Reality*. Cambridge: John Wiley, 1956.

Section IV
Intergroup Relations

Chapter 8

Ethnic Attitudes

Rudolf Kalin[1], Department of Psychology, Queen's University

The term multiculturalism has been used in two senses; one, to refer to the fact of ethnic diversity, and two, to refer to the Canadian government's policy of recognizing and encouraging this diversity. In October 1971, Prime Minister Trudeau announced to the House of Commons a "policy of multiculturalism within a bilingual framework"[2] which was meant to *encourage the retention* of characteristic cultural features by those ethnic groups which desired to do so, and to *encourage the sharing* of these features with others in the larger Canadian society. The prime minister outlined a three-stage argument for promoting multiculturalism. First, the policy's joint goals were to "break down discriminatory attitudes and cultural jealousies" and thus assure "the cultural freedom of Canadians." Second, he asserted that such freedom from discrimination "must be founded on confidence in one's own individual identity; out of this can grow respect for that of others and a willingness to share ideas, attitudes and assumptions." Finally, he proposed that "a vigorous policy of multiculturalism will help create this initial confidence." In short, the prime minister essentially proposed a social psychological theory in which the promotion of multiculturalism leads to increased confidence in one's identity which in turn leads to respect for the identity of others.

A number of questions for research are contained or implied in these various assumptions and policy positions. Two issues emerge as particularly important. First, are Canadians willing to accept cultural diversity as social fact and as government policy? Second, is Prime Minister Trudeau's social psychological theory correct, namely that confidence in one's own identity is a prerequisite for the development of positive attitudes toward others? This theory will be referred to in this chapter as the "multiculturalism assumption."

Several studies have been conducted to date to provide answers to these questions, among which were two national surveys. The first was the Non-official Language Study (O'Bryan, Reitz & Kuplowska, 1976) which examined whether the various ethnic groups were in favour of retaining their own culture and language. The second was the Majority Attitudes Study (Berry, Kalin & Taylor, 1977). It assessed the ethnic attitudes of a national sample of Canadians. The research questions raised by the government's policy will be addressed on the basis of results from these two major studies and some subsequent investigations.

The Acceptance of Multiculturalism Among Other Ethnic Groups

The Non-official Languages Study was an extensive investigation of language and culture retention and was carried out with representative samples of ten ethnic groups (Chinese, Dutch, Germans, Greeks, Hungarians, Italians, Polish, Portuguese, Scandinavians and Ukrainians) in five metropolitan areas (Montreal, Toronto, Winnipeg, Edmonton, Calgary).

Results from this study regarding knowledge and use of non-official languages provided strong evidence that multiculturalism as a social fact is alive and well in Canada. Fifty per cent of the sample was fluent in a non-official language and 55 per cent made use of such a language every day. Knowledge and use varied considerably by ethnic group. Highest fluency rates were shown among Canadians of Greek, Hungarian, Italian, and Chinese origin, lowest among Scandinavian, Ukrainian and Polish Canadians. Use of a non-official language was dramatically different in the various groups. Ninety per cent of the Greek sample reported daily use, while only 8 per cent of the Scandinavian sample did. Non-official language knowledge and use was also strongly affected by the generational status of the respondent. By the third generation virtually no one was fluent anymore in the ancestral language.

Support for the government's policy was measured in two ways: (1) by a direct question of whether the respondent favoured the policy and, (2) by assessing the desire for the retention of non-official languages. According to both indices, support for the government's policy was substantial, but it varied considerably by ethnic group. It was strongest among Chinese, Ukrainians and Greeks and weakest among Scandinavians and Dutch. Not only was there a strongly expressed desire among the various groups to retain their ancestral language, but loss of that language was perceived to be the most serious problem facing the group, more serious than job discrimination, for example. It appears therefore, that ethnic diversity, both as social fact and as government policy is strongly supported among ethnic groups in Canada.

The Psychological Climate for Multiculturalism

In order to examine the views of all Canadians on ethnic diversity a second large-scale investigation was undertaken (Berry et al., 1977). A sample of 1,849 respondents was selected from a national sampling frame. Interviews were conducted in person during June and July 1974. After assessing a number of background characteristics of respondents, the interviews were primarily concerned with measuring attitudes in four domains: attitudes toward a number of ethnic groups in Canada, beliefs regarding cultural diversity, attitudes toward immigration, and prejudice and discrimination.

Selected results from the national survey and several additional studies are presented below in order to assess the psychological climate for multiculturalism in Canada. This is accomplished in two sections. In the first, results indicative of a positive reception of multiculturalism are summarized. The second section outlines results giving rise to concern.

Positive Signs

Ethnic Attitudes

Most attitudes were measured with seven-point Likert-type scales. A score of four on such scales can be taken to represent the neutral point and can therefore be regarded as the dividing line between tolerant and prejudiced responses.[3] The tendency in the total sample was to score in the direction of tolerance on virtually all of the ethnic attitudes. On ethnocentrism, representing a measure of general prejudice (see Adorno et al., 1950), the mean score was 3.53, suggesting more tolerance than prejudice.

Attitudes towards immigrants and immigration were also generally positive. Consequences of immigration were perceived to be positive. Respondents denied with a substantial majority that "English (and French) Canadians would lose their identity," (only 21 per cent and 25 per cent respectively agreed) or that "relations between English and French Canadians would become worse" (only 25 per cent agreed) as a result of immigration. There was, however, some concern that "there would be more unemployment" and that "there would be more political problems" with further immigration. Various types of immigrants were found to be acceptable. Considered as most acceptable were "immigrants who could be useful to this country," "immigrants with a skilled trade," and "immigrants who are highly educated." Only immigrants "from communist countries" and "anyone who wants to immigrate," were not found acceptable.

Multiculturalism attitudes were tapped in four area: (1) multicultural ideology measuring the degree to which respondents were in favour of various ethnic groups retaining their traditional cultures and sharing them with the larger society; (2) perceived consequences of multiculturalism; (3) multicultural programs (for example, the extent to which respondents supported actual or potential multicultural programs—folk festivals, third language broadcasting); (4) behavioural intentions toward multiculturalism (e.g., vote for political candidate who supported multiculturalism).

Results of the survey showed that multicultural attitudes were generally positive. On multicultural ideology, respondents were more in favour of retaining cultural diversity (mean of 4.51) than of assimilation or segregation.[4] For example, only 19 per cent of respondents disagreed with the statement that "it would be good to see all the ethnic groups in Canada retain their cultures." Consequences of multiculturalism were also perceived to be more positive than negative (mean of 4.52), and attitudes toward multicultural programs were on the positive side (mean 4.71). Some programs of course were greeted with greater acceptance than others. Strong positive reaction was given to "community centres" and "folk festivals," while more people disagreed with the use of non-official languages in broadcasting and teaching in regular schools. Behavioural intentions toward multiculturalism were also somewhat less favourable than multiculturalism ideology or program attitudes.

A further positive sign for intergroup harmony appears to be geographic mobility. In secondary analyses of the national survey data, Kalin and Berry (1980) found this factor was associated with ethnic tolerance. Respondents who were mobile in the sense of travel (in and out of Canada) and residential moves had more positive attitudes than sedentary respondents.

Attitudes toward specific ethnic groups were also assessed. Nine groups were selected as attitude objects: English and French Canadians, immigrants in general, Canadian Indians, Germans, Chinese, Ukrainians, Jews, and Italian Canadians. Two additional attitude objects, consisting of ethnic groups mentioned by the respondent were also rated. Each respondent was asked to rate the eleven ethnic groups on ten adjective dimensions, six of which were evaluative, that is, they measured attitudes. Attitudes were generally positive toward all groups. There was no evidence of extreme prejudice against any one group. But respondents did have clear preferences for certain groups over others. These are described in a later section.

Some explicit items dealing with "race" appeared in the attitude measures. It is therefore possible to examine the extent of overt racism. Only 19 per cent of respondents agreed with the statement that "it would be a mistake ever to have coloured people for foremen and leaders over whites." A minority of 33 per cent of the sample agreed that "the purity of the Canadian race would be affected" by further immigration. Only 15 per cent of the sample were ready to reject black immigrants. These results indicate that a great majority of Canadians reject explicitly racist statements. Thus it would be unfair to describe Canadians as racist. There were, on the other hand, substantial minorities who did endorse overtly racist views. To the extent that this minority is vocal and active, ethnic harmony may be threatened.

Mutual Attitudes of French and English Canadians
It is quite common to hear of the conflict between French and English Canadians in public debates and in the news media. Attitudes held by English and French Canadians of each other are therefore of some interest. Results from the national survey were quite surprising. These attitudes were remarkably positive (see Table 5.9 in Berry et al., 1977). English and French Canadians also judged each other as similar. This mutual, perceived

similarity was apparent in two ways. First, respondents rated the eleven ethnic groups on the adjective "similar to me." On this measure, French and English Canadians rated each other as considerably more similar than they did any other group (see Appendix 5.4, Berry et al.). Second, a card-sorting procedure designed to measure perceived similarity also revealed a strong mutual similarity between French and English (see Berry et al., Table 5.2).

A number of the attitude scales administered to respondents contained specific items regarding English-French relations. Only a small minority agreed that immigration would make relations between English and French Canadians worse, or that the English Canadians' (or the French Canadians') voice would become weaker as a result of multiculturalism.

This pattern of results prompted Berry et al. to term French and English Canadians as mutual positive reference groups. The term positive reference group is an elaboration of classical ethnocentrism theory (Sumner, 1906; Adorno et al., 1950; LeVine & Campbell, 1972). In ethnocentrism theory, ingroups and outgroups are distinguished. The basis for distinction between these groups and their relationship to membership groups, however, is not always clear. Merton and Rossi (1957) have argued that a membership group does not always function as an ingroup. It would also appear that not every non-membership group is an outgroup. By borrowing the term *reference group* (e.g. Hyman, 1942; Sherif & Sherif, 1953) these distinctions can be clarified. A *positive reference group* is a group that serves as a model for emulation and whose standards are accepted. A *negative reference group* is a group whose standards are rejected. An ingroup can then be defined as a membership group which also functions as a positive reference group. An outgroup is a non-membership group which usually functions as a negative reference group. There are, however, non-membership groups that serve as positive reference groups. According to Berry et al. English and French Canadians serve as mutual positive reference groups. The primary basis for their conclusion was the high mutual ratings of perceived similarity.

Developmental Trends in Ethnic Attitudes
In a follow-up study to the national survey (Kalin, 1979), some of the same attitudes were studied in a large sample of school children. Knowing the ethnic attitudes of young people is significant for a complete understanding of the climate for multiculturalism. As children are the adults of tomorrow, knowing their attitudes will help us predict the attitudes of Canadians in the near future (assuming, of course, that these attitudes remain relatively stable as children become adults). It is also important to discover developmental trends. Should attitudes toward cultural diversity in general, and toward specific ethnic groups in particular, become less favourable as children grow up, special programs may be called for in the educational curriculum to bring about attitudinal changes favourable to multiculturalism.

The attitude survey of children had two major goals: (1) to compare the ethnic and multicultural attitudes of children with the national adult sample studied by Berry et al., and (2) to discover developmental trends in these attitudes. Respondents were 453 children from Grades 5-13 in public and separate schools in Thunder Bay, Ontario. A questionnaire was administered to obtain biographical information from each child and to measure attitudes including ethnocentrism, perceived consequences of immigration, multicultural ideology, and attitudes toward French, Chinese, Italian Canadians, and "Canadians like me."

The attitudes of the children were on the whole remarkably similar to those of the national adult sample. Some statistically significant differences emerged, but these were quite small. Children were somewhat less ethnocentric and had a more positive multicultural ideology than the adults. At the same time, the children perceived the consequences of immigration to be somewhat more negative than the adult respondents.

The major findings regarding developmental trends are dispayed in Figure 8.1. Ethnocentrism was found to decrease progressively as the grade level of the children increased. Attitudes toward French and Chinese Canadians became more positive with higher grades. In addition to the trends displayed in Figure 8.1, own-group attitudes became less positive. A convenient way to summarize these results is to say that with increasing age, children became progressively less ethnocentric, both in terms of the ethnocentrism measure directly, and in terms of in- and out-group attitudes.

The general trend of decreasing ethnocentrism as children grow older is in line with some previous research (e.g. Davidson, 1976); but it also contradicts the conclusions reached by some that prejudice increases with

Figure 8.1
Developmental Trends in Ethnic Attitudes

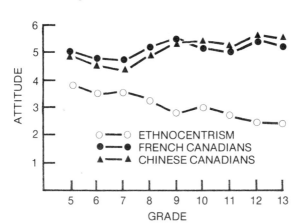

age (Proshansky, 1966; Brand, Ruiz and Padilla, 1974, Ziegler, 1979). Two possible reasons for these discrepant conclusions can be mentioned. First, most of the studies leading to the conclusion that prejudice increases with age were conducted before the 1960s. Times may have changed and schools may have made a concerted effort in recent times to eradicate prejudice. Second, there may also be a sociocultural reason. The conclusion of increasing prejudice was primarily based on studies of prejudice against blacks conducted in the United States. It is possible that in the Canadian multicultural context, ethnic attitudes develop in a more positive direction.

With regard to the main questions asked in the attitude survey of school children, the results provide cause for optimism. Chidren as a group were somewhat less ethnocentric than adults, and of the children, the oldest ones were less ethnocentric. If adolescents maintain their relatively low level of prejudice into adulthood, the next generation of adults would show more tolerance and less prejudice than the current. The climate for the acceptance of multiculturalism should therefore become more favourable.

This prediction should not be treated as a certain outcome, but as an educated guess that is predicated on a number of assumptions. The premise concerning the stability of attitudes over time has already been mentioned. There is also the assumption of inferring developmental trends from cross-sectional, as opposed to longitudinal data. Inasmuch as all grades from 5-13 were represented, the developmental inference seems reasonable. There is finally the possibility that the trends observed indicate merely increasing sophistication of children rather than actual changes in attitudes. The sophistication hypothesis cannot be entirely ruled out but it is not likely to be the whole explanation of observed trends. If it were, adults should be more positive than children, which clearly was not the case.

Signs for Concern

Not all results from the national survey by Berry et al. suggested a positive reception of multiculturalism. There were in fact several signs that some groups in Canada may be the object of prejudice and discrimination. Results also showed that lack of tolerance for ethnic diversity is particularly prevalent in some segments of the Canadian population.

The Perceived Ethnic Hierarchy

It was noted earlier that no extreme prejudice against specific ethnic groups was uncovered in the national survey by Berry et al. But respondents showed a clear preference for some groups over others. This preference hierarchy is displayed in Table 8.1 where twenty-six ethnic groups are ranked in terms of the mean attitude score. The groups appear in two columns. In the left are the nine groups rated by all respondents and on the right the groups nominated by particular respondents and therefore rated by a much smaller number. The attitude score was derived by taking the mean rating of a given group on six evaluative adjectives minus the mean ratings on the same six adjectives across all nine standard target groups. The scores are therefore measures of the attitude toward a particular group *relative* to all the other groups.

Table 8.1
Perceived Ethnic Hierarchy

Standard list of ethnic groups	Mean	N	Rank	Respondent nominated ethnic groups	Mean	N
English	.52	1801	1			
			2	Scottish	.49	186
French	.47	1786	3			
			4	Dutch	.46	138
			5	Scandinavian	.39	94
			6	Irish	.37	142
			7	Belgian	.35	48
			8	Japanese	.13	111
			9	Hungarian	.10	93
			10	Polish	.08	230
Jewish	.04	1717	11			
German	.02	1716	12			
			13	Czech	.02	47
			14	Russian	−.07	79
			15	Yugoslavian	−.09	54
			16	West Indian	−.11	48
Immigrants in general	−.12	1736	17			
Ukrainian	−.13	1601	18			
Italian	−.20	1719	19			
			20	Portuguese	−.25	112
Chinese	−.26	1736	21			
			22	Spanish	−.31	39
			23	Greek	−.36	127
Canadian Indian	−.46	1786	24			
			25	Negro	−.52	51
			26	East Indian	−.95	102

Source: Berry, Kalin & Taylor (1977, p. 106). Reproduced by permission of the Minister of Supply and Services Canada.

Table 8.1 shows that the charter groups were evaluated most favourably. Of the non-charter groups, north Europeans were evaluated relatively favourably (Dutch and Scandinavians) compared to the south and east European groups (Greeks and Poles), who were in turn rated more favourably than several other groups (East Indians, Negroes, Spaniards, Portuguese). It should be noted that, with the exception of the Japanese, all racially different groups appear near the bottom of the evaluative hierarchy.

The perceived ethnic hierarchy revealed in the national survey is quite consistent with the order of preference obtained in other Canadian studies (Goldstein, 1978), or American for that matter (Ehrlich, 1973). According

to Palmer (1976) a similar "pecking order" has been in existence throughout the twentieth century history of Canada. Mackie (see chapter 11 of this
volume) also obtained a very similar hierarchy with different methods and
different subject populations.

Discrimination Against Immigrants
The existence of a perceived ethnic hierarchy suggests that Canadians may
be more willing to interact with members of some groups than others. To
examine whether this is the case, Berry et al. conducted an experiment
within the national survey. The behavioural intentions of respondents
toward charter-group members and immigrants were assessed by asking
them a series of questions regarding their willingness to interact with
various kinds of target persons. The ethnicity of the target person was
varied (immigrant/English or French Canadian, depending on whether the
respondent was English or French Canadian), as was the status (low/high),
and the type of relationship (friendship/business). Each level of every
factor in the experiment was represented by two questions. To assess a
respondent's behavioural intentions toward a low-status immigrant in a
friendship relationship, for example, the following questions were asked:
"Would you be willing to have an immigrant shoemaker (or plumber) as a
close friend of your family?" To represent high status, the occupations of
teacher and dentist were chosen. Behavioural intentions were expressed
on seven-point scales ranging from one to seven.

Results from this experiment are displayed in Figure 8.2. Two major
results are apparent. First, respondents were generally quite willing to
interact with immigrants; but they were more willing to interact with
members of the charter groups. In other words, there was a general and
relative preference expressed for charter-group members over immigrants. The relative preference of one group over the other can be called
discrimination. Discrimination does not mean absolute avoidance of
immigrants, but it does refer to differential behavioural intentions toward
immigrants as compared with members of the charter groups. Second,
responses to English and French Canadians were independent of their
status or the type of relationship. Ratings were similar no matter whether
the target persons were of high or low status, or whether the interaction
was one of friendship or of business. However, both status and type of
relationship were important factors in the respondents' ratings of immigrants. Status appears to be particularly important in behavioural
intentions toward immigrants in business relationships. Canadians seem
to be considerably less willing to seek the services of immigrants in high
status occupations like dentistry and teaching, but relatively more willing
to use immigrant plumbers and shoemakers.

It was reported earlier in this chapter that respondents had a preference
for highly educated and skilled immigrants. When placed into the context

of the experimental findings just reported, we are apparently faced with the following paradox. While Canadians prefer highly educated and skilled immigrants for admission to this country, they may be reluctant to use their services, once these immigrants have arrived. These findings are consistent with earlier ones by Jones and Lambert (1965) who found a general preference for admitting higher status immigrants, but a greater reluctance to use the services of high as compared with low status immigrants. This ambivalence among Canadians may well cause considerable hardship for high status immigrants.

Figure 8.2
Behavioural Intentions Toward Majority Canadians and Immigrants

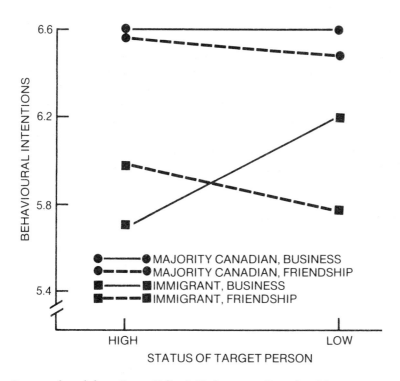

Source: adapted from Berry, Kalin & Taylor, 1977. Reproduced by permission of the Minister of Supply and Services Canada.

Discrimination Against Foreign-Accented Speakers
Since the above findings are based on a survey of opinions, they must be accepted with certain reservations. Responses of opinion questions may represent carefully chosen answers rather than spontaneous attitudes. A way of overcoming such problems is to study reactions to ethnicity that are

less transparently revealed. This is possible by studying responses to speech cues associated with ethnicity.

Research on evaluative reactions to speech cues in fact started in Canada. Lambert, Hodgson, Gardner, and Fillenbaum (1960) introduced a technique they called the "matched guise." In this method, one speaker speaks in different guises and listeners make social evaluations of tape recorded segments of the speech. The guises can be different languages (English and French) or different accents (Québécois and French from France). Lambert et al. (1960) had subjects evaluate the personalities of a series of speakers, who were in fact the guises of bilinguals speaking Canadian French and English. A strong bias against French Canadian guises appeared in the evaluations. Lambert (1967) has argued that evaluations of speech samples may be more likely to reveal listeners' private reactions to other groups than direct attitude questionnaires. The matched guise technique has been used subsequently in a variety of national and cultural contexts (Giles and Powesland, 1975).

There are certain drawbacks to the use of the matched guise technique. One of these is the fact that it may be very difficult, if not impossible, for one speaker to assume realistic guises of certain languages or accents. An alternative method is to expose listeners to *samples of speakers* from particular language communities. This method was followed by Kalin and Rayko (1978) in a study designed to examine reactions to foreign-accented speakers. These researchers wanted to discover the effects of the ethnicity of speakers, as revealed in accents, on judgments of job suitability. University students were asked to act the role of personnel consultants of a large manufacturing enterprise. They had to predict how well each of ten job applicants would do in each of four jobs varying in status (plant cleaner, production assembler, industrial mechanic, and foreman). Information on applicants was provided through brief biographical dossiers and the "consultants" heard thirty-second recordings of each applicant speaking, purportedly from a job interview. Five candidates spoke with an English Canadian accent and five of the speakers were foreign born and spoke fluent English but with a foreign accent (Italian, Greek, Portuguese, West African, Slovac). Ratings of candidates were made on their suitability for each of the four jobs.

The major results of this study are displayed in Figure 8.3 Definite discrimination appeared in favour of English Canadian and against foreign-accented speakers. Foreign-accented applicants, as compared with English Canadian speakers, were rated less suitable for the higher status jobs, but more suitable for the lower status jobs.

Kalin, Rayko and Love (1980) carried out a further investigation to determine reactions to various ethnic accents from different levels of the evaluative hierarchy of ethnic groups in Canada. The highest rated group (English), the lowest rated group (South Asian), one slightly above average group (German), and one below average group (West Indian) were chosen. To remove the possible contrast effects, English Canadians were not included. A preliminary study was also conducted to ascertain whether correct ethnic labels would be assigned to the speech samples presented.

In this preliminary study, subjects listened to sixteen speakers with the four accents, rated them for comprehensibility and tried to identify them. Correct identification ranged from 20 per cent to 94 per cent, but

Figure 8.3
Job Suitability Ratings for English Canadian and Foreign-Accented Speakers

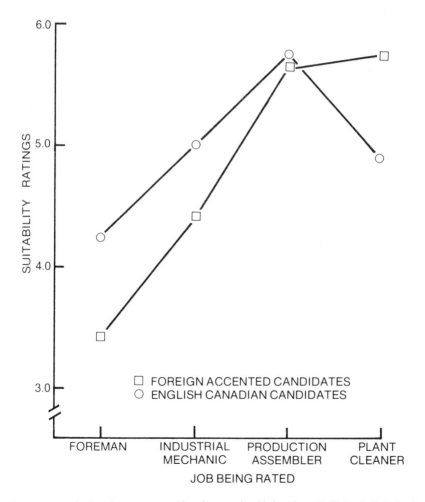

Source: reprinted with permission of authors and publisher from R. Kalin & D.S. Rayko, "Discrimination in evaluative judgments against foreign-accented job candidates" in *Psychological Reports*, 1978, 43, 1203-1209, Figure 1.

were all better than chance. English speakers were rated more comprehensible than all others; German-accented speakers were found to be more comprehensible than South Asians and West Indians.

In the main experiment subjects rated the suitability of the same sixteen speakers for four jobs varying in status. The main results are shown in Figure 8.4.

Figure 8.4
Job Suitability Ratings for Speakers with Four Ethnic Attitudes

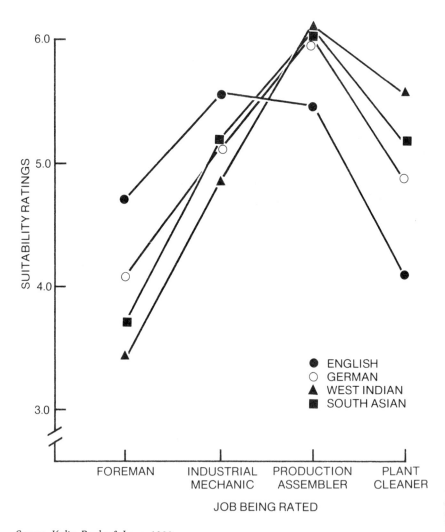

Source: Kalin, Rayko & Love, 1980

For the highest status job (foreman) English accented candidates were rated the most suitable, then German, South Asian and finally West Indian accented candidates. But for the job of least status (industrial plant cleaner) the order of the mean suitability scores was exactly reversed.

The study demonstrated stable discriminations among the speakers with various ethnic accents. This discrimination took the form of favouritism and denigration. Favouritism was indicated by judgments of a group of speakers as suitable for high status jobs and unsuitable for low status jobs. Denigration was indicated by the reversed pattern of judgments. A clear, favouritism hierarchy in the order English, German, South Asian, and West Indian was evident in the judgments. The discrimination was triggererd by the ethnicity of speakers because other possibly relevant factors (background information and speech content) were controlled. Thus discrimination on the basis of ethnicity occurs in Canada and prospects for ethnic harmony are not completely positive.

Such discrimination based on accent difference, however, is by no means unique to Canada. In the United States, Hopper and Williams (1973) found that white compared with black accented speakers were rated as more employable for executive jobs. In England, Giles, Wilson and Conway (in press) found that speakers with a nonstandard (i.e., regional Welsh) accent were rated as more suitable for a relatively low prestige job (production assembler) as compared with standard (R.P., meaning Received Pronunciation, or high prestige English) accents.

Attitudes in Various Segments of the Population
In the national survey by Berry et al. (1977) several background factors of respondents were examined. The two variables which were strongly related to attitudes were ethnicity and socio-economic status. French Canadians, compared with Anglophone Canadians of British or other ethnic background, and persons of lower, as compared with higher socio-economic background were generally less tolerant and more ethnocentric. French Canadians, as well as persons of lower socio-economic status, tended to rate their own group quite highly but they were somewhat negative toward certain other ethnic groups. They also tended to score higher on ethnocentrism and authoritarianism and be more negative in their immigration and multicultural attitudes.

The precise reason for the greater ethnocentrism of French Canadians is difficult to pinpoint. However, it becomes somewhat understandable when we consider the history of French Canada. Since the Conquest, French Canadians have been engulfed in a sea of Anglo-domination. Although they have had certain rights, their culture and language have been threatened constantly. Immigrants have tended to integrate into Anglophone Canada and in recent years the birth rate has declined dramatically among French Canadians. French Canada in fact has been called a "siege culture" (Baker, 1973). Given a concern for cultural survival, the ethnocentric stance of French Canadians may represent a psychological attempt at self-protection.

The greater ethnocentrism among respondents of lower socio-economic status may have a similar explanation. Here the threat may not come from cultural but rather economic insecurity.

Prospects for Multiculturalism

On the basis of results from these various studies, a number of conclusions regarding the prospects for multiculturalism can be drawn. The climate for multiculturalism is clearly not uniformly positive or negative. A number of positive signs emerged. The ethnic groups themselves are in favour of preserving their culture (O'Bryan et al., 1976). Among all Canadians, a majority are in favour of multiculturalism and accepting cultural diversity. Tolerance is the prevalent view and overt racism and extreme prejudice are only shown by a small minority. English-French relations are particularly good. The study of children indicates that multiculturalism may be more acceptable in the next generation than at present.

Results were also obtained, however, that must be taken as negative signs. Good will does not extend equally to all groups. New arrivals in Canada with visible or audible ethnic features can expect some discrimination and prejudice. Racially distinct groups in particular may be the victims of prejudice. Ethnic tolerance is also more forthcoming from some than other segments of society. The greater reluctance to accept cultural diversity among French Canadians and persons of lower socio-economic status requires special attempts to remove cultural and economic insecurity among these segments of society. The suggestion also emerges that ethnic harmony may deteriorate if cultural conflict becomes more pronounced and economic conditions worsen.

An Examination of the Multiculturalism Assumption

The second research question raised by the government's policy was the "multiculturalism assumption." This assumption can be assessed by analyzing the relationship between attitudes toward one's self, or one's own group and those held toward other groups. On a theoretical level, the "multiculturalism assumption" may be contrasted with ethnocentrism theory, which holds that positive self or own-group attitudes are generally associated with negative attitudes toward other groups (LeVine & Campbell, 1972). If ethnocentrism theory were supported, we might have to doubt whether the enhancement of individual identities would promote ethnic tolerance.

Testing the validity of the "multiculturalism assumption" and of ethnocentrism theory is not simple, as these are difficult constructs to define and measure. In their assessment of the two competing theories,

Berry et al. (1977) employed two different measures. The first of these consisted of the respondents' evaluation of their own ethnic group and was based on the assumption that individuals with a strong confidence in their own identity evaluate their own group highly.

Berry et al., examined the relationship between respondents' evaluation of own and other groups. They found at the individual level that the more positively respondents evaluated their own group, the more negatively they rated other ethnic groups. Berry and Kalin (1979) subsequently examined the relationship at the aggregate level. They created an attitude matrix in which the five largest groups in Canada served as attitude object as well as holders of attitudes. There was clear ethnocentrism in the matrix: attitudes toward own group were more positive than attitudes toward other groups. It appears, therefore, that by employing own-group evaluation as a measure of confidence in one's own identity, ethnocentrism theory, but not the multiculturalism assumption, is supported.

By employing a different measure of confidence, however, the multiculturalism assumption received support. Berry et al. (1977, p. 192) developed measures of economic and cultural security as indices of "confidence in one's own identity." Economic security would be indicated if respondents denied that negative economic consequences would follow further immigration, for example. Cultural security was measured only among respondents from the charter groups. High scores would be obtained by denying, for instance, that members of the charter groups would lose their identity as a result of immigration or multiculturalism. When the security measures were related to the attitudes it was found that individuals who were secure in their economic and cultural context were tolerant of other ethnic groups and had generally positive attitudes toward cultural diversity.

These discrepant results highlight the conceptual ambiguities of the multiculturalism assumption. The prime minister's statement and the government's response to Book IV contain several similar yet distinct terms. In addition to "confidence in one's own identity," the phrases "feeling of security in one's particular social context" and "sensitivity to own identity and to the richness of the country" are used. These psychological characteristics are not necessarily equivalent. "Evaluation of one's own group" and cultural and economic security are clearly not measures of the same underlying construct of confidence. This conclusion received empirical support in the national survey where own-group evaluation and the two measures of security were negatively related. Individuals who gave the most positive own-group evaluation were the most insecure. The cluster of attitudes consisting of positive own-group evaluation, insecurity and lack of tolerance for other groups is postulated by the ethnocentrism hypothesis and the theory of the authoritarian personality (Adorno et al., 1950). These theories assert that the positive evaluation by ethnocentric persons of their own group does not result from objective self-appraisal, but from uncritical self-glorification. This glorification, or exaggerated positive evaluation, results from a defense against insecurity.

Admittedly, this type of theorizing is removed somewhat from the results of the national survey by Berry et al. (1977). It does suggest, however, that "confidence in one's own identity" should not be equated with positive self-evaluation. Such self-evaluation may well be the result of defensiveness and is likely to be associated with a lack of tolerance for others. Multiculturalism programs therefore should not foster defensive self-evaluation but promote acceptance of own and other groups.

The point that exclusive attention to one's own ethnic group may in fact increase one's commitment to that group but not promote cultural integration has been argued by Kelner and Kallen (1974). These authors contend that "if cultural interchange is to contribute to full integration into Canadian society, then each must learn about the others' living culture, in order to appreciate human affinities as well as differences" (p. 31). This outward orientation was in fact suggested by the multiculturalism policy itself which encouraged ethnic groups to *share* their own cultural features with others in the larger society.

Ethnic Relations in a Multicultural Context
In chapter 1 of this book it was emphasized that social psychology is influenced by the cultural context in which it takes place. Most of the studies reviewed in the present chapter were avowedly triggered by the fact of ethnic diversity and the ideal of multiculturalism in Canada. Before concluding this chapter it is appropriate to point out how this context may have shaped the approaches taken and the findings obtained in the study of Canadian ethnic relations and how these might be different from a society that de-emphasizes ethnic diversity and aspires to uniculturalism. These issues have been treated extensively by Berry (1979). According to Berry, an approach based on a unicultural model studies a non-dominant group (often termed "subcultural") in relation to the dominant (often termed mainstream) culture. He proposes an alternative model that is cross-cultural, "in which cultural groups are studied in relation to each other and are recognized as fully autonomous and independent elements in the study" (p. 416). Research in a multicultural society should be based on the cross-cultural model. Such an approach was taken by Berry, et al. (1977) in their national survey, and more specifically by Berry and Kalin (1979) who examined the attitudes held by the five largest ethnic groups in Canada toward themselves and each other. The use of a multiple comparison model has also been advocated for the American context by Brand, et al. (1974).

Berry et al. (1977) also pointed out that the simple distinction of ingroup vs. outgroup from classical ethnocentrism theory requires modification when applied to multicultural Canada. These authors found it necessary to employ the terms mutual and unilateral positive reference groups for some non-membership groups who were the objects of positive attitudes. Such positive reference groups may well be discovered in other societies when a multiple comparison approach is taken.

Finally, research into ethnic relations in a multicultural society does not stop with the assessment of specific ethnic attitudes, but is concerned with the evaluation of and readiness for ethnic diversity itself, as was done in several of the studies described in the present chapter. By applying the ideology of multiculturalism prevalent in Canadian society to research in ethnic relations, novel approaches and unexpected findings have become possible and constraints imposed by a unicultural model have been overcome.

FOOTNOTES

[1]While the present author's name appears alone for this chapter, it must be acknowledged that in writing it he relied extensively on the book *Multiculturalism and Ethnic Attitudes in Canada*, of which J.W. Berry and D.M. Taylor were also co-authors. I am heavily indebted to these two colleagues for many of the ideas presented in this chapter.

[2]All direct quotes regarding the multiculturalism policy are from Prime Minister Trudeau's statement to the House of Commons in his response to the Report of the Royal Commission on Bilingualism and Biculturalism, Book IV, as quoted in a press release, October 8, 1971.

[3]To regard four as a neutral point disregards the possibility that some respondents may have a personal neutral point that differs from four for reasons of response bias. As four is halfway between a "Strong Agreement" and a "Strong Disagreement" it appears reasonable to regard it as a general neutral point.

[4]These concepts are described in detail in chapter 12.

REFERENCES

Adorno, T.W., Frenkel-Brunswik, E., Levinson, D.J., Sanford, R.N. *The Authoritarian Personality.* New York: Harper & Row, 1950.

Baker, D.G. Ethnicity development and power: Canada in comparative perspective. Paper presented at the National Conference on Canadian Culture and Ethnic Groups in Canada, Toronto, 1973.

Berry, J.W. Research in Multicultural Societies: Implications of cross-cultural methods. *Journal of Cross-Cultural Psychology*, 1979, *10*, 415-434.

Berry, J.W., Kalin, R., & Taylor, D.M. *Multiculturalism and Ethnic Attitudes in Canada.* Ottawa: Minister of Supply and Services Canada, 1977.

Berry, J.W., and Kalin, R. Reciprocity of inter-ethnic attitudes in a multicultural society. *International Journal of Intercultural Relations*, 1979, *3*, 99-112.

Brand, E.J., Ruiz, N.A., and Padilla, A.M. Ethnic identification and preference. *Psychological Bulletin*, 1974, *81*, 860-890.

Davidson, F.H. Ability to respect persons compared to ethnic prejudice in childhood. *Journal of Personality and Social Psychology*, 1976, *34*, 1256-1267.

Ehrlich, H.J. *The Social Psychology of Prejudice.* New York: Wiley, 1973.

Giles, H., and Powesland, P.F. *Speech Style and Social Evaluation*. London: Academic Press, 1975.

Giles, H., Wilson, P., and Conway, T. Accent and lexical diversity as determinants of impression formation and employment selection. *Language Sciences* (in press).

Goldstein, J. The prestige of Canadian ethnic groups: some new evidence. *Canadian Ethnic Studies*. 1978, *10*, 84-96.

Hopper, R., and Williams, F. Speech characteristics and employability. *Speech Monographs*, 1973, *40*, 296-302.

Hyman, H.H. The psychology of status. *Archives of Psychology*, No. 269, 1942.

Jones, F.E., & Lambert, W.E. Occupational rank and attitudes toward immigrants. *Public Opinion Quarterly*, 1965, *29*, 137-144.

Kalin, R. Ethnic and multicultural attitudes among children in a Canadian city. *Canadian Ethnic Studies*, 1979, *11*, 69-81.

Kalin, R., & Rayko, D.S. Discrimination in evaluative judgments against foreign accented job candidates. *Psychological Reports*, 1978, *43*, 1203-1209.

Kalin, R., and Berry, J.W. Geographic mobility and ethnic tolerance. *Journal of Social Psychology*, 1980.

Kalin, R., Rayko, D.S., & Love, N. The perception and evaluation of job candidates with four different ethnic accents. In H. Giles, W.P. Robinson, & P. Smith (eds.), *Language: Social psychological perspectives*. Oxford: Pergamon Press, 1980.

Kelner, M., and Kallen, E. The multicultural policy: Canada's response to ethnic diversity. *Journal of Comparative Sociology*, 1974, No. 2, 21-34.

Lambert, W.E. The social psychology of bilingualism. *Journal of Social Issues*, 1967, *23*, 91-109.

Lambert, W.E., Hodgson, R.C., Gardner, R.C., and Fillenbaum, S. Evaluational reactions to spoken languages. *Journal of Abnormal and Social Psychology*, 1960, *60*, 44-51.

LeVine, R.A. & Campbell, D.T. *Ethnocentrism: Theories of conflict, ethnic attitudes and group behaviour*. Toronto: Wiley, 1972.

Merton, R.K. & Rossi, A. Contributions to the theory of reference group behaviour. In R.K. Merton (ed.), *Social Theory and Social Structure*. New York: Free Press, 1957.

O'Bryan, K.G., Reitz, J.G., & Kuplowska, O.M. *Non-official Languages: A Study in Canadian Multiculturalism*. Ottawa: Minister of Supply and Services Canada, 1976.

Palmer, H. Reluctant hosts: Anglo-Canadian views of multiculturalism in the twentieth century. In Canadian Consultative Council on Multiculturalism. *Multiculturalism as State Policy*. Ottawa: Minister of Supply and Services Canada, 1976.

Proshansky, H.M. The development of intergroup attitudes. In L.W. Hoffman and M.L. Hoffman (eds.), *Review of Child Development Research*, Vol. 2. New York: Russell Sage, 1966.

Sherif, M. & Sherif, C.W. *Groups in Harmony and Tension*. New York: Harper, 1953.

Sumner, W.G. *Folkways*. New York: Ginn, 1906.

Ziegler, S. Ethnic diversity and children. In W. Michelson, S.V. Levine, and A. Spina (eds.), *The Child in the City: Changes and Challenges*. Toronto: University of Toronto Press, 1979.

Chapter 9

Stereotypes and Intergroup Relations

Donald M. Taylor, Department of Psychology, McGill University

What is a stereotype? Do stereotypes play an important role in intergroup relations? How are they related to prejudice? Is there any truth to stereotypes? Do only bigots use stereotypes? Do they threaten unity in multicultural societies?

In the course of exploring answers to these questions some possibly surprising conclusions will be reached. Specifically, it will be argued that there are some instances where ethnic stereotypes can have socially desirable consequences. This chapter itself is divided into three main sections. The first explains the overall approach and involves a discussion of why stereotypes, as representing a cognitive-social orientation, may be crucial to intergroup relations. In the second section, a definition of stereotype is proposed and its function is examined in detail. The third section outlines a framework developed initially by Taylor and Simard (1979) for thinking about stereotypes and intergroup relations.

A Cognitive-Social Approach to Intergroup Relations

In this chapter a cognitive-social approach to intergroup relations will be emphasized. Before becoming immersed in a detailed examination of stereotypes some discussion of the meaning of the two key concepts, cognitive and social, will help put the chapter in perspective.

A Cognitive Approach

One of the fundamental and enduring issues in all of psychology is the question, "How does the individual use all of his or her past experience to direct behaviour at this precise moment?" In the context of ethnic relations the concern is with understanding how the experiences of members of different groups relate to their behaviour with one another. From a psychoanalytic orientation this might involve a careful analysis of unconscious processes operating in early childhood. Alternatively, a behaviourist would focus more on the entire reinforcement history of the individual. The view adopted in the present chapter is that regardless of the precise theoretical orientation, past experience must be organized and stored cognitively so that it can serve as a guide to behaviour.

The major cognitions in the field of intergroup relations are ethnic stereotypes and ethnic attitudes. The present chapter will focus mainly on the stereotype but, as will become clear, attitudes have a fundamental role to play in stereotyping.

A Social Approach

Normally there would be no need to elaborate a *social* approach in a book on social psychology. Discussion is made necessary because of a bias inherent in most of the theory and research in current social psychology. Social psychology was conceived initially as the discipline that would integrate the study of the individual with the social context. A survey of current social psychology textbooks will reveal that while there has been much attention given to the individual, the social half of the equation has been neglected. That social or group processes are not incorporated in most treatments of more individualistic topics (e.g., person perception, interpersonal attraction) is understandable if not desirable, but for this individualistic orientation to dominate a topic, such as intergroup relations is serious. Take for example a conversation between husband and wife. On the surface there appear to be no group processes operating; it would seem to be an interaction between two individuals. But surely there are times when the wife will be speaking not as an individual but as a representative of women, and the husband perhaps talking from the point of view of men. If group processes have a role to play in such apparently individualistic interactions their operation in intergroup relations must be profound.

A number of American (Sampson, 1977; Steiner, 1974) and European (Billig, 1976; Tajfel, 1972) writers have begun to criticize social psychology for this bias. Taylor and Brown (1979) note that the bias appears at two levels. First, at the empirical level, research concentrates almost exclusively on individuals rather than groups. Second, in terms of theory, the focus is on concepts which describe individual or at best interindividual processes. Taylor and Brown (1979) argue that while the ultimate aim of psychologists is to understand the individual, there is a need to appreciate better the role of group structure and process for understanding individual behaviour.

In his article "Whatever happened to the group in social psychology?" Steiner (1974) suggests that social issues were neglected because the United States was in a period of social tranquillity and hence group processes were not of primary concern. The European writers explain the individualistic bias more in terms of a pervasive ideology. They argue that it is the North American belief in the sanctity and importance of the individual which has led to the neglect of social processes. This latter interpretation is especially important in the present context for it suggests that there may be certain unique properties to Canadian society that may influence the orientation taken in the present chapter.

Canadian research on stereotypes and ethnic group relations has no doubt been influenced by the prevalent individualistic orientation in the United States. However, unlike our neighbours to the south, social issues, especially ethnic group relations, have always been fundamental. This perhaps explains the long-standing interest of Canadian researchers in issues such as ethnic stereotyping. For the same reason there would seem to be a better appreciation of social processes.

Stereotypes: Definitions and Function

Walter Lippman (1922) is credited for applying nomenclature from the printing trade to describe stereotypes as the "picture in the head" we have of others (for major reviews of the stereotype literature see Brigham, 1971; Campbell, 1967; Cauthen, Robinson & Krauss, 1971; Fishman, 1956; Gardner, 1973; Tajfel, 1969).

A sampling of the many definitions of stereotype will illustrate the recurring themes that warrant more detailed comment. Brigham (1971), for example, defines stereotype as "a generalization made about an ethnic group, concerning a trait attribution, which is considered to be unjustified by an observer." An early definition by Katz and Braly (1935) proposed that a stereotype is a rigid impression, conforming very little to the facts and arises from our defining first and observing second. That stereotypes are an inferior cognitive process is reflected in definitions such as the one proposed by Allport (1954) who describes the stereotype as an exaggerated belief about a category, or Middlebrook (1974) who notes that they are often defined as an inaccurate, irrational overgeneralization. Lippman (1922) claimed that the stereotype "precedes the use of reason, is a form of perception, imposes a certain character on the data of our senses before the data reach the intelligence" (p. 98). Finally in a recently published social psychology text, Baron and Byrne (1977) define stereotypes as "clusters of preconceived notions regarding various groups" where there are "strong tendencies to overgeneralize about individuals solely on the basis of their membership in particular racial, ethnic, or religious groups" (p. 155).

Before discussing the adequacy of these definitions it may be instructive to describe the basic procedure for measuring stereotypes since the method represents, in concrete form, the operationalization of the concept stereotype. The basic procedure was developed in 1933 by Katz and Braly, and while there have been several recent innovations (Brigham, 1971; Gardner, Wonnacott & Taylor, 1968; Triandis & Vassiliou, 1967), the basic underlying rationale remains unchanged. Subjects are presented with the name of a particular ethnic group and are asked to check off which of a large number of traits best describes the group in question. Sometimes subjects can choose as many characteristics as they wish, other times only the five most important, but in either case the stereotype is defined by those few characteristics that are checked most frequently by the group of subjects.

In order to place these definitions and assessment procedures in context Table 9.1 presents the four attributes most associated with different ethnic groups as indicated by a number of studies on stereotypes in Canada. Notice that despite wide differences in the subject samples and the particular year the study was conducted, there is a surprising consistency in the stereotypes about certain groups.

Table 9.1
Examples of Research Assessing Stereotypes
of Canadian Groups

Investigators	Subjects	Target Group	Stereotype Attributes
Aboud, F.E., 1973	English Canadians (Quebec)	French Canadian male sociology students	Sensitive, separatist, socialistic, talkative
		French Canadian male	Excitable, colourful, emotional, artistic
	English Canadians (Quebec)	English Canadian male	Materialistic, competitive, conservative, reserved
Aboud, F.E., & Taylor, D.M., 1971	English Canadians (Ontario)	English Canadians	Likeable, competent, proud, ambitious
		French Canadians	Proud, emotional dissenting, demanding
	French Canadians (Quebec)	English Canadians	Educated, dominant, ambitious, authoritarian
		French Canadians	Proud, humane, materialistic, studious
Gardner, R.C., Taylor, D.M. & Feenstra, H.J. 1970	English Canadians (Ontario)	French-speaking people	Artistic, religious, proud, colourful
		English-speaking people	Proud, pleasant, loyal, intelligent
Gardner, R.C., Wonnacott, E.J. & Taylor, D.M. 1968	English Canadians (Ontario)	French Canadians	Talkative, excitable, proud, religious
Kirby, D.M., & Gardner, R.C. 1973	English Canadian Adults (Ontario)	French Canadians	Religious, emotional, talkative, sensitive
		English Canadians	Clean, intelligent, modern, good
		Canadian Indians	Poor, quiet, follower, sensitive
Lay, C.H., & Jackson, D.M. 1972	English Canadians (Manitoba)	French Canadians	Excitable, emotional, impulsive, tenacious

From these various definitions, and the procedures used in their assessment, certain common themes emerge. First, stereotypes refer to the personality characteristics of another group, or one's own group (auto-stereotype). Second, a stereotype refers to people's perceptions or beliefs about others rather than factual statements. Third, the focus is on shared beliefs; that is, a set of characteristics believed by a large number of one group to be true of another. Fourth, stereotypes are described as poor judgments of others since in applying characteristics to the entire group they involve over-categorization and over-generalization.

In this chapter a stereotype will be defined as *consensus among members of one group regarding the attributes of another.* Some of the key elements in this definition are now examined in order to specify precisely how it relates to the four themes common to most definitions.

First it was noted that most definitions, or more accurately the methods derived from them, focus on personality characteristics. There is no need to restrict stereotypes to personality characteristics; surely any set of shared beliefs can be important. If English Canadians believe French Canadians to be separatists, and in return English Canadians are stereo-typed as politically conservative, these represent stereotypes that could affect relations between the two groups just as much as stereotypes about personality characteristics. Social class can be an important element in an ethnic stereotype. For example, La Gaipa (1971) found that his United States subjects associated Negro with unskilled worker, while proprietor and clothing merchants were related to Jewish people. Included in the stereotype, then, should be any set of shared beliefs about a group. Certain Canadian researchers such as Aboud (1973, 1975, 1977), Gardner and Taylor (1969), Mackie (1974) and Mann (1976) have already studied attributes other than the usual personality characteristics.

Stereotypes clearly refer to peoples' perceptions and beliefs, but do these stereotypes have any basis in reality? Many argue that they do not. This position is of course consistent with the prevalent view of stereotypes; they are manufactured judgments which rationalize prejudice. And there is some indication that stereotypes have little basis in reality. Often, for example, conflicting traits are contained in the same stereotype. How can Jewish people be both clannish and always trying to intrude into Gentile society at the same time? (Adorno, Frenkel-Brunswik, Levinson & San-ford, 1950).

These possibilities notwithstanding, the view adopted here is that many stereotypes do contain a "kernal of truth"—a position which is consistent with that of Mackie (1973) whose excellent review addresses this issue in detail. This is not to suggest that stereotypes are accurate and sophisticated cognitive descriptions of a group of individuals. Far from it. But they are often useful characterizations of a group's attributes.

The definition adopted here emphasizes that stereotypes are shared beliefs. This is a central feature of stereotypes but one that is not often acknowledged by researchers in the field. One person's beliefs about a group do not constitute a stereotype. The procedures used for measuring stereotypes make this clear. Only if a number of subjects check the same trait is it included in the stereotype.

This aspect of stereotyping is crucial since it emphasizes the *social* importance of the process. It was argued at the outset that research and theory in social psychology were too individualistic and here we have a prime example. Taking into account the social or shared feature of stereotypes has important implications. A number of group processes must be involved if members of one group attribute precisely the same attributes to another group. There are likely social pressures to conform, and a shared meaning to permit communication within the group, which in turn will enhance ingroup solidarity and create more clearly defined ingroup and outgroup boundaries.

Although this shared feature of stereotypes has been a neglected area of research, the clear exception to this tradition is the work by Gardner and his associates. Gardner (1973) has consistently emphasized the consensual features of stereotyping. Gardner, Kirby and Finley (1973) have demonstrated empirically that the shared feature of stereotypes facilitates communication among ingroup members about an outgroup. Only if there is a consensus that members of group X are backward do statements such as, "Isn't that just like an X?" or "Well, he is an X after all," have any meaning.

Finally, the present definition contains no evaluative pronouncements about the process of stereotyping. This represents somewhat of a departure from tradition since social scientists with some exceptions (e.g., Berry, 1970; Gardner, 1973; Mackie, 1973; Tajfel, 1969; Triandis, 1971) openly condemn the process. Most definitions allude to undesirable features in ethnic stereotypes. They may be referred to as morally wrong, inaccurate, unjustified, over-generalizations, over-categorizations, erroneous casual attributions or arrived at through some inferior cognitive process. In short, stereotypes are viewed as undesirable because they rely on faulty judgmental processes, and because they are the outgrowth of prejudicial motivations.

Why should such a value judgment be associated with the stereotype? One answer perhaps is that researchers react in human ways to psychological processes they view as destructive. Most researchers no doubt believe that characterizing an ethnic group in the form of a stereotype is socially destructive, prejudicial and detrimental to good relations between groups.

But this is only true if one adopts the ideology that ethnic differences lead to intergroup conflict. Such a rationale would be based on the assumption that similarity relates strongly to attraction; a view which has received considerable empirical support (Byrne, 1969). Therefore, cultural differences, especially those that become reified in the form of a stereotype, are not conducive to mutual attraction among members of different ethnic groups. Such a view, of course, is consistent with the often referred to "melting pot" philosophy of cultural integration of the United States.

According to this philosophy, producing homogeneity by eradicating cultural differences enhances the potential for peaceful intergroup relations. Clearly then in terms of the ideology of cultural homogeneity, which has until recently been characteristic of the United States, ethnic stereotypes would be viewed as undesirable.

But Canadian experience is perhaps different somewhat. In chapters 1, 2 and 8 of the present volume, the official policy of the Canadian government regarding multiculturalism has been described. This policy advocates that every ethnic group should be encouraged to retain its ethnic distinctiveness. The multicultural ideology implies that ethnic stereotypes which reflect a group's cultural distinctiveness may be highly desirable and even perhaps necessary for effective relations between groups.

This is not to imply that all forms of stereotyping are desirable but only to suggest that the value judgments which become expressed in the very definition of stereotypes may be linked to the prevalent ideology. Stereotyping is a cognitive process that operates in us all because of the functions it serves and hence the basic definition of stereotype should not contain evaluative judgments.

Having discussed at some length a definition of the ethnic stereotype, there are three fundamental issues about the operation of stereotypes to be addressed in detail. First, do stereotypes play an important role in intergroup relations? Second, how are stereotypes related to prejudice? And finally, what functions do stereotypes serve?

Stereotypes and Intergroup Relations

In raising the issues that stereotypes play an important role in intergroup relations we must confront directly the possibility that stereotypes only exist in the minds and theories of social scientists and in fact have no role to play for normal people in the course of their everyday encounters. Volunteer participants in a study will, if asked by the experimenter, check off personality traits judged to be characteristic of a particular group. But does this mean that people actually use stereotypes when they interact with members of another ethnic group? The point is that in traditional studies which measure stereotypes the subject is given no information whatsoever except for the name of an ethnic group. In such circumstances the subject is forced to rely upon the broadest of generalizations about the group in question. Are we to believe that the same subject would apply these stereotypes in situations where there is an abundance of intimate information about the other person?

The results of a series of experiments (Aboud & Taylor, 1971; Gardner & Taylor, 1968; Mann, 1976; Taylor & Gardner, 1969) on perceptions of ethnic group members suggest that stereotyping is not an artifactual phenomenon but is rather fundamental to the process of intergroup relations. In these experiments individual members of an ethnic group

(French Canadian) were presented to Anglophone subjects by means of tape or video-tape recordings, and it was the subject's task to form an impression of the specific individual ethnic group member. In different conditions in the experiments the stimulus person, whose ethnicity was clear from his accented English, described himself in a way which either (1) was consistent with the stereotype of a French Canadian, (2) was totally inconsistent with the stereotype, or (3) revealed little or no information about himself.

From the results it was evident that while Anglophone subjects did take into account what the speaker said about himself, their judgments were always modified by the group stereotype. Thus, even when the French Canadian speaker indicated he was neither religious, sensitive, proud, nor emotional, the subjects' stereotype seemed to prevent them from taking this at face value. In short the stereotype operated like a cognitive filter, systematically modifying information about an individual from another ethnic group.

The application of stereotypes to *individual* ethnic members was also found by Grant (1978) who explored Anglophone stereotypes of the Irish, among others. He found that the Irish are stereotyped as happy-go-lucky, talkative and pleasure loving. In an interesting design Grant (1978) presented subjects with an Irishman who was described as scientific and ambitious, two traits which were normally not associated with the Irish stereotype. Subjects were of course willing to believe that this particular Irishman was scientific and ambitious but they were also insistent that he was happy-go-lucky, talkative and pleasure loving as well. It would seem that people not only stereotype entire groups, but also apply their stereotypes to individual members of the ethnic group and do this even in the face of contradictory evidence.

There is another feature of stereotyping which points to its potential importance for intergroup relations. The original Katz and Braly study of stereotyping described earlier was conducted in 1933 at Princeton University. Some eighteen years later the study was repeated by Gilbert (1951) again at Princeton. The results showed that the stereotypes of the ten ethnic groups were remarkably unchanged although the stereotypes appeared slightly less crystalized than they did in 1933. The study was again repeated at Princeton in 1969 (Karlins, Coffman & Walters, 1969) and despite some replacement in stereotype traits for certain groups, similar stereotypes emerged. It would seem that once a stereotype becomes formulated it is extremely resistant to change. This observation is supported by data in the Canadian context (Gardner, Wonnacott & Taylor, 1968) where a sample of Anglophone students from Ontario rated French Canadians on a number of personality characteristics. The study was then repeated with a new sample one year later and the correlation between the mean ratings for the two samples was extremely high (.97) indicating that the stereotype included a well-defined set of shared beliefs that are stable over time. Stereotypes, then, are shared cognitions which are stable both over time and, as we have seen, across situations. This feature, along with the fact that people apparently apply their stereotypes to individual ethnic group members, even in the face of contradictory information, suggests that stereotyping is an important phenomenon with profound implications for intergroup relations.

Stereotypes and Prejudice

Prejudice, as the label implies, involves prejudgment, the forming of an opinion prior to being exposed to all the evidence. In this sense the stereotype can be equated with prejudice since stereotypes refer to beliefs about the attributes of members of a group which become applied before account is taken of the actual attributes of the particular individual. If I stereotype Gianetto as emotional even before I meet him, I am being prejudiced.

In another sense, however, stereotyping and prejudice should not be equated. Prejudice usually implies an emotional, attitudinal, or evaluative attribution, and in the case of ethnic groups the attribution is usually negative. As we have seen, negative evaluative overtones are traditionally associated with the stereotype. But the present view is that stereotypes are not synonomous with attitudes and so in a very fundamental sense stereotypes and prejudice are not the same. That is, a stereotype is not by definition a negative attitude. Stereotypes are shared beliefs; attitudes are evaluative orientations.

For example, a community may have a stereotype of a particular group, but some members of the community may have a positive attitude and others a negative attitude toward the group. Many might agree that the Scots are stingy, but they may disagree in their attitudes towards the Scots. This point is supported by studies where stereotypes and attitudes were found to be independent of one another in a Canadian context (see Gardner, Wonnacott & Taylor, 1968; Gardner, Taylor & Feenstra, 1970; Kirby & Gardner, 1973; Lay & Jackson, 1972). For example, Gardner, Wonnacott and Taylor (1968) asked English-speaking university students in Ontario to rate French Canadians on a number of characteristics, some of which were expected to reflect the stereotype, other were highly evaluative. In addition, subjects' evaluative reactions were assessed by means of traditional, well-validated measures of attitude. A factor analysis of the entire battery of scales demonstrated that stereotypes and attitudes are orthogonal. Thus, French Canadians were stereotyped as "religious," "sensitive," "proud," and "emotional," by the majority of subjects. An examination of the attitude scales indicated that this same stereotype was held equally by subjects with a positive and those with a negative attitude toward French Canadians.

This does not mean that stereotypes and attitudes are totally unrelated, but only that they are not equivalent concepts, so that one term cannot be interchanged with the other. What is the relationship between these two concepts? The view taken here is that the stereotype is the vehicle by which attitudes can be expressed. More specifically, there are three ways by which a person can express his or her attitudes through the stereotypes. First, descriptive attributes of the stereotype may be chosen to reflect attitudes so that, to express a negative attitude, negative attributes such as dirty, stupid, and so forth, might be included in the stereotype. But since stereotypes endure over time and across situations, choosing attributes *only* because of their evaluative connotation is unlikely. Choosing attributes on this basis probably only occurs where the intergroup situation has deteriorated to open conflict. The American stereotype of the Japanese before and after Pearl Harbour (Seago, 1947), the stereotype of Germans before and during World War II (Dudycha, 1942) and the stereotype changes which resulted from the Sino-Indian border dispute (Sinha & Upadhyay, 1960) are perhaps examples of this process. However, in most instances, attitudes are not expressed by only choosing attributes for their evaluative meaning with no consideration for their descriptive component.

A second mechanism for expressing attitudes involves a more subtle selection of descriptive stereotype attributes. The traits which form the basis of most group stereotypes have both descriptive and evaluative components (Kirby & Gardner, 1972; Peabody, 1967). Hence, it is possible to maintain the descriptive aspect of a stereotype and at the same time express one's attitudes via the choice of specific evaluative labels. A group might be stereotyped as either bold or rash, generous or extravagant, depending upon attitudes toward the group. The earlier example of the stereotype of Scots illustrates the point; those with positive attitudes might stereotype them as "thrifty," whereas they might be "stingy" to those who hold negative attitudes.

The first two mechanisms for expressing attitudes involve selecting the descriptive content of the stereotype to reflect attitudes directly. In fact, most stereotype labels cannot be freely interchanged depending upon individual attitudes. The third, and most important mechanism, involves maintaining the descriptive attribute of the stereotype independent of the attitude being expressed.

How is this possible? There is no reason to believe that attributes have evaluative connotations independent of the social object being judged. Hence the term "religious" when applied to a priest may mean one thing, and when applied to a French Canadian mean something totally different. People with different attitudes toward French Canadians will then attribute different evaluative connotations to traits such as religious, sensitive, proud and emotional when they are applied to them. While

certain traits are potentially more variable in their meaning than others (see Lamarche, 1975), even traits which seem evaluatively straightforward can have different connotations; loyalty to one's own group is a good thing but loyalty among members of another group is valued negatively.
although attitudes are expressed through the stereotype. Two of the mechanisms for expressing attitudes involve selecting the actual descriptive attributes of the stereotype to reflect attitudes directly; such mechanisms are likely to be applied only where there is open intergroup conflict. A more usual and subtle mechanism for expressing attitudes involves applying a different evaluation to the specific stereotype attributes themselves.

The Function of Stereotypes
There are two important functions to stereotyping. First, stereotypes serve an organizational function and second, they satisfy emotional needs by protecting our self-image.

Stereotypes involve categorization in the sense that the same attributes are applied to all members of a group. This categorization can be functional in two complementary ways. In the case where there is little or no information about an ethnic group, stereotypes "fill in," thus providing an organized perception of the group. More often there is far too much information about a group. In this case the person can categorize in order to reduce the extremely complex environment into manageable units. Thus the categorization involved in stereotyping is a useful guide to behaviour both in situations with a lack of information and ones where there is information "overload."

Moreover, stereotypes can guide behaviour with outgroup members as well as with members of the ingroup. To the extent that an outgroup stereotype has some basis in reality it allows a person to judge how to behave most effectively as well as how to interpret the behaviour of the outgroup member. With regard to ingroup members, the shared stereotype facilitates communication and mutual understanding among members of the ingroup regarding all issues to which the outgroup is relevant.

There are certain important implications that can be drawn from the organizational function served by stereotypes. First, to the extent that stereotypes contain a "kernal of truth" they are reasonable guides to behaviour. Second, stereotyping helps in indirect ways in terms of self-definition. By categorizing others, important contrastive social categories are created which by comparison serve to help us know who we are and where we fit into the complex social environment. Third, if stereotypes are to be truly functional, the form of the categorization should correspond to the context for which it was designed.

People would be expected to have rather complex stereotypes about groups they encounter often in a variety of circumstances as compared to those with whom they have little or no contact. The most complex and sophisticated stereotype then would be retained for one's own group. Complexity would be indicated by several stereotypes referring to sub-groups within the broader group, as well as more attributes generally, and more subtlety with regard to each of the sub-stereotypes. A single broad stereotype with only a few unqualified attributes would be typical for little-known or referred to outgroups. A similar cognitive process is evident if we contrast the complexity of categories an avid skier has for describing snow, with someone who hates winter, for whom snow is simply a burden.

The second important function served by stereotypes is the individual's emotional needs, particularly the need to view oneself positively. This function is related to other psychological concepts such as ego protection, self-image and self-esteem. The underlying theme is that perceptions and cognitions of the environment are designed, in part, to reinforce peoples' own self-image. Most people are inclined to take greater credit for successes than they probably deserve, and are quick to blame anyone but themselves for personal failures.

It is worth noting as well that stereotypes are not the only cognitive process that serve this emotional function. If a person's attitudes toward his or her own group are extremely favourable but attitudes toward an outgroup are less so, this ethnocentric pattern of attitudes indirectly reinforces the view that he/she is a good person. Similarly, in attribution terms, if the person attributes desirable behaviours to his own group as motivated by internal causes but those of the other group to external causes, the person's self-image is enhanced (see Taylor & Jaggi, 1974). When my hockey team does well it is because we played well; if the other team beats us they are just lucky.

Stereotypes operate in the same way. First, the fact that all ingroup members have the same outgroup stereotype reinforces their view that they are correct in their judgments of others. Similarly, if all members share a stereotype of their own group, they can mutually reinforce each other for having these stereotyped attributes. More subtly, stereotypes provide group members with a sense that they "understand" the social world. That is, stereotypes provide ready-made explanations for the behaviour of other groups. Finally, and most directly because attitudes are expressed through stereotypes, an ethnocentric view of the outgroup can be maintained which enhances the esteem of all ingroup members.

Unfortunately, stereotypes are not so neatly arranged that it is possible to say, "This person is stereotyping for organizational purposes whereas this one is only concerned with enhancing his or her self-image." Rather, the two functions operate simultaneously within a single act of stereotyping. The view adopted here is that people have a normal operating balance between the two functions in their use of stereotypes. For most people this probably involves holding stereotypes which maximize the organizational function while still not presenting any threat to the self. So one might, in normal circumstances, stereotype Japanese Canadians as traditional, polite and politically conservative. This stereotype poses no threat to the self-image or the image of the ingroup and serves a useful orientation in dealing with members of that group.

This normal balance operates only when the person is in a psychologically healthy and unthreatened frame of mind. When a person is threatened, the balance of functions for the stereotype changes—the emotional function becomes more important at the expense of the organizational one. What changes might be expected in a threatening situation? Certainly the stereotype might be reduced to only a few negatively valued attributes, the complexity or the relationship among the attributes would be greatly reduced and the application of the attributes to the entire ethnic group would become more rigid and extreme. Under threatening conditions, then, the loss of information noted earlier as the "cost" of stereotyping would reach a threshold point, beyond which the stereotype interferes with effective interaction rather than serving as a useful guide. The present analysis of the functions of stereotypes is highly speculative and research will be required for their confirmation or modification.

Socially Desirable Intergroup Stereotyping

Whether or not stereotypes are viewed as desirable or undesirable would seem to depend upon the ideology associated with ethnicity in the society. In societies where ethnic categorization is viewed as undesirable, where the operating principle is that ethnic differences are the basis of conflict, and where the aim is to produce an ethnically homogeneous society, ethnic stereotypes will be viewed unfavourably. Canada's "multiculturalism policy" encourages members of different ethnic groups to retain their cultural distinctiveness. Ethnic categories are viewed desirably, indeed as essential to the security within the fabric of Canadian society. Preserving ethnic identity not only has political importance, but psychological significance as well, and there has even been some research demonstrating the importance of a secure ethnic identity for good relations between groups (see Berry, Kalin and Taylor, 1977).

Stereotypes can be an important mechanism for recognizing and expressing ethnicity. They refer to a group's major attributes, and to the extent that they are accurate reflections, and refer to positive attributes of the stereotyped group, stereotypes can play a constructive role in intergroup relations. So the claim that stereotypes can have socially desirable consequences refers to situations where the particular intergroup stereotypes satisfy the desires of both groups involved, and where intergroup interaction is not characterized by destructive forms of conflict. More specifically it refers to situations where intergroup stereotypes reflect mutual attraction, even though the members of each group maintain, through stereotypes, their own ethnic group distinctiveness.

The pattern of intergroup stereotyping that gives rise to these socially desirable consequences is represented schematically in Figure 9.1. The column classifications represent the group (I or II) doing the stereotyping while the rows refer to the group being stereotyped. The capital letters in each cell represent specific stereotype attributes which may include traits, beliefs, values, political ideologies and so forth, and the (+) sign is used to indicate a positive attitude expressed through the stereotype in one of the three ways described earlier.

Figure 9.1
Schematic Representation of Situation where Stereotyping May Have Desirable Consequences

Group Doing Stereotyping

		I	II
Group Being Stereotyped	I	ABC+	ABC+
	II	XYZ+	XYZ+

What is depicted in Figure 9.1 then is a situation where each group stereotypes the other in a manner which is consistent with each group's stereotype of itself (autostereotype). Further, members of each group value their own attributes as well as those of the other group. Thus we have a socially desirable intergroup situation where each group retains its own cultural distinctiveness but is attracted to the other group.

The obvious question at this stage is whether the socially desirable stereotyping depicted here actually operates in society. Examples might not seem easy to find. However, they do exist and, if not ideally, at least at a level where mutual tolerance is characteristic of the intergroup situation. It is less difficult to imagine socially desirable stereotyping in other than inter-ethnic group situations. While the discussion has focussed on *ethnic* stereotyping it is clear that stereotyping is a process which is characteristic of social perception in general (see Taylor & Aboud, 1973). Doctors stereotype lawyers and vice versa, as do teachers and students, children and parents, students from different universities, and men and women. In these examples of role stereotyping it is relatively easy to imagine the potential for role distinctiveness co-occurring with mutual tolerance and respect.

In the domain of ethnic stereotyping the relations between the French and English Canadians in Quebec may be illustrative. Although there can be no question that tensions do exist, there is evidence to suggest that in certain contexts and among certain subgroups of English and French Canadians, mutually positive attitudes prevail (see Berry, Kalin & Taylor, 1977). Furthermore, the mutual stereotypes and autostereotypes are well defined. English Canadians stereotype themselves and are stereotyped by French Canadians as conservative, formal and reserved, while French Canadians are stereotyped as sensitive, proud and emotional (Mann, 1976). Thus both groups maintain their cultural uniqueness and at least tolerate each other in the process.

Recent studies by Mann (1976) and Aboud (1973) provide some empirical support for the notion that individuals can be attracted to members of an ethnic group who conform to the stereotype of that group. In Mann's (1976) experiment French and English Canadian actors were videotaped while playing the role of a defence lawyer presenting arguments before a jury in a murder trial. The same arguments were presented in two guises; an "emotional" guise which involved a portrayal of the French Canadian stereotype and a "formal" guise which represented the English Canadian stereotype. The guises were differentiated by means of postures, gestures and voice inflection. English Canadian subjects did not prefer English to French Canadian actors, nor did they favour one guise over the other. Rather, subjects reacted equally favourably to French Canadian actors when they conformed to the French Canadian stereotype and English Canadian actors when they played out their guise. Both French and English Canadian actors who behaved inconsistently with the stereotype of their respective group were rated less favourably.

Aboud (1973) examined the attraction English Canadians felt for members of familiar and unfamiliar ethnic groups. The groups in order of familiarity were English Canadians, French Canadians from Montreal, French Canadians from Northern Quebec, Indians, Eskimos and Hutterites. She found that for unfamiliar ethnic groups, subjects were attracted to individual members who conformed to the stereotype of that group. However, for familiar ethnic groups, subjects favoured individuals who did not conform to the stereotype of that group but were rather similar to themselves. The results were confirmed in a second study using Jewish subjects from Montreal. Taken together these studies indicate that, at least for unfamiliar ethnic groups, individuals are attracted to members of other ethnic groups who conform to the stereotype. That this is not the case for familiar groups serves as a reminder perhaps of the difficulty involved in achieving an intergroup situation where stereotyping has socially desirable consequences.

These examples emphasize personality traits contained in the stereotypes, although Aboud's (1973) studies did focus on aspects of culture and occupation. If further studies were to be conducted which included other components such as the language differences between the two groups, cultural differences which are reflected in every day life (cuisine, theatre, music), differences in emphasis in education (European vs. American) and social philosophy differences (collectivity vs. individual) we may well find that there would emerge an admiration for some of the stereotyped attributes of the other group.

A More Realistic Representation of Socially Desirable Stereotyping
One of the difficulties in finding examples of the ideal situation for stereotyping is that rarely are two groups totally distinctive as is implied in Figure 9.1. In most instances, the concern is with relations between groups who, despite a tendency to live in separate neighbourhoods, nevertheless share the same geographical space. By sharing the same environment such groups come to share important attributes derived from common political, social, educational, and religious institutions. While the focus is usually on the distinctive features, perhaps the shared attributes enhance the probability of positive attitudes between groups developing.

This more realistic context for socially desirable stereotyping is described in Figure 9.2 where the capital letters (ABC) represent more important attributes and the lower case letters (xyz, pqr) are used to denote attributes of lesser importance. The consequences of sharing important attributes and remaining distinct on less important ones may be particularly desirable in contexts where both groups are familiar with each other, where there is a high level of contact and where both groups are interdependent with regard to important shared goals. On the one hand, the shared attributes might facilitate two major social needs of members of the community; the emotional satisfaction which derives from mutual attraction and the achievement of important goals. On the other hand, the unique attributes would permit the development and maintenance of a distinctive group identity, and allow for some novelty and interest in intergroup interaction.

The idea that different ethnic groups in Canada may share certain basic values has been considered by Isajiw (1977). His theoretical position deals with the relationship of technology to ethnicity. The focus is not just on modern industry but rather on an entire set of related values such that the term technological *culture* is adopted. In answer to the question, "Why focus on technological culture?" Isajiw (1977) responds, "Because it is something that, in our society, ethnic groups seem to share more than anything else" (p. 79). We have then one example of what might constitute the shared values depicted as ABC in Figure 9.2.

Figure 9.2
Schematic Representation of Socially Desirable Stereotyping Involving
Both Shared and Distinct Attributes

Group Doing Stereotyping

		I	II
Group Being Stereotyped	I	ABC+ xyz+	ABC+ xyz+
	II	ABC+ pqr+	ABC+ pqr+

The idea that two groups may share certain attributes raises an important question—where do the shared attributes, or where does this "common culture" (ABC in Figure 9.2) come from? For example, English and Italian Canadians living in Toronto may share certain fundamental attributes—beliefs in technological culture, in specific forms of democracy, justice and freedom—while at the same time retain distinctive attributes regarding beliefs about the role of family and interpersonal relationships. But where do the shared beliefs in technological culture, democracy, justice and freedom come from? The answer is that likely the "common culture" comes more from one group than the other. The point is that in most intergroup situations the distribution of power is not equal.

English Canadians are by all accounts the dominant group in Canada. Hence it is this group which over time has defined the "common culture." If the Italian community shares these values it is largely because they have assimilated them rather than having an active role in their creation. Generally, then, it is dominant groups whose attributes define the common culture.

It must be stressed that it is not realistic nor even desirable to contemplate (1) that a minority group will contribute as much to the common culture as a majority group, or (2) that all of a group's values, majority or minority, will be contained in the common culture. Rather, the common culture forms the basis for a shared identity and one which insures participation by all groups in society. Over and above the common culture, group distinctiveness is maintained by attributes a particular group is proud of and hopefully that others respect.

A qualification to be added to Figure 9.2 then is that the common culture (ABC) must involve an agreed upon set of attributes based on contributions from both groups, not those which by default become the common attributes through the natural outcome of social power.

Unequal power relations between groups pose another difficulty which must be noted before one can talk realistically about achieving socially desirable intergroup stereotyping. Two or more groups may have, through mutual contribution, articulated a "common culture." Beyond this the two groups may agree upon their mutual "auto" and "other" stereotypes, and both groups may value their own attributes as well as those of the other groups; however, for one of the groups the attributes in question may be superficial or trivial. Such a situation might take the form of tokenism where a dominant group values selected trivial attributes of the other group as a means of placating that group while protecting its own self-interests.

An example might be the plight of native peoples in North America. Aspects of Amerindian and Inuit culture and art have undergone re-evaluation such that they now comprise a crystallized stereotype which is positively valued by both white society and native peoples. Although this stereotype provides for a positively valued cultural distinctiveness, it may well be that the attributes it consists of are those that white society is willing to entertain, because they are of little importance and in no way threatening in terms of the fundamental rewards society can offer. So white society respects these aspects of the stereotype of native peoples but these attributes may not really permit them to participate more fully in the rewards society can offer.

The appropriate conditions for socially desirable intergroup stereotyping can now be summarized. First, both groups will share a common culture which will become stereotyped as the shared attributes of members of both groups. Beyond this each group will retain and be stereotyped by distinctive attributes that are valued by the person's own group and respected by members of the other group, with the one provision that the distinctive stereotype attributes do not serve as a barrier to full participation in society.

Ethnic stereotypes then in these specific circumstances are socially desirable, indeed perhaps necessary for effective intergroup relations. What must be emphasized is that only when the specific conditions described in Figures 9.1 and 9.2 are present can intergroup stereotyping be viewed in this light. A change in the attitudes expressed through the stereotype, represented schematically by the replacement of plus with minus signs, would produce a less than desirable pattern of intergroup stereotyping. Similarly, changes in the attributes themselves, denoted by the letters in any of the four cells in Figure 9.1 producing a lack of shared perception about stereotyped attributes, would naturally lead to misunderstandings and misattributions in the course of relations between members of different ethnic groups.

Conclusions

At the outset of the chapter a series of questions was posed. The present view of stereotypes implies a set of answers which can be summarized briefly.

What is a stereotype? A stereotype is a consensus among members of one group regarding the attributes of another. It is a socially important process because of its consensual nature; it can refer to any beliefs about a group, not just personality characteristics, and there is no reason to assume that it is necessarily an inferior cognitive process.

Do stereotypes play an important role in intergroup relations? Yes. They are fundamental cognitions which serve organizational and emotional functions. More directly they influence perceptions and judgments of individual ethnic group members even in the face of contradictory information.

How are stereotypes related to prejudice? In one way stereotypes are the same as prejudice in the sense that they both represent prejudgments. In another way they should not be equated. Prejudice implies a negative attitude and this is not necessarily the case for stereotypes.

Is there any truth in stereotypes? While this is a controversial issue the present view is that in many instances there is some truth to stereotypes. The stereotype can be a useful guide to behaviour in intergroup relations; however, in times of conflict where the emotional function of stereotypes becomes predominant, they can seriously detract from intergroup interaction.

Do only bigots use stereotypes? It is clear that the present perspective recognizes everyone uses stereotypes, and that they are a normal cognitive process for organizing the social environment. The prejudicial person may express negative attitudes about a group through the stereotype, but such a person will express these attitudes through a variety of processes including his or her values, attributions, opinions, intentions and behaviour.

Do stereotypes threaten unity in multicultural societies? This is the most difficult question of all. The framework presented in this chapter is based on the premise that a secure ethnic identity is a necessary prerequisite for effective intergroup relations. Preserving ethnic identity and the stereotypes which symbolize this cultural distinctiveness need not be a divisive force. The "common culture" comprised of the fundamental attributes shared by all of society forms the basis for a shared identity. Beyond this, cultural distinctiveness represented cognitively in the form of a stereotype can be maintained. Where a group is proud of this distinctiveness, and is at the same time respectful of the stereotypes of others, it should be possible to attain unity not through diversity but with diversity.

REFERENCES

Aboud, F.E. *Evaluational and information seeking consequences of social discrepancy as applied to ethnic behaviour.* Unpublished doctoral dissertation, McGill University, 1973.

Aboud, F.E. Seeking information about different ethnic groups: The role of motivation and confirmation. *Journal of Applied Social Psychology*, 1975, *5*, 331-341.

Aboud, F.E. The functions of language in Canada: Discussion of paper by J.D. Jackson. In W.H. Coons, D.M. Taylor & M.A. Tremblay (eds.), *The Individual, Language and Society in Canada.* Ottawa: Canada Council, 1977.

Aboud, F.E., & Taylor, D.M. Ethnic and role stereotypes: their relative importance in person perception. *Journal of Social Psychology,* 1971, *85,* 17-27.

Adorno, T.W., Frenkel-Brunswik, E., Levinson, D.J., & Sanford, R.N. *The Authoritarian Personality.* New York; Harper & Row, 1950.

Allport, G.W. *The Nature of Prejudice.* Cambridge: Addison-Wesley, 1954.

Baron, R.A., & Byrne, D. *Social Psychology: Understanding Human Interaction.* Boston: Allyn & Bacon, 1977.

Berry, J.W. A functional approach to the relationship between stereotypes and familiarity. *Australian Journal of Psychology,* 1970, *22,* 29-33.

Berry, J.W., Kalin, R., & Taylor, D.M. *Multiculturalism and Ethnic Attitudes in Canada.* Ottawa: Minister of Supply and Services, Canada, 1977.

Billig, M. *Social Psychology and Intergroup Relations.* London: Academic Press, 1976.

Brigham, J.C. Ethnic stereotypes. *Psychological Bulletin,* 1971, *76,* 15-38.

Byrne, D. Attitudes and attraction. In L. Berkowitz (ed.), *Advances in Experimental Social Psychology,* Vol. 4. New York: Academic Press, 1969.

Campbell, D.T. Stereotypes and the perception of group differences. *American Psychologist,* 1967, *22,* 817-829.

Cauthen, N.R., Robinson, I.E., & Krauss, H.H. Stereotypes: a review of the literature 1926-1968. *Journal of Social Psychology,* 1971, *84,* 103-126.

Dudycha, G.J. The attitudes of college students toward war and the Germans before and during the Second World War. *Journal of Social Psychology,* 1942, *15,* 317-324.

Fishman, J.A. An examination of the process and functioning of social stereotyping. *Journal of Social Psychology,* 1956, *43,* 27-64.

Gardner, R.C. Ethnic stereotypes: The traditional approach, a new look. *Canadian Psychologist,* 1973, *14,* 133-148.

Gardner, R.C., Kirby, D.M., & Finley, J.C. Ethnic stereotypes: the significance of consensus. *Canadian Journal of Behavioural Science,* 1973, *5,* 4-12.

Gardner, R.C., & Taylor, D.M. Ethnic stereotypes: their effects on person perception. *Canadian Journal of Psychology,* 1968, *22,* 267-276.

Gardner, R.C., & Taylor, D.M. Ethnic stereotypes: meaningfulness in ethnic group labels. *Canadian Journal of Behavioural Science.* 1969, *1,* 182-192.

Gardner, R.C., Taylor, D.M., & Feenstra, H.J. Ethnic stereotypes: attitudes or beliefs? *Canadian Journal of Psychology,* 1970, *24,* 321-334.

Gardner, R.C., Wonnacott, E.J., & Taylor, D.M. Ethnic stereotypes: a factor analytic investigation. *Canadian Journal of Psychology.* 1968, *22,* 35-44.

Gilbert, G.M. Stereotype persistence and change among college students. *Journal of Abnormal and Social Psychology,* 1951, *46,* 245-254.

Grant, P.R. *Attribution of an ethnic stereotype.* Unpublished Masters Thesis, University of Waterloo, 1978.

Isajiw, W.W. Olga of wonderland: ethnicity in technological society. *Canadian Ethnic Studies,* 1977, *9,* 77-85.

Karlins, M., Coffman, T.L., & Walters, G. On the fading of social stereotypes: studies in three generations of college students. *Journal of Personality and Social Psychology,* 1969, *13,* 1-16.

Katz, D., & Braly, K. Racial stereotypes of one hundred college students. *Journal of Abnormal and Social Psychology,* 1933, *28,* 280-290.

Katz, D., & Braly, K. Racial prejudice and racial stereotypes. *Journal of Abnormal and Social Psychology,* 1935, *30,* 175-193.

Kirby, D.M., & Gardner, R.C. Ethnic stereotypes: norms on 208 words typically used in their assessment. *Canadian Journal of Psychology*, 1972, *26*, 140-154.

Kirby, D.M., & Gardner, R.C. Ethnic stereotypes: determinants in children and their parents. *Canadian Journal of Psychology*, 1973, *27*, 127-143.

La Gaipa, J.J. Stereotypes and perceived ethnic-role specialization. *Journal of Social Psychology*, 1971, *85*, 285-292.

Lamarche, L. Composition d'une liste d'adjectifs ordonnés selon leur degré de polysémie. Paper presented at Canadian Psychological Association meeting, Quebec, June 1975.

Lay, C.H., & Jackson, D.N. A note on the independence of stereotypes and attitude. *Canadian Journal of Behavioural Science*, 1972, *4*, 146-155.

Lippman, W. *Public Opinion.* New York: Harcourt, Brace, 1922.

Mackie, M. Arriving at "truth" by definition: the case of stereotype inaccuracy. *Social Problems*, 1973, *20*, 431-447.

Mackie, M. Ethnic stereotypes, prejudicial attitudes, and education. *The Alberta Journal of Educational Research*, 1974, *20*, 279-292.

Mann, J.F. *Cognitive, behavioural and situational determinants of ethnic perception.* Unpublished doctoral dissertation. McGill University, 1976.

Middlebrook, P.N. *Social Psychology and Modern Life,* New York: Alfred A. Knopf, 1974.

Peabody, D. Trait inferences: evaluative and descriptive aspects. *Journal of Personality and Social Psychology,* Monograph, 1967, *7*, (4, hole #644).

Sampson, E.E. Psychology and the American Ideal. *Journal of Personality and Social Psychology*, 1977, *35*, 767-782.

Seago, D.W. Stereotypes: before Pearl Harbour and after. *Journal of Psychology*, 1947, *23*, 55-63.

Sinha, A.K.P., & Upadhyay, O.P. Change and persistence in the stereotype of university students toward different ethnic groups during Sino-Indian border dispute. *Journal of Social Psychology*, 1960, *52*, 31-39.

Steiner, I.D. Whatever happened to the group in social psychology? *Journal of Experimental Social Psychology*, 1974, *10*, 94-108.

Tajfel, H. Cognitive aspects of prejudice. *Journal of Social Issues*, 1969, *25*, 79-97.

Tajfel, H. Experiments in a vacuum. In J. Israel & H. Tajfel (eds.), *The Context of Social Psychology: A Critical Assessment.* London: Academic Press, 1972.

Taylor, D.M., & Aboud, F.E. Ethnic Stereotypes: is the concept necessary? *Canadian Psychologist*, 1973, *14*, 330-338.

Taylor, D.M., & Brown, R.J. Towards a more social social psychology. *British Journal of Social and Clinical Psychology*, 1979, *18*, 173-180.

Taylor, D.M., & Gardner, R.C. Ethnic stereotypes: their effects on the perception of communicators of varying credibility. *Canadian Journal of Psychology*, 1969, *23*, 161-173.

Taylor, D.M., & Jaggi, V. Ethnocentrism and causal attribution in a South Indian context. *Journal of Cross-Cultural Psychology*, 1974, *5*, 162-172.

Taylor, D.M., & Simard, L.M. Ethnic identity and intergroup relations. In D.J. Lee (ed.), *Emerging Ethnic Boundaries.* Ottawa: University of Ottawa Press, 1979.

Triandis, H.C. *Attitude and Attitude Change.* New York: Wiley 1971.

Triandis, H.C. & Vassiliou, V. Frequency of contact and stereotyping. *Journal of Personality and Social Psychology*, 1967, *7*, 316-328.

Chapter 10

Intergroup Communication

Lise M. Simard, Département de Psychologie, Université de Montréal

Communication, in the psychological sense, refers to the exchange of information (ideas, experiences) between individuals or groups of individuals. For the information to be transmitted, however, there must exist some shared conventions on the signs or symbols used for conveying the message. Complexity of human social interaction could not be achieved without the richness and flexibility of man's highly sophisticated language system.

To be effective, however, this complex and elaborate system should use symbols shared by the people who want to communicate. What happens when individuals do not speak the same language? What happens in multi-ethnic and multilingual environments where effective social interaction requires the use of a second language? Moreover, more than one communication system may be needed even when native speakers of the same language interact. Labov (1973) for example, would describe the black community as having a language distinct from that of other native English speakers and hence any contact between such groups would involve some form of bilingualism. The work of Bernstein (1971) on restricted and elaborate codes and similar work by Taylor and Clément (1974) with Quebec French supports the same idea. Some form of functional bilingualism is required if any intergroup communication is to take place in a multilingual context. This leads us to a fundamental question: is it possible for members of different linguistic groups to communicate effectively?

Certain delimitations should be made concerning the dimensions of the question to be addressed. First, we intend to limit our discussion of intergroup communication to situations where there is interaction; communication through mass media will not be examined (for a study on this question, see Mousseau-Glaser, 1972). Second, the discussion of the question will also be limited to situations formulated in individualistic terms where we will focus on social interaction and communication among individuals from different ethnolinguistic groups. Finally, the definition of the term "efficient" communication should be stated. In this context, a communication will be judged efficient if the intended information is transmitted, if both interlocutors perceive it as such, and, if the process of communicating was perceived as relatively easy and satisfying by the ones communicating. One criterion of an efficient communication would be that future interaction is perceived as possible and desirable by the two participants, given that opportunity for such interaction prevails.

The situation in Montreal provides a good starting point for testing the possibility of interaction between members of different linguistic groups. In this context the second language for each group is an official national language which already possesses a highly ascribed status outside Canada. This, along with the historical context of Canada, suggests that extensive interaction should occur between members of the two groups at all social levels. To achieve this, each group receives instruction in both French and English at primary and secondary school. Thus, each child receives from seven to twelve years of second language training.

The fact that French and English are languages of highly ascribed status should be a motivating factor for members of each group to learn and use the language of the other; however, there exists little interaction between the French and English populations. Lieberson (1965) used census data to examine trends in the ability of Montreal's population to communicate with one another between 1921 and 1961, and concluded that there has been no increase in linguistic communication during the period examined. In order to test this parallel existence more directly, Simard and Taylor (1973) questioned people about their social contacts. Students from a French university and from an English university were asked to record detailed information concerning their conversations for the previous twenty-four hours in terms of where they took place, topic of conversation, ethnic group of the "other," and language spoken. Of the 1,008 social encounters recorded 99.9 per cent were with members of the same language group. It may still be accurate to describe Montreal in terms of "two solitudes" (cf. MacLennan, 1945; Mailhiot, 1956).

Why is there so little interaction between French and English Canadians despite the fact that they share the same social environment? This question brings us back to another one that was stated earlier in this chapter: is it possible for members of different linguistic groups to communicate effectively? This question relates to at least two different dimensions: competence and motivation. That is, for intergroup communication to become a reality, people should be competent enough in the other language and must be motivated enough to use that competence.

Linguistic Incompeten̦ce as a Barrier to Intergroup Communication

Is it possible to attain sufficient linguistic competence in another language so that members of different linguistic groups can communicate effectively? Some researchers have suggested that failures to communicate may arise when two people share the same language but not similar cultural or cognitive frames of reference (Gatbonton and Tucker, 1971; Triandis, 1960; 1977). That is, the individual's values and traditions would bias his transmission or reception of information.

In order to study whether bilinguals could communicate equally well with native speakers from both linguistic groups, Tucker & Gedalof (1970) studied how well bilinguals of French Canadian parentage communicated with monolingual English or French speakers. The technique used to measure communication is known as the "cloze procedure" (Taylor, 1959) which requires participants to fill in the missing words in a paragraph from which every fifth word has been deleted. The bilingual speakers performed significantly better with the French speakers than with the English and the authors suggested that distinctive French Canadian cultural values and traditions may have influenced their ability to communicate with peers whose surface linguistic code they appeared to share. Since an obvious limitation to this study is the degree of bilinguality of the participants, d'Anglejan and Tucker (1973) repeated the experiment using experienced professional translators selected by the Translators' Society of Quebec. In spite of their sophistication in both languages, the translators' performance, again, suggested that cognitive differences underlying the surface codes may have affected communication.

Other studies have focussed, not on written communication, but rather on verbal communication taken in the course of interaction because it was felt that such a setting might be more important for the study of cross-cultural communication. Furthermore, these studies were designed to test whether traditional second language education is sufficient for effective interaction. The test purposely avoided participants who might have had special second language training (e.g. immersion, experience in another country) and instead focussed on people from multilingual environments who were products of the normal second language training programs in their respective school systems.

The general research strategy made use of the paradigm developed by Glucksberg, Krauss and Weisberg (1966) which involves two participants who must co-operate in performing an experimental task. One of the participants is designated as the speaker and his/her task is to describe a stimulus to a listener. The listener is given six stimuli, one of which is identical to the stimulus being described by the speaker. The listener's task is to decide as quickly as possible which of the six stimuli is the one actually being described by the speaker. The speed and accuracy with which the speaker and listener perform this task serves as a measure of communicational efficiency.

Surprising results emerged from the experiments of this type. In the first experiment, tape-recorded descriptions served as simulated speakers and native speakers of French decoded messages given by English speakers as efficiently as native speakers of English (Taylor and Gardner, 1970a). In a second experiment conducted in the Philippines (Taylor and Gardner, 1970b), videotaped messages were given to Chinese and Filipino listeners. Again there was efficient cross-cultural communication even though a second language had to be used as the medium of communication.

These result suggested that cross-cultural communication could be efficient; however, a second important finding emerged in both studies which tempered this conclusion. Whereas subjects who heard messages delivered by members of their own ethnic group expected that they would perform well on the experimental task, those in the mixed ethnic conditions revealed negative expectations. Such expectations no doubt serve as an important deterrent to cross-cultural interaction.

The preceding studies had a serious limitation in that the situation was highly artificial. The use of recorded messages provided good experimental control, but some of the language adjustment typically required in cross-cultural communication may have been lost by this procedure. That is, when two people from different ethnolinguistic groups meet they must consciously or unconsciously choose the most effective language or blend of languages to use before any real communication can take place.

In an attempt to deal with this limitation, communicational efficiency was assessed among French Canadian and English Canadian factory workers who met in an actual face-to-face situation (Taylor and Simard, 1972). The use of an actual dyadic situation not only simulated reality better but also allowed for monitoring the language adjustment process that is required for cross-cultural communication. The results again demonstrated that cross-cultural communication can be as efficient as within-group communication. Furthermore, in the mixed ethnic conditions French and English were used almost equally, indicating a setting of reciprocal bilingualism where neither language was dominant over the other. Finally, neither group expressed negative expectations regarding their ability to communicate across cultures.

An important problem associated with this type of research concerns the motivating conditions under which communication takes place. In each case, participants were forced to communicate in order to solve an experimental problem and the time pressures did not allow for spontaneous communication patterns to develop. Furthermore, these same pressures precluded the possibility for communication on topics other than the immediate task at hand. Simard and Taylor (1973) attempted to deal with some of the limitations of the earlier studies. In this experiment, three conditions were used to vary the extent to which the participants were forced to communicate. In one condition, communication among the two participants was necessary to complete the task; in the second condition communication was optional, and in the final condition, communication was completely unrelated to the problem-solving task. After completing the task, the two participants were left by themselves and the use of a hidden tape-recorder made it possible to assess the development of spontaneous patterns of communication.

As might be expected, the three experimental task conditions did influence the amount of communication. However, there were no interactions between this variable and the ethnic composition of the pairs. Thus, mixed ethnic pairs reacted to the situational variables in the same fashion as the same ethnic pairs; the mixed ethnic pairs did not take longer to begin communicating nor did they talk less than the same ethnic pairs. Ethnic composition also did not affect the topics discussed. This is striking since it might be expected that the mixed ethnic pairs would not take a chance on choosing a new topic and would attempt to facilitate communication by talking most about the task at hand. In mixed ethnic groupings, French and English were used almost equally, and language choice was usually determined by the person who initiated the communication.

Motivational Barriers to Intergroup Communication

Assuming that people are able to function in the other language, what factors might stop them from doing so? Why would people choose to avoid cross-cultural communication? As yet there is no well-defined set of motivational factors which have been related to cross-cultural communication; however, an exploration of intergroup communication as it happens outside the laboratory may provide some insights into the basis for poor motivation. Research has already shown that attitudes and motivation influence the extent to which another language is learned (see Gardner, Chapter 6 of this volume); what about the extent to which another language is used after some learning has taken place?

Linguistic Competence versus Social Competence

It has been suggested that in order to achieve an efficient and satisfying communication a speaker should not only achieve a certain linguistic competence but should also attain a certain level of social competence, that is, should know the rules about how to speak about certain topics in particular situations (Hymes, 1971; Segalowitz, 1976; Taylor and Simard, 1975). In second language training, however, the formal rules of a language are stressed while the application of specific styles of the language to different situations is seldom included in the curriculum. Many second language speakers control only the formal speech style which corresponds most closely to the classroom register (Morin, Picard, Pupier & Santerre, 1974) and are consequently unable to vary their manner of speaking in a way that is appropriate for different situations.

Segalowitz (1976) hypothesized that such people may find themselves socially isolated from the interlocutor because of their inability to interpret completely the social messages conveyed to them by means of the speech style variation and their inability to respond appropriately. The second language interaction with native speakers will then be uncomfortable and negative reactions toward the communicative situation and their interlocutor may develop. Segalowitz explored this question in an experiment where English-speaking Montrealers with non-native but nonetheless functional skills in French were asked to interact with a French inter-locutor who used very formal and careful speech in one condition and relatively casual and informal speech in another.

The results supported the predictions. In the casual native language condition subjects felt more relaxed, believed they were better understood and found it easier to express themselves, compared to the formal native language condition, but the pattern was reversed in the second language condition. Moreover, in terms of subjects' evaluations of the impression they conveyed to their "listener," participants thought they appeared relatively less intelligent and self-confident in the casual second language condition than in the formal one, whereas the reverse was true in the native language condition. The most disturbing result, however, concerns the effect of the speech style change on the speaking subjects' evaluations of their interlocutors on personality characteristics. In the second language condition, the speaking subjects rated their interlocutor less positively in the casual conditions than in the formal one whereas this difference was reversed when they used the native language.

These results suggest a lack of motivation felt by many second language speakers to use their linguistic skills. As soon as these speakers get out of the classroom situation and need to use a more casual type of speech, they not only find themselves in an uncomfortable and unpleasant situation, but they also perceive their interlocutor in a less favourable way than they would a native speaker or a second language speaker in a formal situation.

Actual Competence versus Perceived Competence

The study of linguistic and social competence is important from two points of view: first, as an *actual* competence evaluated by some external judges (for example, psycholinguists, sociolinguists and social psychologists) on some objective criteria, and second, as a *perceived* competence evaluated by the speaker and the listener on more subjective criteria. Linguists have developed various methods to measure actual linguistic competence, i.e., the variation we encounter in first language speech (Bickerton, 1971; Cedergren and Sankoff, 1974; Labov, 1969). However, these techniques have yet to be applied to the analysis of second language speech (Segalo-witz, 1977). Work in this area has been initiated by Gatbonton (1978) who used a method derived from Bickerton (1971) to study speech variability or actual competence at the phonological level for second language speakers. This method appears to hold some promise for identifying the various stages through which second language learners pass in moving from the least native-like stage of mastery to the most native-like one.

Most of the time, however, measures of bilingualism are measures of perceived competence, that is, how well individuals evaluate their com-petence on some subjective criteria (census data, for example). Individuals, then, will evaluate their level of competence to decide whether it is sufficient or not for effective intergroup communication. Individuals who, independent of their actual competence, perceive that they do not attain a functional level will obviously not be motivated to communicate.

This perception of competence or incompetence has some implications for intergroup communication. First, it would be important to be able to compare the actual competence with the perceived competence. Many individuals may be persuaded that they do not attain the functional level when, in fact, they do. Second, it would be important to find out the criteria used by people to evaluate their competence: they may be realistic or they may not. The fact that Anglophones consistently report that they are less competent in their second language than Francophones perceived themselves to be (e.g., Census of Canada, 1973; Lamy, 1976; Taylor, Simard and Papineau, 1978), may be for them an important motivational barrier for not engaging in intergroup communication or for using mainly English when such encounters occur, independently of whether they have attained a functional level or not.

Psychological Processes in Intergroup Communication

Individuals will change their speech style depending on the characteristics of the social situation. For example, a mother will address her child in one way and the neighbour's child, in another way. Theoretical work in the area of speech diversity provides a taxonomy of factors such as setting, topic and listener which influence a speaker's verbal output (Ervin-Tripp, 1964; Hymes, 1972). But why do speech modifications occur in the first place and what are their effects on intergroup communication?

In an attempt to deal with these issues, Giles, Taylor and Bourhis (1973) proposed a social psychological model which examines one motivation for speech modification—interpersonal accommodation—where a speaker makes certain linguistic adjustments in the direction of his partner as a means of facilitating social attraction.

Interpersonal Accommodation

This accommodation model has, as its basis, research on similarity-attraction (Byrne, 1971) which suggests that as A becomes more similar to B, it increases the likelihood that B will favourably evaluate A. Interpersonal accommodation through speech involves the reduction of linguistic dissimilarities between members of a dyad such as in the case where A matches B's speech rate, accent, vocal intensities or length of utterance. The greater the speaker's need to gain another's approval or attraction the greater the magnitude of accommodation or convergence. Conversely, should the speaker feel the need to increase social distance with his listener, then it is suggested that he will modify his speech style away from the other, or, diverge (see Giles, 1973). The accommodation model proposes that convergent behaviour is a dissimilarity reducing tactic allowing the speaker to be more favourably evaluated than if he maintained his regular speech habits in the face of the other.

Two hypotheses can be derived from this model: (1) the greater the effort in accommodation perceived from a speaker the more favourably he will be evaluated by the listener, and (2) the more the latter will accommodate back to this person. To test these hypotheses with regard to bilingual accomodation in Quebec, Giles, Taylor and Bourhis (1973) had a taped French Canadian (FC) stimulus speaker provide a message to bilingual English Canadians (EC) in either French (no accommodation), a mixture of French and English (partial accommodation) or English (full accommodation). It was found that the FC was perceived more favourably in terms of considerateness and in his effort to bridge the cultural gap the more he accommodated to the EC listeners. Moreover, when the subjects were given the opportunity to return a communication to their FC partner, those who were spoken to in English accommodated the most (i.e., spoke French), followed by the mixed language condition and least by those who were spoken to in French. A study by Simard, Taylor & Giles (1976) has shown that such patterns are also in evidence when the roles of the two ethnolinguistic groups are reversed. These findings complement those of other studies done in a number of cultural settings which have shown that in ethnic interaction people react more favourably to persons from another group who accommodate (converge) to them in accent, speech rates, dialect or language than to speakers who do not (Bourhis, Giles and Lambert, 1975; Doise, Sinclair and Bourhis, 1976; Giles and Smith, 1979; Harris and Baudin, 1973).

The results reported thus far would suggest that in an intergroup communication situation, the more a person would accommodate linguistically the more that person would be perceived as considerate and interested in breaking down cultural barriers, and the more the listener would be likely to accommodate in return. Beside the fact that an optimal level of accommodation may exist (Giles and Smith, 1979), cross-cultural communication in a real context suggests the need for further elaborations of the accommodation model in that attributed motives underlying accommodative or non-accommodative behaviours should be taken into account.

Causal Attribution

Heider (1958) suggests that we understand a person's behaviour, and hence evaluate the person himself, in terms of the motives and intentions that we attribute as the cause of his actions. The implication of attribution theory to the present context is that a listener can attribute accommodation and non-accommodation each in a variety of ways: (1) lack of ability or appropriate repertoire range, (2) the existence of external pressure to

Figure 10.1
A Revised Version of the Accommodation Model (Simard, Taylor & Giles, 1976)

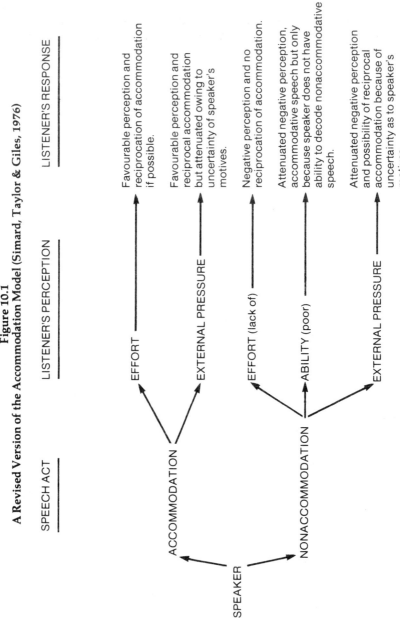

maintain a native speech style, or (3) a lack of effort to reduce dissimilarities between them.

A study, designed primarily to determine whether accommodation is perceived differentially depending on the attributed motives, examined whether the attribution factors of ability, effort and external pressure influenced listeners' reactions to accommodative and non-accommodative speech acts (Simard, Taylor & Giles, 1976). The results suggested an elaboration of the accommodation model, a schematic representation of which appears in Fig. 10.1. It proposes that the perception of accommodation produces positive speaker evaluation and reciprocal accommodation but a qualification needs to be considered if accommodation is attributed to external pressures; listeners decode such an accommodating message less effectively and are less prepared to return an accommodating communication than when the convergence was attributed to effort. Non-accommodation is likely to foster a relatively unfavourable speaker evaluation and induce the listener to maintain his regular speech style. However, when this behaviour is attributed to a lack of language ability or to external pressures rather than to a lack of effort then qualifications again have to be made in that the act may not be perceived or reacted to quite so negatively.

This model highlights the various factors that might explain the lack of intergroup communication in Canada. First, if interpersonal convergence is perceived generally favourably, and non-convergence generally received unfavourably, the repeated non-convergence of certain members might be upsetting and lead to a complete break in the communication process. Second, causal attributions seem to play an important role in understanding the motivational factors underlying intergroup communication. More specifically, the same behaviour by members of two different ethno-linguistic groups may generate different causal attributions depending on (1) whose members are the object of the attribution and (2) whose members are making the attribution.

These latter generalizations were supported by an interesting experiment (Sandilands and Corston Fleury, 1979). The authors created a mixed language situation with two bilinguals and one unilingual in which the bilinguals switch to the language not understood by the unilingual. They presented this situation to French-speaking subjects and to English-speaking subjects in order to analyze the motivations attributed to the bilinguals by the unilingual. Results indicated that Anglophones attributed more hostile motives to the bilingual than did the Francophones. However, both Francophone and Anglophone subjects made different attributions depending on whether the language switch was initiated by an Anglophone or Francophone bilingual.

It is clear that a look at attribution processes as they operate in *both* interlocutors will be necessary to understand the motivational aspects of intergroup communication. The study of attributional factors would probably be most revealing in the cases of non-accommodative behaviour. The following section will examine more closely such divergent behaviours and the possible motivational reasons behind them.

Preservation of Intergroup Distinctiveness

Although individuals in intergroup communication may wish to converge linguistically towards each other in order to reduce the psychological distance between them, in other circumstances, they may choose not only to maintain their own speech style but to accentuate the difference between themselves and others (Bourhis, Giles and Lambert, 1975; Doise, Sinclair and Bourhis, 1976). These speech shifts away from the interlocutor's style have been termed "speech divergence" (Giles, 1973). Tajfel's theory of intergroup relations (Tajfel, 1974; 1978) provides a framework for understanding these non-accommodative behaviours.

Tajfel proposed four interrelated processes as the foundation for the theory: social categorization, social comparison, social identity and psychological distinctiveness. Social categorization is described as a fundamental process whereby individuals not only categorize the social environment, but then use these categorizations as a basis for action. When members of different groups are in contact, they compare themselves on dimensions which are important to them. These intergroup social comparisons will lead people to look for, and even create, dimensions on which they can make themselves positively distinct from the other group(s). This perception of positive distinctiveness by the members of a group will insure that they have a positive social identity.

Social identity involves these aspects of an individual's self-image which derive from the social categories to which he/she perceives himself/herself to belong. In the case of ethnic identity, the focus will be on that aspect of an individual's self-definition which is derived from membership in a particular ethnolinguistic group (Taylor and Simard, 1979). How is the ethnic identity (see Aboud, chapter 3 and Lambert, chapter 4, of this volume) of a person related to cross-cultural communication?

Inhabitants of bicultural or multicultural communities have to balance the anticipated social and instrumental rewards for getting to know the other ethnolinguistic group(s) better with the possible costs of endangering their own identity. Initial research in the Canadian context indicated that French and English Canadians maintain distinct and separate patterns of identity (Taylor, Simard and Aboud, 1972) and that for both groups, language, even more than cultural heritage, emerges as the major determinant of this identity (Taylor, Bassili and Aboud, 1973). That language is perceived as the major dimension of ethnic identity has been found also with Francophone children who live in a multi-ethnic area of Montreal (Simard, Mercier and De Brouin-Gareau, 1979) as well as in

Wales with adult populations (Bourhis, Giles and Tajfel, 1973; Giles, Taylor and Bourhis, 1977). If language is an important subjective dimension of ethnic identity, it is also an objective one. It might be expected then that in situations where ethnic group membership is a salient issue, language divergence may be an important strategy for making oneself psychologically distinct from members of other groups.

Research on this issue corroborates this hypothesis. For example, a phonological analysis of French Canadian learners of English showed that those who identified strongly with Quebec nationalism were more divergent in certain of their English pronunciations than those who identified less closely with Quebec's nationalism (Segalowitz and Gatbonton, 1977). These findings parallel those of Labov (1963) who found that speakers with greater centralization of certain vowels in their mother tongue English had different feelings of group identification from those with less centralization. In Wales, in a language laboratory setting, Welsh participants who valued highly their national language and group membership diverged by accentuating their Welsh accent when responding to a threatening English interlocutor. In contrast, Welsh subjects who did not value their group membership as highly converged in the same circumstances (Bourhis and Giles, 1977). In a more recent Belgian study, a somewhat similar situation was set up which resulted in Flemish participants diverging from a Walloon (French) speaker by means of an actual language shift (Bourhis, Giles, Leyens and Tajfel, 1979).

It has been assumed that learning or speaking a second language has for the most part positive social consequences. This view has been questioned recently (e.g., Bourhis, 1979; Segalowitz, 1977; Taylor and Simard, 1975). Lambert (1977) has found it useful to distinguish between "additive" and "subtractive" bilingualism. In additive bilingualism, one is adding a second, socially relevant language to one's repertory of skills; in such cases, no perceived threat to identity seems imminent. Contrast this, however, with situations where becoming bilingual subtracts from and threatens the existence of the native language. In such circumstances, it would make sense for French Canadians to choose some of the following strategies: (1) not to become bilingual (2) not to interact with English Canadians or (3) not to accommodate if they do interact since second language speaking could be detrimental to autonomy and to the maintenance of a strong ethnic identity.

Intergroup Communication in Real Social Interaction
Communication does not happen in a vacuum: at least two persons and some information to be shared are involved in the process. Therefore, communication will be more successful and can lead potentially to future interaction if real needs to communicate exist between people. Circumstances that appear to offer such needs are friendship and work situations.

An examination of interactions between persons of different ethnolinguistic groups in these situations would help to understand the process of intergroup communication. What is going on in these interactions? What are the feelings and expectations of the persons involved? What language(s) is (are) spoken with what effects on the efficiency and satisfaction dimensions?

Although answers to such questions would be extremely useful, there are not many studies that examine cross-cultural interaction between two people. Two reasons for this are the paucity of intergroup interactions and the difficulty of studying social interactions outside the laboratory. Nonetheless, some exploratory studies of cross-cultural communication have been conducted.

Intergroup Communication and Friendship

What are the processes involved in social contacts between members of different ethnolinguistic groups? More specifically, when contacts are of the associative and informal kind such as in friendship, are the processes of intergroup attraction unique or are they only special instances of the more general processes of interpersonal attraction? For example, the one constant theme in the literature on factors involved in social attraction has been that attraction is mainly a function of the similarity which exists between one person and another (e.g. Byrne, 1971; Berscheid & Walster, 1978). Do the same patterns generalize to cross-cultural attraction? What about the similarity of people in terms of the language they speak? This requires special emphasis in the present context as language is not only a cue to ethnic difference, but also the medium which permits communication in a friendship exchange. The fact that the two groups speak different languages would seem initially to be an overpowering variable. While some evidence reviewed previously suggests that communication by means of a second language may pose difficulties there is also reason to question whether language per se is a serious deterrent to cross-cultural interaction (Taylor and Simard, 1975).

Other questions would also be important for cross-cultural friendship: are people generally motivated to meet other people? Do they generally find other people interesting? Do they expect other people to find them interesting? Is it easy to meet new people who have the potential to become one's close friends? Who is actually selected among the naturally large number of potential acquaintances, and how and where do these encounters take place? Such basic questions, while important for within-group interaction, may have even greater implications for contact with members of a different ethnic group. If forming new acquaintances is difficult generally, and if the specific difficulties can be isolated, this may provide some insights into which problems become enhanced when cross-cultural friendship is attempted.

Research on the topic however is virtually non-existent. The studies I am about to describe attempted, at an exploratory level, to answer such questions by investigating the process of forming social acquaintances with special emphasis on the social contacts formed across ethnolinguistic boundaries (Simard, in press). The research strategy involved assessing informal social interaction among members of the *same ethnic group* and contrasting this with the processes as they operate with members of *different ethnic groups*. Specifically two studies were conducted both with French and English Canadians. The first study assessed peoples' *perceptions* and *expectations* about forming new acquaintances; the second study was a field experiment and focussed on the *behaviour* of people in the process of forming new acquaintances.

General results of the first study indicated that people *perceive* it to be relatively easy to form new acquaintances but do not initiate such contacts with extreme frequency. When contact does occur, it is perceived to be under external situational control. The places people regard as providing situations conducive to forming new acquaintances are ones that are somewhat structured and where a person has clear expectations about what type of person will be encountered (e.g., own university, parties, work). More specifically, both French and English Canadian participants perceive that forming acquaintances occurs less often and with more overall difficulty with members of the other group. The dimensions that are perceived as specially more difficult include aspects such as gaining the interest of members of the other group, becoming interested in such persons, and knowing how to initiate and sustain a conversation.

In terms of the perceived importance of similarity for attraction, every dimension of those examined (e.g., sociodemographical characteristics, personality traits) is perceived as more important when applied to a member from the other group. Members from the other group then must be *more* similar to a person than members from his/her own group on a variety of dimensions in order to be considered as a potential acquaintance. The difference in the importance given to specific dimensions of similarity by the two groups is also revealing. Consistent with the attraction literature, similarity of attitudes emerged as the most important factor. But the most interesting judgment of similarity is the importance attributed to similarity of *Language*. At one level, this finding can be interpreted as merely reflecting peoples' perceptions that it is necessary to share a common language for effective social interaction. However, the participants were specifically asked about the importance of having a potential friend speak their (the subjects') own language and this is what both the Francophone and Anglophone participants judged to be important: that the *other person* speak their own language.

These data do not seem to imply, however, that the participants are unable to function in their second language. To the questions of how well they understand and speak both languages it is true that they perceived themselves as more competent in their own language, and that Francophones perceived themselves as more competent in their second language than the Anglophones. However, a comparison of perceived competence in the other language as compared to own language reveals that the participants do not perceive themselves as totally incompetent in their second language. Moreover, they agree that in their second language they are even more competent in the skill of understanding than that of speaking. Thus, if similarity of language was important only for communicative efficiency, interaction could still take place since each can understand the other in the other's language. But the main indication that similarity of language involves more than sharing the same linguistic code is provided by the French Canadians who perceive themselves as quite bilingual but, at the same time, demand that an Anglophone speak French in order to be considered as a potential friend.

It seems then that similarity of language is important, but not merely because it is necessary for effective communication. It may be that for people in a bicultural environment the degree of second language capability reflects social intentions. Learning the language of another group is behavioural evidence that the person is interested in communicating with members of the other language group. That people will interpret language learning as reflecting social intentions has been suggested in studies of accommodation among French and English Canadians (e.g. Giles, Taylor and Bourhis, 1973; Simard, Taylor and Giles, 1976). Similarity of language may also be perceived as important in terms of what it means to a person to be speaking in his own language. As suggested earlier, language is a very important component of ethnic identity. Thus, insisting on speaking one's own language is assuring the recognition of one's own ethnic group. This reason might be particularly important for French Canadians who are surrounded by English speakers in the North American context. These tentative interpretations suggest that two persons must be able to speak each other's language, that is, both must be bilingual before there exists a potential basis for friendship.

There were several isolated findings which, when considered together, converge to produce a profile of cultural differences between French and English Canadians. For example, French Canadians perceive that it is easy to make friends with English Canadians, feel it is under their control, have relatively good second language skills and yet report not forming many acquaintances with members of the other group. Such a profile provides further corroboration of the interpretation made earlier: namely that French Canadians for reasons of non-accommodation and ethnic identity are not particularly motivated for cross-cultural interaction. English Canadians, on the other hand, *seem* relatively motivated to form acquaintances with members of the other group but do not have the same degree of second language capability and feel that they do not control the forming of acquaintances but need the appropriate external circumstances. Given these cultural profiles, neither French Canadians nor English Canadians are likely to initiate any change in the direction of increased social contact. Unless there is a change in environment for English people or a change in motivation by French people, a parallel social existence will continue.

To test whether the perceptions and expectations just presented have a basis in reality was the concern of a second study in a natural context. The task for the Francophone and Anglophone participants in this field study was to form an acquaintanceship with a person to whom they felt attracted, and who had the potential eventually to become a friend. Every participant was asked to meet either a person of his or her own ethnic group or a person from the other ethnic group, but never both. Subjects were not permitted to explain to the potential acquaintance that they were taking part in an experiment and were required to approach this person in the manner in which they normally form social acquaintances. Participants were also required to obtain the name and telephone number of this person. There were two reasons for this latter requirement. First, it allowed for a check as to whether or not the participant actually met the person, and second, the requirement ensured that the encounter reached some level of intimacy, that is, sufficient for it to be appropriate to ask for the telephone number. Subjects were given two weeks to complete the task and were asked to report behavioural and perceptual data regarding the actual encounter on a guide sheet.

The results of this second study indicated that forming new acquaintances may be more difficult than would be expected from the results of the first study. Ony one-third of the subjects completed the task. This is an unusually low percentage of completion considering that for most laboratory experiments, close to 100 per cent of subjects will complete the task. The expectation that forming new acquaintances with members of the other group is more difficult than with own group members was corroborated. Both French and English Canadians succeeded more often in forming acquaintances with members of their own group. After having completed the task, however, subjects reported no special difficulties with the encounters they had with members from the other group and found them as rewarding and as interesting as encounters formed among one's own group.

People's strategies for forming the new acquaintances reveal another potential problem for intergroup interaction. Although the experiment provided participants with a reason to initiate contact with others, and although they were pressured because of the time allotted to complete the task, half the people still relied on external circumstances rather than initiating contact themselves. It seems that forming new acquaintances by waiting for accommodating external social circumstances must be a well-anchored strategy. As these social circumstances were not operating, increased social contact might not be achieved by solely providing them with the linguistic competence and motivating them to initiate the process. In light of the present findings, it would seem profitable somehow to provide people with the social situations which facilitate the formation of new intergroup friendships.

An important aspect of people's strategy for meeting new acquaintances concerns the language chosen for communication with a member of a different ethnolinguistic group. In the present study, the number of inter-ethnic encounters where both languages were spoken is relatively high, although much higher for Francophones who met an English person (50 per cent) than for Anglophones who met French people (25 per cent). Many more English (64.3 per cent) than French participants (27.3 per cent) confined the communication to their own native language for the entire interaction. In fact English Canadians accommodated fully (i.e. spoke French) to their French Canadian acquaintances only 10 per cent of the time. This would seem to be an especially ethnocentric form of behaviour since both groups perceive it as important that members of other groups accommodate linguistically to them. While the imbalance of French and English usage can be attributed to language competence differences between the two groups, the question still remains as to why these differences in language ability exist.

Intergroup Communication and the Work Environment
Certain results from the study previously described (Simard, in press) suggested that the work setting may be conducive to forming cross-cultural friendships. While we still do not have data to evaluate this suggestion, we can look at a few studies conducted in the work field in Quebec to find out what is happening in terms of intergroup communication. It should be remembered that although the division between the two major language groups is well defined at the institutional level (Vallée and Dufour, 1974), this division is not so clear in the economic domain (Gendron, 1972). Since the two ethnic groups have to work with and for each other, can we expect social interaction in the work situation? According to Hughes (1970), it seems not. In his analysis of the work situation, Hughes defines two dimensions of communication in the labour and industrial sphere, the horizontal dimension, i.e., between people of the same level of business, and the vertical one as in employer-employee relations. He observed that top level managers and technicians communicated among themselves and with their peers in other organizations most often in English since it was characteristic of Montreal that the top management and technical personnel were monolingual Anglophones. At the middle level and toward the lower ranks of industrial and commercial

organization, the personnel were almost completely French speaking and again horizontal communication was found among them. When vertical communication is needed, few bilinguals translate and channel the information downward and upward. Hughes notes that with Francophones who operate at the managerial or professional level, French will be used for horizontal communication and bilingual executive assistants will be employed to communicate with the world at large. In a study (Taylor, Simard and McKirnan, 1978) of twelve hundred managers from a large corporation in Eastern Canada, certain interesting results emerged in terms of the vertical-horizontal dimensions. That is, managers had generally more positive attitudes regarding communication with peers and subordinates (horizontal and vertical downwards) than they did with superiors (vertical upwards). These findings represent a potential important paradox. While all managers feel their relationship with subordinates to be excellent, the fact that they feel upward communication to be less than ideal indicates a general misconception as most of these managers are themselves subordinate to higher managers. An important differential effect that would need to be examined more closely emerged for the ethnicity of the participants: Francophones felt even less positive about communication with superiors than did their Anglophone counterparts.

If contact is minimal in the work setting it is obvious that some Anglophones and Francophones do meet in time. What happens on these occasions? Can they communicate effectively, what are the perceived language skills of those interacting, what language(s) is (are) used, is the use of two languages perceived as affecting interaction? After a detailed analysis of the work environment, the Gendron Commission Report (1972) gave us some of the answers by reporting that Francophones' competence in English is dramatically higher than Anglophones' competence in French. In terms of language use, the Report concludes that "in the inter-relationships in mixed conversation groups, English-speaking persons concede much less to French than do French-speaking persons to English" (p. 93). Moreover, "the desire of French-speaking people to see a change in the situation and improvement in the lot of their language is beyond question" (p. 138). Recently, Quebec's language legislation (Bill 101) which makes French the official language in Quebec, addressed itself directly to this issue. This situation is very intriguing for social psychologists and a few colleagues and myself began to make some exploratory incursions in the fascinating setting of the work environment.

Results from an actual face-to-face situation involving workers from a large industry demonstrated that cross-cultural communication was as efficient as within group communication. The workers, who were not chosen on their bilingual skills, evidenced reciprocal bilingualism, French and English were used almost equally and positive attitudes about communication were evidenced. It is possible, however, that mixed ethnic pairs, in order to communicate as quickly and as accurately as same ethnic pairs, extended more effort in doing so and that the artificial environment of the laboratory experiment encouraged the subjects to make this effort whereas communication in more natural encounters would have been avoided (Taylor & Simard, 1972).

What was needed then to verify these speculations was a study of patterns of language use in a natural work setting where functioning in two languages was a possible event. This setting was provided by a special program in which a number of Francophone and Anglophone managers were required to interact while engaged in real-life activities. Among the various issues to be examined (Taylor, Simard and Papineau, 1978) were the patterns of language use which emerged during the formal and informal interactions among participants and the feelings these generated. In all situations more Francophones accommodated by speaking English than did their Anglophone counterparts. What effect did this pattern of language use have on participants' perceptions of their interactions in term of effectiveness and personal satisfaction? Francophone and Anglophone participants were as satisfied regarding the proportion of time the two languages were spoken. However, all participants felt that the balance of French and English was more personally satisfying than it was effective. These results suggest that participants were quite willing to tolerate less than total efficiency in order to maintain good interpersonal relations.

Does the fact that Francophone participants were as satisfied as Anglophones regarding the proportion of time French was spoken, despite the tendency for the English language to be used more, imply that Francophones favour the dominant use of English? The answer would seem negative when the present results are considered in an historical perspective. In the past (see Gendron, 1972), the English language totally dominated intergroup interaction such that, even when Francophones were in the majority, English was spoken to the virtual exclusion of French. Francophone participants in the present study were probably responding favourably to the fact that the balance has become more equitable, even though complete parity has not been achieved.

Anglophones were as approving as Francophones in their responses to the balance of French and English spoken. At one level, this may not be surprising given that more English was spoken than would be expected on the basis of the ethnic composition of the participants. On the other hand, if it is true that the present findings reflect an increase in the use of French, and if this increase was perceived by the English-speaking participants, there would be some indication that Anglophone executives are not negatively disposed to this development. Whether such favourable attitudes would continue, with an even greater increase in the use of French, is an empirical issue, one that should deserve immediate attention in light of the potential for effective interaction in the future.

If cultural similarity is important for efficient and satisfying communication (Triandis, 1960; 1977), another problem is threatening the potential for intergroup communication in the work setting. In two studies previously described (Simard, Taylor and McKirnan, 1978; Taylor, Simard and Papineau, 1978), Francophones perceived important cultural differences related to the way each group approaches and executes its job, while Anglophones did not. These different perceptions, whether they are real or not, have important implications for intergroup communication at work. Although the present findings are based on the experiences of a select group of people and hence there is reluctance to generalize to other segments of society, the sample represents people who are collectively significant in terms of intergroup relations and as such, their responses may serve as an important barometer of future attitudes throughout Quebec society.

In summary, if at first sight the work environment would appear as one of the facilitating circumstances for intergroup communication, this is not fully corroborated by the few studies on the topic. The pessimism resulting from the overall examinations of the early 1970s seem to have somewhat attenuated, but recent investigations still pinpoint some existing potential barriers to intergroup communication in the work environment.

REFERENCES

Bernstein, B. *Class, Codes and Control*. London: Routledge and Kegan Paul, 1971.
Berscheid, E. and Walster, E. *Interpersonal Attraction* (2nd ed.). Reading: Addison-Wesley, 1978.
Bickerton, D. Inherent variability and variable rules. *Foundations of Language*, 1971, 7, 457-492.
Bourhis, R.Y. Language in ethnic interaction: a social psychological approach. In H. Giles and B. Saint-Jacques (eds.), *Language and Ethnic Relations*. Oxford: Pergamon Press, 1979.
Bourhis, R.Y. and Giles, H. The language of intergroup distinctiveness. In H. Giles (ed.), *Language, Ethnicity, and Intergroup Relations*. London: Academic Press, 1977.
Bourhis, R.Y., Giles, H., and Lambert, W.E. Social consequences of accommodating one's style of speech: a cross-national investigation. *International Journal of the Sociology of Language*, 1975, 6, 55-72.
Bourhis, R.Y., Giles, H., Leyens, J.P., and Tajfel, H. Psycholinguistic distinctiveness: language divergence in Belgium. In H. Giles and R. St. Clair (eds.), *Language and Social Psychology*. Oxford: Basil Blackwell, 1979.
Bourhis, R.Y., Giles H., and Tajfel, H. Language as a determinant of Welsh Identity. *European Journal of Social Psychology*, 1973, 3, 447-460.
Byrne, D. *The Attraction Paradigm*. New York: Academic Press, 1971.
Cedergren, H. and Sankoff, D. Variable rules: performance as a statistical reflection of competence. *Language*, 1974, 50, 333-335.
Census of Canada. *Population: official language and language most often spoken at home*. Statistics Canada. Catalogue 92-726, Vol. 1, Part 3, August 1973.

D'Anglejan, A. and Tucker, G.R. Communicating across cultures: an empirical investigation. *Journal of Cross-Cultural Psychology*, 1973, *4*, 121-130.

Doise, W., Sinclair, A., and Bourhis, R.Y. Evaluation of accent convergence and divergence in cooperative and competitive intergroup situations. *British Journal of Social and Clinical Psychology*, 1976, *15*, 247-252.

Ervin-Tripp, S.M. An analysis of the interaction of language, topic and listener. In supplement to *American Anthropologist*, 1964, *66*, 86-102.

Gatbonton, E. Patterned phonetic variability in second-language speech: a gradual diffusion model. *Canadian Modern Language Review*, 1978, *34*, 335-347.

Gatbonton, E.C. and Tucker, G.R. Cultural orientation and the study of foreign literature. *TESOL Quarterly*, 1971, *5*, 137-143.

Gendron, J.D. *The position of the French language in Québec: Book 1. The language of work* (Report of the commission of inquiry on the French language rights in Québec). Québec: Government of Québec, 1972.

Giles, H. Accent mobility: a model and some data. *Anthropological Linguistics*, 1973, *15*, 87-105.

Giles, H. and Smith, P.M. Accommodation theory: optimal levels of convergence. In H. Giles and R. St. Clair (eds.), *Language and Social Psychology*. Oxford: Basil Blackwell, 1979.

Giles, H., Taylor, D.M., and Bourhis, R.Y. Towards a theory of interpersonal accommodation through language: some Canadian data. *Language in Society*, 1973, *2*, 177-192.

Giles, H., Taylor, D.M., and Bourhis, R.Y. Dimensions of Welsh Identity. *European Journal of Social Psychology*, 1977, *7*, 29-39.

Glucksberg, S., Krauss, R.M., and Weisberg, R. Referential communication in nursery school children: method and some preliminary findings. *Journal of Experimental Child Psychology*, 1966, *3*, 333-342.

Harris, M.B. and Baudin, H. The language of altruism: the effects of language, dress and ethnic group. *Journal of Social Psychology*, 1973, *97*, 37-41.

Heider, F. *The psychology of interpersonal relations*. New York: Wiley, 1958.

Hughes, E.C. The linguistic division of labor in industrial and urban societies. *Georgetown Monograph Series on Languages and Linguistics*, 1970, *23*, 103-119.

Hymes, D. On communicative competence. Philadelphia: University of Philadelphia Press. (Reprinted in J. Price and J. Holmes (eds.), *Sociolinguistics*. Harmondsworth, England: Penguin Books, 1971.)

Hymes, D. Models of the interaction of language and social life. In J.J. Gumperz and D. Hymes (eds.), *Directions in Sociolinguistics*. New York: Holt, Rinehart and Winston, 1972.

Labov, W. The social motivation of sound change. *Word*, 1963, *19*, 273-309.

Labov, W. Contraction, deletion and inherent variability of the English copula. *Language*, 1969, *45*, 715-762.

Labov, W. The logic of nonstandard English. In J.J. De Stefano (ed.), *Language, Society and Education: A profile of Black English*. Worthington: Charles A. Jones, 1973.

Lambert, W.E. The effects of bilingualism in the individual: cognitive and sociocultural consequences. In P.A. Hornby (ed.), *Bilingualism: Psychological, Social, and Educational Implications*. New York: Academic Press, 1977.

Lamy, P. Bilingualism in Montreal: linguistic interference and communicational effectiveness. *Papers in Linguistics*, 1976, *9*, 1-14.

Lieberson, S. Bilingualism in Montreal: A demographic analysis. *American Journal of Sociology*, 1965, *71*, 10-25.

MacLennan, H. *Two Solitudes*. New York: Dwell, Sloan, Pearce, 1945.

Mailhiot, B. La psychologie des relations interethniques à Montréal. *Contributions à l'étude des sciences de l'homme*, 1956, *3*, 7-24.

Morin, Y.C., Picard, M., Pupier, P., et Santerre, L. *Le français de la région de Montréal.* Montréal: Les Presses de l'Université du Québec, 1974.

Mousseau-Glaser, M. Consommation des mass-media: Biculturalisme des mass-media. *Revue Canadienne de Sociologie et d'Anthropologie*, 1972, *9*, 325-346.

Sandilands, M.L. and N. Corston Fleury. Unilinguals in *des milieux bilingues: Une analyse* of attributions. *Canadian Journal of Behavioural Science*, 1979, *11*, 164-168.

Segalowitz, N. Communicative incompetence and the non-fluent bilingual. *Canadian Journal of Behavioural Science*, 1976, *8*, 122-131.

Segalowitz, N. Bilingualism and social behaviour. In W.H. Coons, D.M. Taylor and M.A. Tremblay (eds.), *The Individual, Language and Society in Canada.* Ottawa: The Canada Council, 1977.

Segalowitz, N. Cross-cultural study of bilingual development. In H.C. Triandis, L. Lonner and A. Heron (eds.), *Handbook of Cross-cultural Psychology.* Boston: Allyn and Bacon, 1978.

Segalowitz, N. and Gatbonton, E. Studies of the nonfluent bilingual. In P.A. Hornby (ed.), *Bilingualism: Psychological, Social, and Educational Implications.* New York: Academic Press, 1977.

Simard, L. Cross-cultural interaction: Potential invisible barriers. *Journal of Social Psychology*, in press.

Simard, L. and Taylor, D.M. The potential for cross-cultural communication in a dyadic situation. *Canadian Journal of Behavioural Science*, 1973, *5*, 211-225.

Simard, L.M., Mercier, E., et De Brouin-Gareau, L. Dimensions de l'identité ethnique dans une ville multiculturelle, mimeo. Université de Montréal, 1979.

Simard, L.M., Taylor, D.M., and Giles, H. Attribution processes and interpersonal accommodation in a bilingual setting. *Language and Speech*, 1976, *19*, 374-387.

Simard, L.M., Taylor, D.M., and McKirnan, D.J. Intergroup relations in a work environment: the role of perceived cultural differences. Paper presented at the annual meeting of the Canadian Psychological Association, Ottawa, 1978.

Tajfel, H., Social identity and intergroup behavior. *Social Science Information*, 1974, *13*, 65-93.

Tajfel, H. (ed.), *Differentiation Between Social Groups: Studies in Intergroup Behavior.* London: Academic Press, 1978.

Taylor, D.M., Bassili, J.N., and Aboud, F.E. Dimensions of ethnic identity: an example from Quebec. *Journal of Social Psychology*, 1973, *89*, 185-192.

Taylor, D.M. and Clément, R. Normative reactions to styles of Quebec French. *Anthropological Linguistics*, 1974, *16*, 202-217.

Taylor, D.M. and Gardner, R.C. Bicultural communication: a study of communicational efficiency and person perception. *Canadian Journal of Behavioural Science*, 1970a, *2*, 67-81.

Taylor, D.M. and Gardner, R.C. The role of stereotypes in communication between ethnic groups in the Philippines. *Social Forces*, 1970b, *49*, 271-283.

Taylor, D.M. and Simard, L. The role of bilingualism in cross-cultural communication. *Journal of Cross-cultural Psychology*, 1972, *3*, 101-108.

Taylor, D.M. and Simard, L.M. Social interaction in a bilingual setting. *Canadian Psychological Review*, 1975, *16*, 240-254.

Taylor, D.M. and Simard, L.M. Ethnic identity and intergroup relations. In D. Juteau-Lee (ed.), *Frontières ethniques en devenir.* Ottawa: Presse de l'Université d'Ottawa, 1979.

Taylor, D.M., Simard, L.M., and Aboud, F.E. Ethnic Identification in Canada: a cross-cultural investigation. *Canadian Journal of Behavioural Science*, 1972, *4*, 13-20.

Taylor, D.M., Simard, L.M., and McKirnan, D.J. Alienation, frustration and relative deprivation among managers. McGill University, mimeo, 1978.

Taylor, D.M., Simard, L.M., and Papineau, D. Perceptions of cultural differences and language use: a field study in a bilingual envirnoment. *Canadian Journal of Behavioural Science*, 1978, *10*, 181-191.

Taylor, W. Inferences about language communality: Cloze procedure. In I. de Sola Pool (ed.), *Trends in Content Analyses*. Urbana, Illinois: University Press, 1959, pp. 78-88.

Triandis, H.C. Cognitive similarity and communication in a dyad. *Human Relations*, 1960, *13*, 175-183.

Triandis, H.C. *Interpersonal Behavior*. Monterey: Brooks/Cole, 1977.

Tucker, G.R. and Gedalof, H. Bilinguals as linguistic mediators. *Psychonomic Science*, 1970, *20*, 369-370.

Vallee, F.G. and Dufour, A. The bilingual belt: a garrotte for the French? *Laurentian University Review*, 1974, *6*, 19-44.

Chapter 11

Ethnic Relations in the Prairies

Marlene Mackie, Department of Sociology, University of Calgary

Sociologists agree that ethnicity and regionalism are fundamental dimensions of Canadian society. Although considerable variation exists among groups, many Canadians continue to cherish their allegiance to their ancestral origins and to practice traditions which they have adapted to the conditions of their new country. The frequent description of Canadian society as an "ethnic mosaic" recognizes that the fact of Canadian citizenship or residence does not obliterate people's ties with their homeland. Indeed, until the passage of the Canadian Citizenship Act in 1947, the legal status of Canadians was very ambiguous. Before that time, native-born Canadians' citizenship was British and "nationality" referred to male ancestor's place of origin outside this continent.

A second major source of Canadian diversity stems from regional variation (Hiller, 1976). Significant differences exist in the geography, climate, economic resources, and history of the traditionally delineated regional units of British Columbia, the Prairies, Ontario, Quebec, the Atlantic Provinces, and the Territories. Although it would be a mistake to assume that the people within a given region are homogeneous, Canadians generally do identify themselves as belonging to a particular region and think of themselves as Westerners, or Maritimers, and so forth.

This chapter will focus upon ethnicity as it operates within the context of one region: the prairie region of Alberta, Saskatchewan, and Manitoba. It will emphasize two features which distinguish this region from the rest of the country. First, the prairie region is the most ethnically diverse segment of Canada. Approximately half the population is composed of people whose origin is neither British nor French. This strong representation of what the Royal Commission on Bilingualism and Biculturalism (1970) termed the "third force" means that the relationship between multiculturalism and bilingualism is a matter of considerable debate in Western Canada. Second, interprovincial immigration patterns differ and the Prairies have a much lower percentage of foreign-born residents than do Quebec and Ontario. Most of the prairie foreign-born arrived prior to World War II. Therefore, the major problem is the maintenance of ethnic identity among established groups rather than the assimilation of newcomers.

Regional Characteristics of the Prairie Provinces

The terminology used to denote collectively the provinces of Alberta, Saskatchewan, and Manitoba—Western Canada or the Prairie Provinces—is not very accurate. Strictly speaking, Western Canada also includes British Columbia. However, British Columbia is sufficiently different from the other three western provinces to be considered a separate region. Only a small part of the area of these three provinces is actually prairie. Even though these labels are unsatisfactory, they are more familiar than the logical innovations which geographers have devised such as "the Western Interior of Canada" and "ALSAMA" (Kaye & Moodie, 1973, p. 17).

A region is a geographical area whose population shares a common history, some similarity in lifestyles and interests, and consequently, a regional identity (Lautt, 1973, p. 125). Therefore, an understanding of the contemporary dynamics of ethnic relations in the Prairies requires at least some knowledge of the geography and history of this area.

Geography of Isolation

The Prairie Provinces are bounded by the Rocky Mountains to the west, the Canadian Shield to the north and east, and the American plains to the south. Isolation is the "outstanding characteristic of this landlocked Canadian region" (Kaye & Moodie, 1973, p. 28). It is separated from the populated areas of Eastern Canada by a thousand miles of mostly unsettled wilderness and from the coastal areas of British Columbia by five hundred miles of mountains and plateaus. Although northern development has advanced in recent years, the boreal forests and barren ground have made agriculture and intensive settlement impossible. Though geography has not imposed barriers to the south, the artificial political boundary of the United States has produced isolation of another sort (Kaye & Moodie, 1973, pp. 28-29).

As we shall see, the geographical isolation of Western Canada was a major factor in shaping the historical course of ethnic settlement. Moreover, physical isolation brought with it psychological isolation from the rest of Canada. Despite the development of modern comunication and transportation systems, many Western Canadians continue to feel alienated from the economic and power centres of Eastern Canada. Associated with this sentiment of "being different" are ethnic concerns which are somewhat at variance with those of the other regions.

Population Distribution

Examination of the geographic dispersion of the population provides another indication of the distinctiveness of the Prairie Provinces. Canada contains a territory of 3,851,809 square miles. The Prairie Provinces occupy 19.6 per cent of this territory. Because of variations in climate, terrain, and history, the 1971 Canadian population of 21,568,311 was unevenly distributed among the provinces. Ontario and Quebec contained 35.7 per cent and 27.9 per cent of the population, respectively. The Prairie Provinces together contained 16.5 per cent (Manitoba 4.6 per cent, Saskatchewan 4.3 per cent, Alberta 7.6 per cent) (Statistics Canada, 1971 Census of Canada, Vol. 1, Part 1, Cat. 92-702).

The urban-rural population distribution is another source of regional variation which is relevant to ethnicity. Today, the Prairie Provinces are quite highly urbanized. Canada, as a whole, is 76.1 per cent urban, Manitoba is 70 per cent urban, Saskatchewan is 53 per cent urban, and Alberta is 74 per cent urban. However, significantly more prairie people do live on farms: Canada 6.6 per cent, Manitoba 13 per cent, Saskatchewan 25 per cent, Alberta 14 per cent (Statistics Canada, 1971 Census of Canada, Vol. 1, Part 1, Cat. 92-709).

The factors of a relatively small population and a greater percentage of economic concentration in agriculture and other primary industries are important differences between the prairie region and the rest of Canada.

The Settlement of the Prairies

The settlement of the West is an important segment of Canadian history. Although this chapter cannot deal with all the issues and details involved in this interesting story, more can be learned from such sources as Dawson's (1936) early work, the Royal Commission on Bilingualism and Biculturalism, Book IV: The Cultural Contribution of the Other Ethnic Groups (1970), and Palmer (1977).

The British North America Act of 1867 gave the British and the French the privilege of perpetuating their languages and cultures. According to the first available census figures in 1871, only 8 per cent of the

Canadian population belonged to ethnic groups other than the two "charter" (Porter, 1965) groups. Less than one per cent of the Canadian population at that time was Indian and Eskimo. The 1867 Confederation did not include the Prairie Provinces. Modern prairie history begins in 1870, at which time Manitoba became a province and the Northwest Territories (which included Saskatchewan and Alberta) were created. (It was not until 1905 that Saskatchewan and Alberta joined Canadian Confederation as provinces.) The year 1870 also marks the beginning of commercial agriculture which gradually displaced fur trading as the economic base of the Prairies. By 1885, the Canadian Pacific Railway had forged a link between the Maritimes and the Pacific Ocean. The population of the prairie area rapidly increased, especially between 1896 and 1914, when emigration from Europe to North America produced the most immense mass movement of people in modern history.

Several factors were responsible for the arrival of large numbers of people in the West between 1896 and the beginning of World War I. The Canadian government and in particular, its Minister of the Interior, Clifford Sifton, pursued a policy of actively seeking to attract settlers from the United States, Britain, and continental Europe (Hall, 1977), one reason being that more people were leaving Canada than entering it. Also, it was important to Eastern Canadian financial interests that the West be securely established as an agricultural territory. Conditions in Europe—diminishing economic opportunities for rapidly rising populations, religious and political persecution of minorities—encouraged many to seek a home elsewhere. In addition, events such as the Yukon gold rush, the completion of railways, and the closing of the American frontier coincided and as a result attracted more than three million immigrants to Canada between 1896 and 1914 (Royal Commission, 1970, p. 22).

There are two significant facts about the ethnic composition of the 1901 Canadian population (which was less than 5,500,000). First, while 12 per cent had backgrounds other than British or French, 29 per cent of Manitoba's population, 53 per cent of Saskatchewan's population, and 46 per cent of Alberta's population fell into this category. Second, the numerical domination of the British was well established in the West, as well as in Canada as a whole (Canada, 57 per cent; Manitoba, 64 per cent; Saskatchewan, 44 per cent; Alberta, 48 per cent) (Kalbach, 1978, p. 97). The government had made special efforts to attract emigrants from the United States and Great Britain. These newcomers were joined by settlers from Eastern Canada.

The outbreak of World War I cut off emigration to Canada and it was not until 1923 when another, though smaller, wave of immigration began. This phase, which continued until the Depression years, was less important for Western Canada than the 1896-1914 wave. These later immigrants tended to settle in Eastern Canadian cities. During the Depression of the 1930s, government action ended the flow of immigrants into Canada.

Substantial immigration did not resume until the end of World War II. By this time, Canada had become more urbanized and industrialized. The majority of emigrants located in towns and cities, particularly those of Eastern Canada.

The opening and settlement of the Prairie Provinces is relevant for understanding contemporary ethnic relations for three reasons: (1) the ethnic origins of the immigrants who came to Western Canada in search of the free land and political and religious freedom promised to them by the Canadian government; (2) the geographic location of these groups within the prairie region; (3) the attitudes of the British majority towards non-British immigrants. Each of these topics will be discussed in turn.

Ethnic Origins of the Early Prairie Settlers

Because the waves of immigration to Canada after World War I had considerably less impact on the Prairies than the initial influx of newcomers between 1896 and 1914, the specific origins of these early settlers shaped ethnic relations within the region and between the region and Canada as a whole. Athough post-World War II immigrants from many other parts of the world form part of the current scene, it is descendants of the early settlers and their compatriots, later drawn to this region by the existence of people from their homelands, who dominate contemporary ethnic relations.

The immigration policies of Sifton had a great deal to do with what sort of people came to Western Canada (Hall, 1977). Very few immigrants were specifically excluded. However, Sifton was seeking people who could make a success out of farming on the Prairies. Anglo-Saxon and Scandinavian farmers from western United States were considered particularly desirable. The greatest promotional expenditures were made in Great Britain. In 1902-1903, $205,000 was spent in Britain to entice potential immigrants (Hall, 1977, p. 71). Sifton was interested especially in farmers from northern England and Scotland, but not people from urban English areas, Ireland or Wales. Continental Europe was a third area of emphasis. Steamship agents receiving bonuses for sending immigrants to Canada, sent large numbers of Galicians (Ukrainians), Doukhobors, and Scandinavians. Group or colony settlement of the Ukrainians and Doukhobors was permitted because they were viewed as promising farmers who might not otherwise come. Between 1901 and 1921, the number of Ukrainians in the Prairie Provinces increased from 5,600 to 96,000. Nearly 8,000 Doukhobors from Russia settled in Saskatchewan (Royal Commission, 1970, p. 23).

Southern Europeans (particularly Italians), Jews, Orientals and blacks were thought to be useless as farmers. Most of the Italians and Jews who did come to Canada settled in the Eastern cities. However, some Italian labourers worked on construction of western railroads. A number of Jews located in Winnipeg and in the Manitoba farming community (Royal Commission, 1970, p. 24). Although the other groups mentioned above were simply not encouraged to come to Canada, active discrimination in the form of a head tax ($500 in 1903) was practiced against Chinese immigrants (Hall, 1977). In order to make way for agrarian expansion, the Indians were displaced to isolated reservations.

When the 1911 ethnic composition of the Prairie Provinces is compared with that of Canada as a whole, some differences clearly emerge. Although the concentration of British in Canada and the provinces is quite similar, the French were underrepresented in the Prairies. The non-British, non-French population in Canada was only 16 per cent. However, it was 37 per cent in Alberta, 40 per cent in Saskatchewan, and 33 per cent in Manitoba. The Prairies had considerably more West Europeans from countries other than Britian and France (Scandinavians and Germans) and a high representation of East Europeans (Russians, Ukrainians, Poles). Finally, the indigenous Indians and Eskimos were mostly located in the West (Royal Commission, 1970, Tables A-4, A-16, A-18, A-20).

The disparate ethnic composition of the Prairies, in conjunction with the region's geographic isolation from the eastern centres of power, and its economic role as an "investment frontier" to eastern financial interests, set the stage for differences in perspective between the prairie region and Canada as a whole. Canada's need for immigrants to settle the West set the country on the road to cultural pluralism. Newcomers were warned that if they moved on to the United States, they would be forced to assimilate (Baker, 1977, p. 117). On the other hand, they were encouraged to retain their cultural identities if they remained in Canada. The concentration of the "third force" pioneers in the West gave this region a crucial role in the modern multiculturalism debate of the 1960s and 1970s.

Ethnic Spatial Settlement Patterns
The persistance of cultural heterogeneity in the western region is partly explained by the spatial concentration of people of shared ethnicity (Schlichtmann, 1977). Immigrants of common ancestry tended to cluster in the same locality.

There were many reasons for block settlement. In the early years, the federal government encouraged this practice. Specific territories were set aside for certain groups such as the Mennonites, Icelanders, and Doukhobors, though this policy was eventually changed as political pressure built up to Canadianize or assimilate aliens (Lehr, 1977). The availability of suitable, unallocated land determined where newcomers could settle. Many pioneers naturally chose to locate close to people of their own kind for friendly human contact and mutual assistance in a strange, harsh environment. Geographers have shown that this pattern operated whether people migrated from the old country as a group, whether migration was chain-like with settlers from a particular region attracting newcomers from the same region, or whether independent migrants later gravitated toward people of their own cultural background. In some cases, block settlement represented a consciously motivated attempt to preserve cultural heritage. This statement applies to the Mennonites, Doukhobors, and to some extent, the French Canadians (Schlichtmann, 1977, p. 11). Finally, the hostility of outsiders sometimes caused pioneers with the same background to cluster together. The following are some examples of ethnic block settlements: the Mennonites in Saskatchewan and Manitoba, the Doukhobors in Saskatchewan, the Icelanders in the Lake Winnipeg area of Manitoba, the French in north-central Saskatchewan, the Ukrainians from central Alberta through to southeastern Manitoba.

British Attitudes towards Non-British Immigrants

Although the British North America Act recognized the British-French cultural duality in Canada, the cultural role of the other groups was not explicitly considered. Sifton's immigration policies were designed to attract successful agriculturalists, regardless of their nationality. Every device was used to lure people to the West, including promises of protection of their culture. As hundreds of thousands of immigrants poured into Canada, his policies became a major public issue (Palmer, 1975, pp. 16 ff). Strong sentiments developed against the entry of central, southern, and eastern European and Oriental immigrants. Anti-German feelings reached the point of hysteria during World War I. Because the ethnic minorities were considered a threat to the culture of the Prairies, conviction grew that these groups must be assimilated to the predominant British culture. "They must not be allowed to speak their own language, be led by priests of their own faith, or to read newspapers in their own language" (Rea, 1977, p. 6). The agent of this ideology of "Anglo-conformity" was the public school system (Berry, Kalin & Taylor, 1977, p. 10). However, according to Berry et al. (1977, p. 11), there were two reasons why this ideology did not succeed. First, the other ethnic groups were simply too numerous to be absorbed into the British lifestyle. Their geographic concentration in homogeneous communities added to their strength. Second, the long history of racism and discrimination in English-speaking Canada meant that outsiders were excluded. "Such exclusion may have been a significant factor in the development of ingroup feelings among the 'other ethnic' groups" (Berry et al., 1977, p. 11). That is, the discrimination experienced by these groups tightened their bonds to one another and their allegiances to their cultures.

Current Ethnic Characteristics

The purpose of this section is to consider what can be learned about contemporary[1] ethnic relations in the prairie region by comparing its population characteristics with those of the other provinces. Three types of demographic data will be examined: ethnic origins of the population, foreign-born by immigration period, and mother tongue.

Ethnic Origins

The census figures given in Table 11.1 provide information on the ethnic composition of Canada and the provinces for 1971. One factor that stands out in the table is that there is considerable variability in ethnic composition across Canada (cf., Hiller, 1976). The two "charter groups" are unevenly distributed across Canada. The British are strongly represented in the Atlantic Provinces (with the exception of New Brunswick), while comparatively few live in Quebec. They constitute approximately the same proportion of the prairie region as in the Canadian population as a whole. The British are the strongest single group in every province except Quebec. The French, on the other hand, tend to be concentrated in Quebec and New Brunswick. Although 28.7 per cent of the nation's population is French Canadian, they make up only 8.9 per cent of the Manitoba population and approximately 6 per cent of the other two Prairie Provinces. However, percentages can be misleading. About 240,000 French Canadians live in the prairie region.

Considerable differences exist among Canadian regions in the representation of the "other ethnic" groups. One-quarter of the national population is non-British and non-French. None of the Atlantic Provinces has an "other ethnic" group population over 13 per cent. The presence of the "third element" is strong in Ontario and British Columbia. However, the non-charter groups make up nearly one-half of the prairie region population. The pattern established by the pioneer settlement of these groups in the West continues today.

Table 11.1
Ethnic Origin of the Population of Canada and the Provinces,
by Percentage, 1971

| | ETHNIC CLASSIFICATION | | |
	British	French	Other
CANADA	44.6%	28.7%	26.7%
British Columbia	57.8	4.4	37.8
Alberta	46.7	5.8	47.5
Saskatchewan	42.1	6.1	51.8
Manitoba	41.9	8.9	49.2
Ontario	59.3	9.6	31.1
Quebec	10.8	79.1	10.1
New Brunswick	57.7	37.1	5.2
Nova Scotia	77.5	10.1	12.4
Prince Edward Island	82.7	13.8	3.5
Newfoundland	93.9	3.0	3.1

Source: Statistics Canada, *Perspective Canada: A Compendium of Social Statistics*, 1974, Table 13.7. Reproduced by permission of the Minister of Supply and Services Canada.

Native-Born and Foreign-Born Populations

Establishing what proportion of a region's population was born in Canada and what proportion was born elsewhere provides a very good indication of the probable ethnic concerns within that area. A region with many first-generation immigrants will have people who display many signs of their ethnic heritage. Although a great deal depends on the particular background of the immigrants, that region may well be facing problems of prejudice and discrimination against the newcomers. On the other hand, the character of ethnic relations in a Canadian region where a high percentage of its population is native-born should be quite different. Here, we would expect to find ethnic groups long established in this country to be somewhat preoccupied with the problem of keeping alive their ethnic heritage.

According to the 1971 census, 15.3 per cent of the Canadian population is foreign-born (Canadian Immigration and Population Study, 1974, p. 13). Most of these people (71 per cent) arrived after World War II. Hiller (1976) has demonstrated, moreover, that this foreign-born segment is not distributed evenly across Canada. The pattern has been for those recent newcomers to locate in the urban centres of Eastern Canada, especially Ontario where more than half live. The Atlantic Provinces contain only 2 per cent. Sixteen per cent of Canadians born elsewhere live in the three Prairie Provinces, a proportion approximately equal to British Columbia's share and one-third of Ontario's share. It was the prairie cities, not farms, which attracted post–World War II immigrants. In general, the major problem in the prairie region should be maintenance of ethnic identity among groups which have been established there for some time.

Table 11.2
Percentage Distribution of the Population, by Mother Tongue,
Canada and the Provinces, 1971

Area	% English	% French	% Other
CANADA	60.1	26.9	13.0
British Columbia	82.7	1.8	15.5
Alberta	77.6	2.9	19.5
Saskatchewan	74.1	3.4	22.5
Manitoba	67.1	6.1	26.8
Ontario	77.5	6.3	16.2
Quebec	13.1	80.7	6.2
New Brunswick	64.7	34.0	1.3
Nova Scotia	93.0	5.0	2.0
Prince Edward Island	92.3	6.6	1.1
Newfoundland	98.5	0.7	0.8

Source: Canadian Immigration and Population Study, *Immigration and Population Statistics,* 1974, Table 6.2, p. 80. Reproduced by permission of the Minister of Supply and Services Canada.

Mother Tongue
Mother tongue is defined by the census as "the language first spoken in childhood and still understood." Legally, Canada is a bilingual nation and most of the population speak one of the two official languages, English or French. However, according to the 1971 census, 13 per cent have another mother tongue and 7 per cent use another language at home (Statistics Canada, 1974, p. 257). Table 11.2 shows the mother tongue by Canadian and provincial populations. Two conclusions may be drawn from this table. First, the dominance of the English and French languages suggests that national origin statistics may exaggerate the contemporary vitality of ethnicity. Secondly, Canadians who understand a third language tend to be located in the West. More than 20 per cent of the people in the prairie region fall into that category. Few describe French as their mother tongue. English is clearly the dominant language in the West.

Ethnic Identity in the Prairie Region
In order to understand the contemporary dynamics of ethnicity in the West, these questions must be addressed: How much does ethnicity matter to groups which have been established in Canada for some time? Is ethnicity more important to some groups than to others? If group variation does exist, what factors are responsible?

Definition of Ethnic Identity
Isajiw (1975) defines ethnic identity as

> commitment to a social grouping of common ancestry, existing within a larger society of different ancestral origins, and characterized by sharing of some common values, behavioural patterns or symbols different from those of the larger society (p. 129).

This definition involves several important ideas. Ethnic identity concerns the degree of an individual's attachment to his/her ancestral group. Because the definition focusses on people who belong to ethnic groups with traditions different from those of the containing society, it directs attention to the relationship between the concepts of "ethnic identification," on the one hand, and the concepts of "assimilation" and "integration," on the other. "Assimilation implies almost total absorption into another linguistic and cultural group" (Royal Commission, 1970, p. 5) and the forfeiture of ethnic identity. The culture of assimilated members of an ethnic group is indistinguishable from the dominant Canadian culture. Although integration means that the person participates comfortably in Canadian social life (O'Bryan, Reitz & Kuplowska, 1976, p. 4), ethnic identity is not lost.

Finally, Isajiw's definition suggests that there are a variety of ways in which an individual may be committed to an ethnic group. In other words, ethnic identity is multidimensional. Minimum commitment is simply acknowledgment of common ancestry (Isajiw, 1975, p. 135). For example, a person views himself/herself as a German Canadian or a Ukrainian Canadian. Other dimensions include choice of marriage partners or friends from within the ethnic group; language use; membership in ethnic religious groups and/or ethnic organizations; consumption of ethnic publications; promotion of parochial education (Driedger, 1975).

Ethnic Identity in Canada

Although Rose (1976, p. 16) argues that "a fairly high degree of ethnic consciousness seems to be a 'normal' feature of human society," the level of ethnic identity does vary between societies. For a variety of reasons, ethnic consciousness in Canada could be expected to be relatively high. Unlike the United States with its "melting pot" ideology, which attempted to minimize ethnic differentiation, Canada has adopted cultural pluralism. Despite the ideology of "Anglo-conformity," the force of events resulted in ethnic groups becoming major components of Canadian society. Official recognition of ethnic differences continues today in the government's bilingualism and multiculturalism policies. Also, differences among ethnic groups in such considerations as time of arrival in Canada, level of education, similarities with British culture, and the value placed on achievement led to an uneven opportunity structure (Isajiw, 1975, p. 132). Therefore, ethnicity in Canada is bound up with social class (Pineo, 1977); ethnic stratification is a fact of life in our society. Finally, the rural settlement patterns of the early immigrants fostered ethnic identity in a way that the urban patterns of immigrants to the United States did not. The legal support for multiculturalism, the diversity of ethnic groups, the rural settlement patterns, and the hinterland mentality of the isolated western provinces should produce particularly strong awareness of ethnic roots in this part of the country.

Group Variation in Ethnic Identity

Studies show that Canadian ethnic groups differ in their assimilation into the wider society and their attachment to their original cultures.

> The Scandinavians were the fastest in their rate of assimilation. The Dutch, Germans and Poles assimilated quite quickly, while Ukrainians, Hungarians, Italians and Chinese tended to be less likely to lose rapidly their ethnic distinctiveness (O'Bryan et al. 1976, p. 8).

To a large extent, these variations in rate of assimilation resulted from the experiences which the groups had in their early years in this country. The factors which encouraged rapid assimilation include either early arrival in

Canada in the opening of the West or arrival after World War II; an original culture which was similar to Anglo traditions, language, and values; lack of prejudice and discrimination by outsiders; and scattered, rather than block, residential patterns.

Sociologists have found that the contemporary social organization of a group is a good predictor of whether ancestral roots still have a vital meaning or whether identification lies with the dominant society. Especially useful here is Breton's (1964) concept of "institutional completeness." To state the extreme case, if an ethnic community is complete in the sense that it can satisfy its members' needs for education, work, food, social assistance, religion, etc., its members have little need for contacts with the larger society. The more institutions an ethnic community possesses, the greater is the probability its members will maintain their ethnic identity.

Empirical Studies of Ethnic Identity in the Prairie Region

Driedger (1975) administered questionnaires to 1,560 University of Manitoba students representing seven groups: British, French, Germans, Jews, Poles, Scandinavians, and Ukrainians. The first purpose of the study was to test whether ethnic identity is multidimensional in terms of the factors of language use, religion, endogamy (ingroup marriage), parochial education, choice of ingroup friends, ethnic media, and ethnic voluntary organizations. In other words, the study examined Breton's notion of "institutional completeness." A second purpose was to determine whether different ethnic identity factors were emphasized by the representatives of different ethnic groups.

Driedger found that ethnic identification is indeed multidimensional. For this student sample, types of commitment to ethnic groups involved all of the components listed above except ethnic media. As expected, different components were emphasized by different ethnic groups. Endogamy, organizations, parochial education, and friends were important to Jews. The French and Ukrainians stressed language, while religion was important to the Germans. The Poles and Scandinavians scored low on all six factors. Finally, comparison of groups on composite scores made up of the scores on the six types of commitment allowed Driedger to rank the ethnic groups in terms of ethnic identification. The Jews and French ranked highest, while the Scandinavians and Poles ranked lowest.

Frideres and Goldenberg (1977) compared the relative importance of ethnic identity, regional identity, and national identity for 213 students at a large Western Canadian university. The questionnaire used five different types of questions. For example, the students were asked how often they thought about being Canadian or being members of particular ethnic groups and whether they felt their fate was bound up with the fate of Canada and the fate of their ethnic group. In measuring ethnic identity, Frideres and Goldenberg focussed at the level of the minimum symbolism of "acknowledgment of common ancestry." This differs from Driedger's multidimensional approach. These researchers concluded that their sample had a low ethnic identity, a high regional identity, and a very high national identity. In other words, being Canadian and Western Canadian were more important to them than their ethnic ancestry. These results were not affected by the students' age, sex, fathers' occupation, number of places where they had resided, or region where most of their lives had been spent. In order to explain the unexpectedly low level of ethnic identity, the authors suggest that "the apparent 'surge' of ethnicity in Canadian society might be that it is primarily a result of the exploitation by well-organized (established) ethnic groups of the new 'cultural' programs currently being initiated" (p. 99). Because these organizations involve older people, they felt that an older sample might display more interest in their ethnic background. However, the next study to be discussed did not support this "age" hypothesis.

Mackie (1978) examined the ethnic identification of a Calgary, Alberta sample of 885 adults. Two major hypotheses were tested. First, it was predicted that ethnicity would be an important matter to these Western Canadians. Second, it was hypothesized that the salience of ethnicity would vary by the type of question used to measure it. The second hypothesis was based on the assumption that a person has many identities (e.g., ethnic identity, family identity, occupational identity) and that their relative importance varies with the individual's current circumstances. For example, at work, a person's occupational identity is usually salient, while his/her family identity remains latent. In order to test these predictions, the sample was asked two types of questions. The direct question, which asked which ethnic group, if any, the respondent identified with, focussed attention on ethnicity. The indirect question was widely separated from the direct question in a questionnaire which dealt with many matters and seemingly had nothing to do with ethnicity. It simply asked respondents to provide twenty answers to the question "Who Am I?" The two questions provided a comparison of *solicited* ethnic identity and *volunteered ethnic* identity.

The replies to both questions failed to support the first hypothesis. Only one-third of the respondents said they identified with any ethnic group. On the "Who Am I?" question, 3 per cent mentioned ethnic ancestry (compared with 18 per cent who mentioned religion, 10 per cent nationality, 4 per cent local community, and 2 per cent region). The above difference between the levels of solicited and volunteered ethnic identity supported the second hypothesis. Ethnicity was more salient for immigrants to Canada than for the native-born. Among the latter, no differences were found by sex, age, or education. However, ethnicity and nationality did matter more to upper-middle-class than to working-class respondents.[2]

At the present moment, the evidence available on the question of ethnic identity in the western region is somewhat confusing. On the one hand, the organizations which represent the various ethnic groups strongly support the Canadian governmental policy on multiculturalism, particularly as it pertains to the preservation of their own groups' traditions (Berry et al., 1977). A study of representatives of the ten largest non-official language groups in five Canadian cities (including Winnipeg and Edmonton) reported that an overwhelming majority of all groups supported retention of their languages (O'Bryan et al., 1976). However, both the Frideres and Goldenberg and Mackie studies found that ethnicity was not a vital concern in their respondents' everyday lives. Some of the contradiction can undoubtedly be explained in terms of differences between organizations and individuals, and differences in the salience of ethnic identity under varying circumstances. Nevertheless, more research is required to resolve the issue.

Inter-Group Attitudes and Behaviour

Theoretical Concepts

One type of inter-group attitude is prejudice. Prejudice is a negative attitude toward the members of specific groups which causes the holder of the attitude to evaluate group members unfavourably. The target of prejudice is disliked on the basis of group membership, not individual characteristics or behaviour.

While prejudice refers to an attitude, discrimination refers to behaviour. Discrimination is negative behaviour directed towards members of disliked groups because of their group membership. Although discrimination is often the result of prejudice, the relationship between attitude and behaviour is not always that obvious. Prejudiced people may or may not translate their feelings into action. On the other hand, an unprejudiced person may treat a group member in a discriminatory fashion simply because such treatment is customary in his or her community. Prairie region studies which deal with more than one ethnic group at a time tend to focus on prejudicial attitudes, rather than discriminatory behaviour.

Studies Dealing with Prejudice

Studies of prejudice in the prairie region provide some answers to three questions: How prejudiced are Western Canadians? Which ethnic groups are the targets of prejudice? How do western ethnic attitudes compare with those in the rest of Canada?

Mackie (1974) examined the attitudes of 290 Edmonton, Alberta adults[3] towards twenty-four groups. A questionnaire was administered which measured prejudice by means of the Bogardus (1925) Social Distance Scale. Respondents were asked to which of the following types of social contact they would admit the average member of each of the ethnic groups:

1. to close kinship by marriage
2. to my club as personal friends
3. to my street as neighbours
4. to employment in my occupation
5. to citizenship in my country
6. as visitors only to my country
7. would exclude from my country

The social distance quotient (SDQ) for a given group was determined by computing the mean of the number beside the most intimate relationship permitted by respondents. A small SDQ denotes low social distance. The results are shown in Table 11.3.

The order of the groups listed in Table 11.3 facilitates comparison of the relative position of the various groups. Canadians received the top ranking. With the exception of the Ukrainians and Poles, the first eleven positions were accorded to Western European groups. Groups of non-Caucasian racial origin occupy the bottom one-third of the positions. Less social distance was expressed towards blacks than towards Orientals or Canadian Indians. The Hutterites occupy the last rank. However, the social distance expressed towards the Hutterites undoubtedly partially reflects respondents' compliance with the Hutterites' own desire to remain apart from the rest of society.

With one exception, other studies agree with the relative positions of ethnic groups reported by Mackie. Hirabayashi (1963) also used social distance scales with an Edmonton sample. A rank order correlation of .94 between Hirabayashi's and Mackie's results indicates remarkable stability in the rank accorded these twenty-four groups. A national study conducted by Berry et al. (1977) measured evaluation of ethnic groups in an entirely different manner. However, when the relative positions of the eight groups which overlap between their study and Mackie's are compared for the prairie segment of their sample, the rank order correlation is .92. An important exception to this pattern has been reported by Labovitz's (1974) and Frideres's (1975) studies of Western Canadian university students. These researchers (unlike Mackie and Berry et al.) found that more prejudice existed against French Canadians than Canadian Indians.

Although the respondents in all of the above studies clearly preferred some groups to others, the actual level of prejudice does not seem to be high. Most studies find native Indians to be one of the least preferred groups. However, Gibbins and Ponting (1976) conclude that "a vast reservoir of hostility" towards Indians does *not* exist in their Alberta sample. The SDQs shown in Table 11.3 suggest agreement with Berry et al.'s conclusion that "in general respondents appeared to be at least tolerant of 'other ethnic' groups and there was no evidence of extreme ethnic prejudice" (p. 125).

Table 11.3
Ethnic Group Ranking by Alberta Sample,
N=290

Ethnic Group	Social Distance Quotients
Canadians	1.10
British	1.30
Americans	1.39
Dutch	1.41
Norwegians	1.42
Swedes	1.43
Germans	1.59
French Canadians	1.67
Ukrainians	1.67
Poles	1.71
French	1.74
Hungarians	1.84
Italians	2.07
Blacks	2.21
Jews	2.22
Russians	2.28
Chinese	2.32
Japanese	2.34
West Indians	2.34
Eskimos	2.40
Indians (India)	2.46
North American Indians	2.50
Metis	2.63
Hutterites	3.68

Source: "Ethnic stereotypes and prejudice: Alberta Indians, Hutterites, and Ukrainians" by Marlene Mackie in *Canadian Ethnic Studies*, 1974, Table 3, p. 48.

Berry et al.'s (1977) national study provides some answers concerning the comparison of prairie ethnic attitudes to those in other Canadian regions. English Canadians were evaluated more favourably in the Atlantic provinces and Quebec and less favourably in British Columbia and Ontario than they were in the Prairies. French Canadians were regarded more positively in Quebec, the Atlantic provinces, and Ontario than they were in the Prairies and British Columbia. The prairie sample was least favourable of all the regions in their attitudes towards Canadian Indians. Both German Canadians and Ukrainian Canadians received their most positive evaluations from prairie respondents. Prairie attitudes towards Chinese Canadians, Jewish Canadians, and Italian Canadians were relatively positive compared with most of the other regions. In some cases, a positive prairie attitude seemed to be associated with familiarity with a group, e.g., the Germans and Ukrainians. However, the most negative attitudes were expressed towards native Indians by the prairie sample and the Indians are concentrated in the West.

Studies Dealing with Discrimination
Although the 1960 Canadian Bill of Rights and provincial human rights legislation forbid differential treatment of individuals on the basis of race

and nationality, discrimination continues to exist. Discrimination is documented in complaints lodged with human rights agencies, in newspaper reports of incidents involving recent immigrants from countries such as India, and in scholarly studies of groups such as the Canadian Indians and the Hutterites. The study described below deals with discrimination against eighteen prairie ethnic groups, allowing us to examine the comparative treatment of these groups and to reach some conclusions concerning the relationship between prejudice and discrimination.

Frideres (1973) studied the *perceived* discrimination of 984 adult post-war immigrants in Calgary and Edmonton. These respondents were asked whether or not they had personally experienced discrimination on the basis of their ethnicity since coming to Alberta. Notice that perceived discrimination is not the same as actual discrimination. Although the initiator of an act which a respondent believed to be discriminatory may not have intended to discriminate, the belief of the respondent is what counts. Frideres argues that perceived discrimination underestimates the actual incidence of discrimination because to acknowledge that one has been the victim of discrimination is damaging to one's self-concept. In other words, such incidents are probably *under*-reported.

Frideres was interested in measuring how much discrimination was experienced by the various ethnic groups, as well as the specific forms which discrimination took. He also wanted to see what relationships existed between discrimination and education, marital status, age, number of years in Canada, occupation, income, and employment status. Finally, he determined whether amount of perceived discrimination was related to the cultural homogeneity of the groups. According to his definition, a group "high" in cultural homogeneity is "high" in endogamy, mother tongue retention, and religion retention.

One-fifth of all the post-war immigrants claimed to have been discriminated against since their arrival in Alberta. The two main types of discrimination were employment and social barriers. Different proportions of the various ethnic groups reported discrimination. These eight groups claimed the highest levels: Jewish, 64 per cent; Asian, 58 per cent; Italian, 52 per cent; Yugoslavian, 52 per cent; Austrian, 48 per cent; Ukrainian, 44 per cent; British, 24 per cent; German, 22 per cent. The term "British" is rather misleading; these persons holding British citizenship were not necessarily white Anglo-Saxons.

Frideres found that groups highest in cultural homogeneity were also the groups reporting the most discrimination, though the causality underlying such an association is not clear. If Frideres's results are compared with those in Table 11.3, it becomes apparent that the groups which experience the most discriminatory behaviour are also among the least highly evaluated groups.

The analysis of the correlates of discrimination shows that marital status and employment status during the last year were not related. Immigrants high in educational attainments and income reported less discrimination than those with less education and income. People in both high status and low status occupations reported more discrimination than those in medium status occupations. Younger immigrants were more prone to report discrimination than older immigrants. Finally, time of arrival in Canada showed an interesting relationship to perceived discrimination. Among those who came immediately after World War II, a high proportion claimed discrimination. The numbers reporting discrimination decreased between 1946 and 1960 and increased again in the period 1960-1970. The recent upsurge in complaints may well stem from the passage of the Canadian Bill of Rights and the widely reported activities of the Royal Commission on Bilingualism and Biculturalism. Both these events have highlighted ethnic issues and the rights of ethnic groups.

Conclusions

The immense size of Canada, its geographical barriers and the pattern of its history have all resulted in a nation made up of regions with somewhat distinctive characteristics. Although the integration of the regions into the Canadian confederation under the aegis of the federal government means many shared concerns, the uniqueness of their situations must also be understood. The completion of two recent nationwide studies—O'Bryan et al., *Non-Official Languages* (1976) and Berry et al., *Multiculturalism and Ethnic Attitudes in Canada* (1977)—means that Canadian scholars are now in a position to begin to make systematic regional comparisons on the question of ethnicity which go beyond census data.

The basic patterns of contemporary ethnic relations in the prairie region were established with the waves of immigrants who opened the West. Today, the ethnic flavour of the Prairies stems from the descendants of these pioneers rather than from recent immigrants. The diversity of the peoples attracted to free homesteads makes the West the modern stronghold of "third element" groups. The vicissitudes of these groups during their early years in Canada, including the dominant society's attitudes towards them, have a great deal to do with the extent of their current assimilation into Canadian society, as well as their related levels of ethnic identification. Contemporary evaluations of the various ethnic groups bear a remarkable resemblance to turn-of-the-century attitudes.

Several ethnic-related issues are of paramount importance for the prairie region. The two national studies (referred to above) report that maintenance of their own ethnic identity and traditions is a vital concern which the western region group representatives share with those else-where in Canada. However, these objectives are not easily attained by groups separated by three generations from personal experience with these traditions. Moreover, the indifference of many individuals towards their ethnic roots contrasts sharply with the positions taken by ethnic organizations. The manner in which the federal government implements its policy of recognizing the special rights of the two charter groups within the context of multiculturalism will have far-reaching implications for the prairie region. A final issue for the future concerns the demands of native Indian organizations for drastic improvement of their lot. Although the discussion of indigenous peoples has been left to chapter 12, the Indians who belong neither to the charter nor to the "third element" groups are an important feature of ethnic relations in the western provinces.

FOOTNOTES

[1] The most recent data available derive from the 1971 census.

[2] When the 635 responses of native-born Canadians were analyzed, the following ethnic identifications were claimed: none, 75%; British, 14.2%; German, 3.2%; French, 2.4%; Ukrainian, 1.6%; Scandinavian, 1.3%; Italian, 0.8%; Polish, 0.5%; Japanese, 0.3%; Dutch, 0.3%; Russian, 0.2%, Hungarian, 0.2%.

[3] The original study measured the attitudes of 590 respondents. Subsamples of 300 and 290 completed somewhat different questionnaires. For simplicity's sake, only the latter subsample is discussed here.

REFERENCES

Baker, D.G. Ethnicity, development and power: Canada in comparative perspective. In W. Isajiw (ed.), *Identities: The Impact of Ethnicity on Canadian Society.* Toronto: Peter Martin Associates, 1977.

Berry, J.W., Kalin, R., & Taylor, D.M. *Multiculturalism and Ethnic Attitudes in Canada.* Ottawa: Supply and Services Canada, 1977.

Bogardus, E.S. Measuring social distance. *Journal of Applied Sociology,* 1925, *9,* 299-308.

Breton, R. Institutional completeness of ethnic communities and personal relations to immigrants. *American Journal of Sociology,* 1964, *70,* 193-205.

Canadian Immigration and Population Study. *Immigration and Population Statistics.* Ottawa: Manpower and Immigration, 1974.

Dawson, C.A. *Group Settlement: Ethnic Communities in Western Canada.* Toronto: Macmillan, 1936.

Driedger, L. In search of cultural identity factors. *The Canadian Review of Sociology and Anthropology,* 1975, *12*(2), 150-162.

Frideres, J.S. Discrimination in Western Canada. *Race,* 1973, *15*(2), 213-222.

Frideres, J.S. Prejudice towards minority groups: ethnicity or class. *Ethnicity,* 1975, *2,* 34-42.

Frideres, J.S. & Goldenberg, S. Hyphenated Canadians: Comparative analysis of ethnic, regional and national identification of western Canadian university students. *The Journal of Ethnic Studies,* 1977, *5*(2), 91-100.

Gibbins, R. & Ponting, J.R. Public opinion and Canadian Indians: a preliminary probe. *Canadian Ethnic Studies,* 1976, *8*(2), 1-17.

Hall, D.J. Clifford Sifton: Immigration and settlement policy, 1896-1905. In H. Palmer (ed.), *The Settlement of the West.* Calgary: Comprint Publishing, 1977.

Hiller, H.H. *Canadian Society: A Sociological Analysis.* Scarborough: Prentice-Hall, 1976.

Hirabayashi, G.K. Social distance and the modernizing Metis. In Card, B.Y., Hirabayashi, G.K., & French, C.L. *The Metis in Alberta Society*. Edmonton: University of Alberta, 1963.

Isajiw, W.W. The process of maintenance of ethnic identity: the Canadian context. In P.M. Migus (ed.), *Sounds Canadian: Languages and Cultures in Multi-Ethnic Society*. Toronto: Peter Martin Associates, 1975.

Kalbach, W.E. Growth and distribution of Canada's ethnic populations, 1871-1971. In L. Driedger (ed.), *The Canadian Ethnic Mosaic: A Quest for Identity*. Toronto: McClelland and Stewart, 1978.

Kaye, B. & Moodie, D.W. Geographical perspectives on the Canadian plains. In R. Allen (ed.), *A Region of the Mind*. Regina: Canadian Plains Research Centre, 1973.

Labovitz, S. Some evidence of Canadian ethnic, racial, and sexual antagonism. *The Canadian Review of Sociology and Anthropology*, 1974, *11*(3), 247-254.

Lautt, M.L. Sociology and the Canadian plains. In R. Allen (ed.), *A Region of the Mind*. Regina: Canadian Plains Research Centre, 1973.

Lehr, J.C. The government and the immigrant: perspectives on Ukrainian block settlement in the Canadian west. *Canadian Ethnic Studies*, 1977, *9*(2), 42-52.

Mackie, M. Ethnic stereotypes and prejudice: Alberta Indians, Hutterites, and Ukrainians. *Canadian Ethnic Studies*, 1974, *6*(1-2), 39-52.

Mackie, M. Ethnicity and nationality: how much do they matter to western Canadians? *Canadian Ethnic Studies*, 1978, *10*(2), 118-129.

O'Bryan, K.G., Reitz, J.G., & Kuplowska, O.M. *Non-Official Languages: A Study in Canadian Multiculturalism*. Ottawa: Supply and Services Canada, 1976.

Palmer, H. (ed.) *Immigration and the Rise of Multiculturalism*. Toronto: Copp Clark, 1975.

Palmer, H. (ed.) *The Settlement of the West*, Calgary: Comprint Publishing, 1977.

Pineo, P.C. The social standing of ethnic and racial groupings. *The Canadian Review of Sociology and Anthropology*, 1977, *14*(2), 147-157.

Porter, J. *The Vertical Mosaic*. Toronto: University of Toronto Press, 1965.

Rea, J.E. My main line is the kiddies ... make them good Christians and good Canadians, which is the same thing. In W. Isajiw, (ed.), *Identities: The Impact of Ethnicity on Canadian Society*. Toronto: Peter Martin Associates, 1977.

Report of the Royal Commission on Bilingualism and Biculturalism. Book IV. *The Cultural Contribution of the Other Ethnic Groups*. Ottawa: Queen's Printer, 1970.

Rose, J.D. *Peoples: The Ethnic Dimension in Human Relations*. Chicago: Rand McNally, 1976.

Schlichtmann, H. Ethnic themes in geographical research on western Canada. *Canadian Ethnic Studies*, 1977, *9*(2), 9-41.

Statistics Canada. *Perspective Canada: A Compendium of Social Statistics*. Ottawa: Information Canada, 1974.

Statistics Canada. *Perspective Canada II: A Compendium of Social Statistics*. Ottawa: Supply and Services Canada, 1977.

Chapter 12

Native Peoples and the Larger Society

John W. Berry, Department of Psychology, Queen's University

In this chapter the relationships between two broad categories of people are considered—those who were in Canada before the first arrival of Europeans and those who came after. The former are referred to as "native" (a non-pejorative term which refers to their early presence here); and the latter as the "larger society" (a term indicating their present numerical and political dominance in the country as a whole). Although some may view this distinction as inherently ethnocentric or racist, it does describes fairly accurately the present psychological reality of importance to native peoples.

Some may also argue that these two groups are too diverse to produce two simple categories. Native peoples are varied by traditional culture (Inuit, Indian and their numerous linguistic and ecological variations), legal status ("status" Indians, "non-status" Indians and Metis), and degree of acculturation ("bush" or "land" oriented, town or white oriented). Similarly, the larger society is multicultural, increasingly multiracial, and regionally diverse. It is only possible to lump such variation into two categories if there is some valid reason for doing so. There seem to be five such reasons: historical, geographic, cultural, economic and legal.

Historically, a dual view of ethnic relations was dominant in the minds of the two groups (Jaenen, 1976). The legacy of the early European writers is that a "we-they" view of people in Canada still persists (Chamberlin, 1975, ch. 3). This was reinforced *then* by the geographic fact that the two peoples inhabited different continents, and *now* by the strong tendency for native peoples to reside in more northern areas of the country. The duality was further reinforced by the readily observed cultural differences between the groups both on first contact and at present. Economic factors, too, play a role particularly in recent times since native peoples clearly occupy the lowest levels of the economic ladder. Finally, and perhaps most importantly, native peoples have been and still are the object of special laws which tend to identify them as a group and to set them apart from the larger society.

Acculturation and Intergroup Relations

Although the concept and acculturation in principle could be employed in all studies of intergroup relations, it usually appears only in anthropologically oriented studies of native, immigrant, or Third World peoples. In essence, it refers to the transfer of cultural elements between two groups in contact; but it can also refer to the transfer of behavioural or other psychological features (Berry, 1979).

Three Elements of Acculturation

Three elements of acculturation may be distinguished: *contact, conflict* and *adaptation* (Berry, 1980). The first is necessary, the second probable and the third inevitable. At the core of the notion of acculturation is the contact between two groups which can occur through trade, invasion, enslavement, educational or missionary activity, or through telecommunications. Without contact there is no acculturation. Such variables as the nature, purpose, duration, and permanence of contact all shape the ensuing acculturation. The least acculturation may take place where there was no purpose (contact was accidental) or where contact is the result of mutually desired trade, or where it is short-lived; the greatest acculturation will take place where the purpose is a deliberate penetration of a society (e.g., by invasion, education and evangelization) over a long period of time (by settlement). Clearly, acculturation is likely to be great in the present case of native life, with the largest flow of culture from the dominant European to the non-dominant native peoples. However, for the initial period of contact (Bailey, 1937, ch. 10), the cultural transfer was fairly balanced; Europeans acquired perhaps more from native peoples (e.g., food and transportation) than vice versa.

Conflict is common, but not inevitable, in cultural and psychological systems. Conflict can be defined as incompatibility between two systems, whether it becomes expressed (overt) or not. Although not all differences are incompatible, many are. For example, hunting and agriculture cannot both take place on the same territory, nor can monotheistic and animistic belief systems be held simultaneously by an individual.

Three Varieties of Adaptation

Conflicts require solutions and the term *adaptation* is used here to refer to varieties of resolution of acculturation conflict. Three varieties are outlined; *adjustment, reaction* and *withdrawal* (Berry, 1980). In the case of adjustment, changes are made which reduce the conflict by making cultural or behavioural features more similar; homogenization (as in the "melting pot") or assimilation of one group into another are examples of such adjustment. In the case of *reaction,* changes are made which attempt to reduce the conflict by retaliating against the source of the conflict: native political organization or aggression are examples of such reaction. In the case of *withdrawal* changes are made which essentially remove one element from the contact arena; moving back to the reserve or setting up "nativistic" communities are examples of this mode. The nature of intergroup relations in Canadian society will depend upon which adaptive mode is pursued.

Four Modes of Acculturation
One way to conceptualize these three forms of adaptation in social and psychological terms is illustrated in Figure 12.1. We begin by recognizing two questions of crucial importance to all groups and individuals undergoing acculturation: "Is my identity and culture of value and to be retained?" "Are positive relations with the larger (dominant) society to be sought?" For the sake of our conceptual analysis, dichotomous answers ("yes" or "no") are provided, yielding the four-fold classification in Figure 12.1.

Figure 12.1
Adaptive Options in Intergroup Relations as a Function
of Response to Two Questions.

		Is Identity and Culture of Value and to be Retained?	
		"Yes"	"No"
Are Positive Relations with the Larger Society to be Sought?	"Yes"	Integration	Assimilation
	"No"	Segregation	Deculturation

Here, instead of one positive type (adjustment), we have two which are distinguished by the contrasting value placed on identity and cultural retention; these are *assimilation* and *integration,* and are conceptually distinct. Assimilation means relinquishing one's identity and culture, and moving *into* the larger society. Integration involves retaining one's identity and culture, and moving to *join* the larger society. The term integration implies both the maintenance of the integrity of one's culture and identity, and the movement to become an integral part of a larger societal framework.

In the lower row of Figure 12.1, the two "negative" options are indicated. One of these is *segregation,* and refers to both the group's withdrawal away from the larger society (self-segregation), and to the exclusion of the group by the larger society (imposed segregation).

Deculturation is difficult to define precisely, because it is accompanied by a good deal of collective and individual confusion and anxiety. It is characterized by striking out against the larger society (moving *against* or *reaction),* by feelings of *marginality* and *alienation* and loss of identity, and what has been termed *acculturative stress.* In deculturation groups are out of cultural and psychological contact with either their traditional culture or the larger society. When imposed by the larger society, it is tantamount to ethnocide. For whatever reason it results, it constitutes the classical situation of "marginality."

Early Relations Between Native Peoples and Europeans
It is only in the context of first contact that much of present day relations may be understood. The writings of Jaenen (1976), Bailey (1937) and

Trigger (1976) are particularly important for describing this early context. One famous dictum (Parkman, 1899, p. 131) stated that "Spanish civilization crushed the Indian; English civilization scorned and neglected him; French civilization embraced and cherished him." In commenting on the validity of this dictum, Jaenen points out two facts. First, it was the Europeans who sailed from Europe to the Western Hemisphere, not the other way around, and Europeans assumed that Europe was the centre of the world. Moreover, the very claim of "discovery" is inherently ethnocentric. There likely was a generally shared denigration of native peoples among early Europeans. Secondly, if there were any real differences among the three groups of Europeans, it was not due to any lack of ethnocentrism on the part of some, but to the specific nature of their economic relations with native peoples. As Jaenen argues, the agricultural English found it necessary to displace native groups, while the French were dependent on native peoples for safety, sustenance and the pursuit of the fur trade. Thus the attitudes of the French may have reflected a lower degree of conflict between them and native peoples in New France. Put in other terms (Trigger, 1976, p. 3), relationships were largely symbiotic in Canada where the French were trading, but involved subjugation in the United States where the British were busy establishing colonial settlements.

French Views of Native Peoples
However, early French behaviour was not free of ethnocentric values and discriminatory acts. Slavery was not uncommon, and was justified by the argument that "the imperfect must be subject to the perfect" (Jaenen, 1976; p. 15), a view borrowed from the Spanish. In an analysis of this kind of rationale, Washburn (1959) has noted that there were numerous moral and legal justifications for acting toward Amerindians in a discriminatory fashion, including their supposed treachery and barbarism.

Other views were that native peoples were "the living representation of ancient Europeans who were retarded in their development" (Jaenen, 1976, p. 22) or that they were "like immature children who required European tutelage in order to realize their full capacities" (Jaenen, 1976; p. 26). Views such as these implied that with tutelage (see Honigmann and Honigmann, 1965) and care, Amerindian peoples might be able to realize their full potential. In keeping with these attitudes, the French policy held the native peoples capable of assimilation into French culture, and accordingly set up educational and religious programs for their inclusion. Contemporary descriptions portrayed native peoples as "backward or less evolved, different in degree but not in kind ... therefore capable with education and training to rise ... to a status of equality with the ruling group" (Jaenen, 1976; p. 153). There were, however, also very positive descriptions in the contemporary literature.

Failure of the assimilation policy led to an opposite reaction, that of discrimination (Jaenen, 1976; p. 159), which never became dominant, however, or passed into official legislation. By 1685 "the missionaries had abandoned all hope of assimilating the Amerindians and making Frenchmen of them" (Jaenen, 1976, p. 183). The net result appears to have been an attitude of tolerance qualified by a degree of mystery about why the native peoples didn't adopt their "obviously" better way of life.

British Views of Native Peoples
Early British views are largely documented for the culture areas now within the United States borders. Attitudes towards the Iroquois nations in the Northern United States and Southern Canada were generally positive. However, they must be taken in the context of the military alliance then established between the British and the Iroquois. But they do illustrate that the sweeping generalization by Parkman (1899) described earlier, may be in need of qualification.

Native Views of Europeans
The Amerindian views of Europeans are much less well documented, since literacy was not widespread among native peoples. But, we may surmise that the failure of the assimilation policy indicated a negative attitude toward the French lifestyle, if not toward the French as a people. More specific statements of native peoples disapproving of intermarriage and the placing of native children can be found (Jaenen, 1976, p. 163), and in keeping with an earlier observation, native peoples in the seventeenth century "seem to have stereotyped the Englishman as a farmer or town-dweller, whose activities gradually drove the original agriculturalists deeper into the hinterland, whereas the stereotype of the Frenchman was a trader or soldier laden with baubles and brandy who asked only for furs and hospitality" (Jaenen, 1976, p. 19).

Lurie (1959, p. 57) and Trigger (1976, p. 843) have both pointed out, however, that Amerindian responses to the presence of Europeans varied widely, depending upon the particular native lifestyle, the particular European needs, and the interaction (match or mismatch) between them. Thus, we are directed away from sweeping generalizations toward a consideration of more local contact situations.

The Current Intergroup Arena
The present setting for intergroup relations in Canada is best characterized by Berger's (1977) observation that what is basically a *homeland* for the native peoples serves as a *frontier* for the larger society. This characterization is true for all but the urban setting (Brody, 1971; Dosman, 1972) which constitutes a special context for intergroup relations. However, whether in the city or elsewhere in Canada, one overriding truth is inescapable: the native peoples are a colonized people, occupying a dependent position that is largely outside the framework of the larger society.

The Situation of Native Peoples
Native peoples in general are economically poor, occupy housing of minimal standards, and have had little success in moving through the educational systems of the larger society (Hawthorn, 1967; Berry, Evans, and Rawlinson 1971; Bowd, 1977). They have experienced governmental policies which have kept them segregated on reservations, but more recently are facing assimilation policies. At the same time, economic, educational, religious, and telecommunications policies and programs of various institutions have placed enormous assimilation pressures on native peoples, but attitudes in the general population of the larger society have often been negative and discriminatory. With these contrary purposes, pressures, policies and programs, it is no wonder that a state of conflict exists between the native peoples and the larger society. And given the relative economic and political strengths, it is no wonder that one dominates and the other is dependent.

The resolution to this conflict may be considered in relation to the four adaptive options outlined earlier (Figure 12.1): assimilation, segregation, integration, and deculturation. Clearly the four options are all still possible; although assimilation has been evident, as well as segregation, neither has become fully dominant. Similarly, deculturation is present (mainly in urban areas) and integration is now a general cultural policy. Which option is taken will depend to some extent upon the nature of the local contact arena and on the nature of the local intergroup attitudes. It may also depend on whether Metis, Indians or Inuit are involved.

The Metis Situation
In general, the Metis have had the most contact (both cultural and genetic) and now live in greater proximity to the larger society, while the Inuit are lower on both measures; the Indian population, while highly varied on these measures, are probably intermediate.

Recent accounts of the Metis as a people (Anderson and Anderson, 1977; Sawchuk, 1978; Sealey and Lussier, 1975) emphasize their sense of peoplehood, of themselves as a "nation." They are not simply leftovers, the result of occasional meeting of native peoples and early Europeans; rather, they view themselves (Adams, 1975) and are viewed by others as one distinct element in the Canadian mosaic. They, along with the "non-status" Indian population of Canada (those native peoples not legally recognized as Indian by the federal government), are organized into many provincial associations, and one national one, the Native Council of Canada, and one proceeding with native claims against the federal government. Although highly assimilated in some respects (language and dress) in some parts of the country, and somewhat deculturated (mainly in urban areas), these recent signs of national development will probably lead to their eventual integration, rather than to self-segregation.

The Inuit Situation

The Inuit are much less exposed to the larger society, and while their sense of peoplehood is equally strong, it is more retained than regained. Recent inroads by the federal government, however, have placed them in a highly dependent position (Brody, 1975; Paine, 1977). Indeed, in Paine's view, (1977, p. 3) they are now experiencing "welfare colonialism" in contrast to an older economic form which began with the whalers and continued with the arrival of missionaries and the Hudson's Bay Company. Only in the major centres, (Frobisher Bay and Inuvik; Honigmann and Honigmann, 1965, 1970) is there evidence of major deculturation and assimilation. And while there have been moves "back to the land" by some groups (the self-segregation option) there is every likelihood that integration will be the predominant mode. This appears to be the option currently espoused by the national political organization, the Inuit Tapirisat (Eskimo Brotherhood) of Canada (Inuit Tapirisat of Canada, 1975).

The Indian Situation

There is much greater variation in the current condition of the various Indian peoples. In northern reaches the situation is similar to that of the Inuit. Minimal contact and a retained identity have been reinforced by agreements for self-government (the James Bay Agreement for the Cree), or by demands for recognition as a "nation" within confederation (the Dene Declaration, see Watkins, 1977). In southern areas (for example, the Iroquois and Huron of Ontario and Quebec) extensive assimilation has taken place among most, but is accompanied among some by a reaffirmation of traditional identity and cultural values (e.g., the Longhouse). In mid-northern and many western areas (N.W. Ontario and Prairies) an intermediate level of acculturation has created dramatic social and personal problems of adaptation (see later section on acculturative stress) and evidence of deculturation.

Although highly varied, some common policies are being pursued by the National Indian Brotherhood, usually in cooperation with the many provincial associations. One is in the area of education (National Indian Brotherhood, 1972) in which full native control is sought over the educational institutions attended by native children. It is argued that existing schools are instruments of assimilation and even of deculturation; only with full control can identity and culture be retained and developed. Necessary features of the larger society such as training in the official languages and assuming economic roles are incorporated, thereby leaning away from self-segregation toward integration.

Native Peoples' Orientations to the Larger Society
Public Statements
Perhaps the two best single sources of public statements by individual native peoples are the injunction hearings to stop the James Bay Hydro-

electric project (in the Quebec Inuit and Cree areas, see Richardson, 1975), and the public inquiry into the MacKenzie Valley Pipeline project (Berger, 1977; Watkins, 1977). For policy statements, the "Red Paper" (Citizen Plus) of the Indian Chiefs of Alberta (1970), the National Indian Brotherhood statement on Education (1972), and the Dene Declaration of the Joint General Assembly of the Indian Brotherhood of the NWT and the Metis Association of the NWT are all articulate and forceful documents.

Although there are many variations, and some specific contradictions among these sources (Cardinal, 1969; 1977), the overall thrust of them is toward integration; they seek to avoid assimilation in the economic or educational spheres; they decry the deculturation of the individuals and groups who are lost between the two worlds, and they apparently want to avoid segregation, both of the imposed and chosen variety. The Dene Declaration exemplified these features by insisting on the right to be regarded as an independent nation and have self-determination within Canada.

In the National Indian Brotherhood education policy statement (1972, p. 25) an attack was made upon the older use of the term "integration," since it really meant assimilation; however, it is clear from the total statement that "integration" (in the sense of "mingling the best elements of a wide range of human differences") is the goal of Indian education.

With respect to individual statements, the report by Berger (1977) contains many statements illustrating the pursuit of native collective goals within the larger framework, and the strong distaste for assimilation and deculturation. The new arrangements being sought are in all cases, *within* Confederation and in cooperation with the larger society. This is the nature of the Cree and Inuit settlement in Quebec, and of the Inuit proposal in the high Arctic (Inuit Tapirisat of Canada, 1975). It is also the orientation of the Dene.

Two somewhat more aggressive statements should be mentioned here which do not fit this general picture. One is by Wuttunee (1971); he has argued forcefully against special government treatment of native peoples (especially when it "supports little red dictators" p. 8). Instead, he favours a form of assimilation, arguing that among Indians, "there are many who are not perpetual alcoholics and who are prepared to become taxpayers" (p. 11). He notes that many Indians have already assimilated and others must accept this challenge. This position has not found much support among other native peoples; however, it is important to note that assimilation has indeed been proposed and apparently rejected.

Another somewhat aggressive view has been well articulated by Waubageshig (1970). A fundamental dichotomy between the colonizer and the colonized is attended by *violence* (rather than by conflict, as in our scheme of acculturation) between the two parties. In the view of Waubageshig, this violence occurs during the process of colonization, and will occur during the process of decolonization. Violence is predicted to occur in the form of "armed struggle" (p. 80) and will take place over land rights. While it is true that there has been some use of arms in the past few years and some sit-ins have taken place, the level of violence has generally been below that expected by Waubageshig. Whether this is due to the moderate positions taken by native or by government negotiators is not clear. However, there does appear to be an agreeable basis for negotiating and re-negotiating lands and treaties (Government of Canada, 1977) at the present time. Thus we may conclude that the more extreme options of assimilation and of rejection based upon violent conflict appear to lack support in the native community at large.

Community Studies

Field work by anthropologists, and others, usually uncover this generally positive orientation toward integration (Vallee, 1967; Smith, 1974, 1975; Brody, 1975; Stymeist, 1975; Paine, 1977). For example, with respect to occupational preferences of northern native youth (Smith, 1974) there is a clear preference for occupations within the economic structure of the larger society (airline pilot, radio-operator, banker, lawyer, doctor), and a rejection of some which are more traditional (hunter and trapper) and of others of general low status (garbageman, janitor, labourer). At the same time, these youth are interested in maintaining local ties, for example by keeping a home in the settlement. Further work by Smith (1975) on pluralism in the MacKenzie Delta noted the presence of a "hostile dependency" (Smith, 1975, p. 68); dependency upon the larger society is recognized by the native peoples and it is resented, for it is acknowledged as leading to eventual assimilation or to deculturation. Unable to pursue self-segregation, and wishing to avoid cultural loss, integration appears to be accepted.

In more southern areas, two field studies (Brody, 1971; Stymeist, 1975) document a more deculturated community situation, but obviously one which is not valued or desired by the native peoples caught in that situation. In Brody's view this problem might be reduced by improving the socio-economic position of native peoples (perhaps by matching traditional economic activities with contemporary economic roles) and by changing native education to meet more adequately their contemporary needs.

Attitude Surveys

Few studies have attempted to elicit individual attitudes of native peoples with formal attitude scales. However, in a series of studies (Berry, 1975, 1976) nine samples of native peoples were drawn to represent varying kinds of traditional culture and degrees of acculturation. These were two Cree samples from James Bay, three Ojibway from Northwestern Ontario, two Carrier from northern plateau British Columbia, and two Tsimshian from coastal British Columbia. Interviews were conducted by members of the respondents' own group, in either the traditional language or in English, whichever was preferred.

Three attitude scales were employed, which were derived from earlier studies by Sommerlad & Berry (1970) and Berry (1970) with Australian Aborigines. The scales were designed to assess three of the four options outlined in Figure 12.1: assimilation, integration and segregation; the latter scale assessed attitudes toward self-segregation and was termed the rejection scale.

Results in the nine samples indicate an overall preference for integration, with assimilation and self-segregation less preferred. However, there are wide-ranging differences among the samples. Not surprisingly, those samples most acculturated (highest level of formal education and wage employment) were relatively more in favour of assimilation than self-segregation, while those least acculturated showed a relative preference for self-segregation over assimilation; however, in all cases, integration remained the most preferred. Another result was that those cultures which were traditionally more similar to the larger society (in terms of being settled in permanent relatively high density communities, and being socially and politically stratified) were relatively more in favour of assimilation than those which were traditionally nomadic and egalitarian.

The results of these attutide studies indicate that integration is generally being endorsed at the individual level. However, wide individual differences (and some community differences) are detected in survey work which are masked in the other, more general, sources of evidence. Nevertheless, if any general statement may be made about the orientation of native peoples toward the larger society, it is that deculturation is uncomfortable, assimilation is threatening, and self-segregation is politically unrealistic; integration remains as the probable option, not only by default, but is actually valued as the option most supportive of the goals of native peoples.

Orientations of the Larger Society Toward Native Peoples

According to Berger (1977) "Euro-Canadian society has refused to take Native culture seriously" (p. 85). In essence, native people have been placed outside the framework of daily life; "Indians are regarded as outsiders, as people who have no real place in the community" (Stymeist, 1975, p. 62). Patterson (1972, pp. 39-40) traces this situation from 1876 (the date of the first Indian Act), noting that "from the point of view of the European, the Indian had become irrelevant" (p. 40).

The present seems to be characterized by transition. On the one hand, contemporary analysis (Berger, 1977) still finds evidence for the perception of native peoples as outsiders. On the other hand, native peoples are more and more "asserting themselves to regain as much control as possible of the decision-making processes which shape their political, economic, and social affairs" (Patterson, 1977, p. 40), thus forcing their interests onto the awareness of the larger society. In the view of Gibbins and Ponting (1967a, p. 1), Indians have now moved out of this "period of irrelevance." The response by the larger society to this new assertiveness will be of critical importance to intergroup relations in Canada; what do we know about current orientations which will help us to predict the likely course of events?

In the past, there has been clear evidence of segregation (e.g., reserve policy), as well as governmental policies (e.g., earlier education policy) which have been clearly assimilationist in their orientation and programs, while others (the multiculturalism policy) have promoted integration. A number of attitude surveys have demonstrated wide ranges of individual attitudes toward native peoples, attitudes which appear to vary with region, degree of contact and ethnicity.

Public Statements
The primary policy instrument used by the larger society in their dealings with native peoples has been the Indian Act (with versions dated from 1876 to 1951); this is now under discussion, with a view to revision (Government of Canada, 1978). The Indian Act has placed native peoples in a bind: one feature of the Act segregated them, another placed them on a dependency relationship and yet another created a framework for assimilation.

The situation was obviously unsatisfactory to both native peoples and the larger society, and led to the White Paper of 1969. That proposal noted that "to be an Indian today is to be someone apart . . . to lack power . . . to be without a job, a good house . . . without knowledge, training or technical skill, and above all, without those feelings of dignity and self-confidence that a man must have if he is to walk with his head held high" (Government of Canada, 1969, p. 3). It continued: "Obviously the course of history must be changed. To be an Indian must be to be free—free to develop Indian cultures in an environment of legal, social and economic equality with other Canadians" (p. 3).

The specific proposals were viewed by the government as leading toward integration, but were viewed by native peoples as leading toward assimilation, and were vehemently rejected. Current proposals (Government of Canada, 1978) for discussion are a renewed attempt based upon the activities of a joint working committee of the National Indian Brotherhood and the Federal Cabinet. Proposals are in the areas of "tribal government," education, land claims, hunting and fishing rights, and the thorny question of membership in the band. The thrust of these proposals is clearly in the direction of native self-determination; as such they should lead away from assimilation and deculturation, toward integration and segregation. Which of these latter two will predominate will depend largely upon the orientations of the native peoples themselves.

Community Studies

Community studies may be represented by the work of the Honigmanns (1965, 1970) in two Arctic towns, and by Stymeist (1975) in a northwestern Ontario community. Working in Frobisher Bay and Inuvik, John and Irma Honigmann have done extensive work on the general question of cultural and personal change in the face of the northern penetration of Euro-Canadian society.

One of the principal concepts employed in the description of group relations is that of *tutelage* (Honigmann and Honigmann, 1965, ch. 5). Tutelage can be relatively informal, where the individual learns about Euro-Canadian ways by imitation or trial and error; and it can be more formal, where deliberate instruction and reinforcement are provided by Euro-Canadian society.

The expected outcome of tutelage is, of course, that the Inuit will learn to be more like the white man: "Euro-Canadians believe they have no course but to develop the Eskimo as rapidly as feasible to white standards, language, skills and sophistication" (Honigmann and Honigmann, 1965, p. 160). The only alternative which is seen is generally unacceptable: "To leave the Eskimo alone or to his traditional life, they reject out of hand as manifestly impractical and immoral" (Honigmann and Honigmann, 1965, p. 160). In terms of the four options, the Euro-Canadians apparently view assimilation as the appropriate goal, and dismiss segregation; not even considered are integration or deculturation.

In their writings, the Honigmanns show evidence of subscribing to tutelage as the appropriate role relationship, and they have been taken to task for it (Paine, 1977, ch. 5). Essentially Paine argues that rather than "filling a social vacuum" (Honigmann and Honigmann, 1965, p. 227) by assuming the role of tutor, the Euro-Canadian has taken a position of superiority over the Inuit, which "has become a vexing factor in white-Inuit relations" (Paine 1977, p. 79). He points out that among the barren land Inuit (Vallee, 1962, p. 129) and in the MacKenzie Valley (Parsons, 1970, p. 38), relations with Euro-Canadians have also placed the Inuit in a childlike role. We may conclude that right across Arctic Canada Euro-Canadians have generally subscribed to paternalistic assimilation in interacting with Inuit.

In the study of Ojibway relationships with the larger society in northwestern, Ontario, Stymeist (1975, p. 6) noted a strong division between the town's people and the Indians. This division was based upon a perception of a great difference between the two groups and a general denigration of native peoples by the larger society; and these have led to a pronounced acceptance of segregation. Although he found that "relatively few whites are actively and openly prejudiced against native people" (p. 80), and that indeed native people are respected for certain qualities (knowledge of bush life, and ability to survive in the harsh environment), it was not difficult to elicit "a stock of complaints made in a serious or half-serious tone: Indians are dirty; they smell bad; they are lazy; they won't work; they are all drunks; they live off welfare; they are given too much, and so on" (Stymeist 1975, pp. 75-76). Such inconsistent attitudes suggest some degree of uncertainty about how to view native peoples; on the one hand they are unacceptable because of some perceived features of their lifestyle, but on the other hand they are admired. Perhaps a combined sense of pity and distaste, rather than hatred, is the real meaning to be attached to this ambivalence.

Such prejudice has led to discrimination and exclusion, as documented by Stymeist (1975). Segregation appears to operate in full force in this town. Across Canada the generality of such prejudice and exclusion, of course, can be assessed only by broad survey analyses.

Attitude Surveys

Two national studies have been conducted which have attempted to assess attitudes toward native peoples in the larger society (Berry, Kalin and Taylor, 1977; Gibbins and Ponting, 1976a). In addition, one study assessed attitudes in two communities (Berry, 1976) employing the same scales which were used to assess Amerindian attitudes (reported in the previous section); coincidentally one of these communities had also been studied by Stymeist (1975). The opportunity exists, therefore, to compare results by the two approaches.

The Gibbins and Ponting (1976a) study focussed exclusively upon attitudes toward Indians. One of their main scales is the Indian Sympathy Index (ISI). A sample of 1,832 respondents aged eighteen years or more was randomly selected from the Canadian population living south of the 60th parallel. Interviews were face-to-face, and were conducted in the respondent's home, in their preferred official language (French or English) in the period January to March, 1976.

Results from the survey led Gibbins and Ponting to conclude that "Canadian Indians do not face a markedly hostile public" (Gibbins and Ponting, 1976b , p. 40). There was no evidence of extreme negative attitudes or of a "white backlash." Moreover, respondents in the larger society showed general sympathy for the pursuit of land claims by Indians; a majority (60 per cent) agreed that "all" or "many" Indian land claims were valid. The general conclusion was that "Canadians are surprisingly attuned to native issues, and that the conflict between the needs of the native people and the priorities of contemporary Canadians may not be as acute as is sometimes assumed" (p. 40).

However, there were individual and group differences in this general picture. Quebec respondents were more sympathetic than those from Saskatchewan and Alberta. Those who were more knowledgeable about Indian people were *no* different in attitudes from those who possessed very little knowledge. Furthermore, personal contact made no difference

(Gibbins and Ponting, 1977), and correlations between ISI scores and respondents' education and income also proved to be non-significant. (Gibbins and Ponting, 1976a).

In the national survey by Berry, Kalin and Taylor (1977) (See chapter 8 for more extensive description), Canadian Indians were not the specific focus of study, but served as one attitude object among many in a general study of multicultural and ethnic attitudes. This context difference may affect respondents' orientations: in one study Indians were the sole focus of the study, while in the other, Indians were judged in a context of many other groups. Thus direct comparisons of results of the two studies should be made with caution. Two main sections of the study were concerned with Canadian Indians. In the first, a card-sorting task, respondents revealed how similar they thought Canadian Indians and Eskimo and Metis were to "myself." For English Canadian respondents, Canadian Indians had a similarity rank of 4 of 27, Eskimos rank 5 and Metis rank 9. For French Canadian respondents Canadian Indians were also ranked 4, Eskimos ranked 6 and Metis 11.

A second section of the study assessed the attitudes and stereotypes of various groups held by the respondents. The group Canadian Indians was included among eight others, and respondents were asked to rate them on ten adjectives using a seven-point scale. In the total sample Canadian Indians were rated particularly high on the scales "Canadian and "stick together" and particularly low on "hard-working," "clean," "similar-to-me," "wealthy," and "well-known-to-me." No other group had as many low ratings.

Using an overall evaluation score, Indians were at the bottom of the evaluative hierarchy of ethnic groups. However, they were not uniformly or substantially low on all ratings. For example, while they were lowest on rating of "hardworking," they were second highest on "Canadian" (after English Canadian), and they were third highest on "interesting."

The third attitude study to be considered is that of Berry (1976). As part of the study assessing attitudes of Canadian Indians in nine communities, attitudes in two non-native samples were assessed employing the same scales. However, instead of asking Indians how they viewed the three options, the Euro-Canadian respondents were asked to indicate how, in their view, Indian peoples should relate to the larger society. Thus the assimilation and integration scales retained the meaning but the self-segregation scale changed to imposed segregation. One community was in southern Ontario and had no native peoples in or nearby. The other, in northwestern Ontario was in fact the same town studied by Stymeist (1975). Samples were stratified by age and sex, and were taken at random.

Results indicated that both communities do not consider segregation to be acceptable. The option most favoured was assimilation, with integration being second. Clearly there is a conflict between the views of

Euro-Canadians and native peoples. There is also an apparent discrepancy between the results of Stymeist (1975) and those of Berry (1976) for one of these towns. It will be recalled that Stymeist found segregation and discrimination to be implicitly accepted in the northwestern Ontario town, although "relatively few whites are actively and openly prejudiced against native people" (Stymeist, 1975, p. 80). In contrast, assimilation was most strongly indicated in the study by Berry (1976). This difference may be due to a contrast in focus; in one study the interest was on actual behaviour, while on the other the focus was on attitudes and beliefs.

Conclusions

Given the range of evidence presented in this chapter—historical, political, community and individual—how can native peoples and the larger society reorganize their relationships to suit both parties best? And what social and psychological changes are necessary to accomplish this reorganization?

The contemporary political demands and statements by native peoples and policies enunciated by the federal government provide the start for answering these questions. Fortunately there is reasonably widespread agreement among the parties at the policy level, although conflict still persists over specific programs and policy implementation. This area of agreement may be broadly characterized as integration; the maintenance and continuing development of native peoples as a culturally distinct set of peoples within the framework of the larger society. Of course agreement about integration will not definitely ensure the improvement of intergroup relations if integration is the course adopted; agreement may be necessary, but may not be a sufficient condition for success. However, our starting point should be integration; the others are clearly unacceptable to either or both of the groups in contact.

The basic question is *how* to go about pursuing integration in order to bring about mutually positive attitudes between native peoples and the larger society and to avoid acculturative stress. Integration, of course, means *contact*; and the social psychological literature on contact indicates that group contact leads to mutual acceptance only under certain conditions. Two of the more important conditions for our present discussion are the equality of status of the two groups, and the avoidance of conflict over scarce resources.

As we noted earlier, there is both a vast status differential between the native peoples and the larger society and a developing conflict over natural resources in the North (and over what might be called "welfare resources" in the South). Clearly, if integration and contact are to have their intended beneficial effects, rather than the opposite, these two conditions of contact will have to be managed. The two obvious implications are that status inequality must be reduced, and resource conflicts must be settled before intergroup attitudes will improve. And it is probable that the stresses of contact will also be reduced with these two changes. At the present time, many native groups believe that the recognition of Aboriginal Rights generally (and land claims specifically) both will resolve resource conflict and improve their status as a people, in economic and cultural terms (see Watkins, 1977); and the larger society seems to be sympathetic to this request (Gibbins & Ponting, 1976b). We thus observe, at the present time, an important consensus about both ends and means, which offers Canadians a unique opportunity to improve relationships between native peoples and the larger society.

REFERENCES

Adams, H. *Prison of Grass: Canada from the Native Point of View.* Toronto: New Press, 1975.

Anderson, D.R. and Anderson, A.M. *The Metis People of Canada: A History.* Edmonton: Alberta Federation of Metis Settlement Associations, 1977.

Bailey, A.G. *The Conflict of European and Eastern Algonkian Cultures.* St. John: New Brunswick Museum Monograph Series, No. 2, 1937.

Berger, T.R. *Northern Frontier, Northern Homeland,* Vol 1. Ottawa: Supply and Services, 1977.

Berry, J.W. Marginality, stress and ethnic identification in an acculturated Aboriginal community. *Journal of Cross-Cultural Psychology,* 1970, *1,* 239-252.

Berry, J.W. Amerindian attitudes toward assimilation: multicultural policy and reality in Canada. *Man and Life,* 1975, *1,* 47-60.

Berry, J.W. *Human Ecology and Cognitive Style.* New York: Sage/Halsted, 1976.

Berry, J.W. Social and cultural change. In H.C. Triandis and R. Brislin (eds.), *Handbook of Cross-Cultural Psychology,* Vol 5. Boston: Allyn & Bacon, 1979.

Berry, J.W. Acculturation as varieties of adaptation. In A. Padilla (ed.), *Psychology of Acculturation.* Washington, AAAS, 1980.

Berry, J.W., Evans, C. and Rawlinson, H. *Post Secondary Educational Opportunity for the Ontario Indian Population.* Toronto: Queen's Printer, 1971.

Berry, J.W., Kalin, R. and Taylor, D. *Multiculturalism and Ethnic Attitudes in Canada.* Ottawa: Minister of Supply and Services Canada, 1977.

Bowd, A. Ten years after the Hawthorn Report: changing psychological implications for the education of Canadian native peoples. *Canadian Psychological Review,* 1977, *18,* 332-345.

Brody, H. *Indians on Skid Row.* Ottawa: Indian and Northern Affairs, 1971.

Brody, H. *The Peoples' Land: Eskimos and Whites in the Eastern Arctic.* Markham: Penguin, 1975.

Cardinal, H. *The Unjust Society.* Edmonton: Hurtig, 1969.

Cardinal, H. *The Rebirth of Canada's Indians.* Edmonton: Hurtig, 1977.

Chamberlain, J.E. *The Harrowing of Eden: White Attitudes Toward North American Natives.* Toronto: Fitzhenry & Whiteside, 1975.

Dosman, E.J. *Indians: The Urban Dilemma.* Toronto: McClelland and Stewart, 1972.

Gibbins, R. and Ponting, J.R. Public opinion and Canadian Indians: a preliminary probe. *Canadian Ethnic Studies,* 1976a, *8,* 1-17.

Gibbins, R. and Ponting, J.R. Indians and Indian issues: what do Canadians think? *Canadian Association in Support of Native Peoples Bulletin,* 1976b, 38-43.

Gibbins, R. and Ponting, J.R. Prairie Canadians' orientations toward Indians. *Prairie Forum.* 1977, *2,* 57-81.

Government of Canada. *Indian Policy.* Ottawa: Indian and Northern Affairs, 1969.

Government of Canada. *Native Claims: Policy, Process and Perspectives.* Ottawa: Indian and Northern Affairs, 1977.

Government of Canada. Discussion paper for the Indian Act Revision. *Indian News,* November, 1978.

Hawthorn, H.B. (ed.) *A Survey of the Contemporary Indians of Canada.* Ottawa: Indian Affairs Branch, 1967.

Honigmann, J.J. and Honigmann, I. *Eskimo Townsmen.* Ottawa: Canadian Research Centre for Anthropology, 1965.

Honigmann, J.J. and Honigmann, I. *Arctic Townsmen.* Ottawa: Canadian Research Centre for Anthropology, 1970.

Indian Chiefs of Alberta. *Citizen Plus: A Presentation to the Government of Canada,* 1970. (Reprinted in Waubageshig (ed.), *The Only Good Indian.* Toronto: New Press, 1970, pp. 5-40.)

Inuit Tapirisat of Canada. *Nunavut—Our Land.* Ottawa: ITC, 1975.

Jaenen, C.J. *Friend and Foe.* Toronto: McClelland and Stewart, 1976.

Lurie, N. Indian cultural adjustment to European civilization. In J.M. Smith (ed.), *Seventeenth Century America,* Chapel Hill: University of North Carolina Press, 1959.

National Indian Brotherhood. *Indian Control of Indian Education.* Ottawa: NIB, 1972.

Paine, R. (ed.) The White Arctic: Anthropological Essays on Tutelage and Ethnicity. St. Johns: Memorial University of Newfoundland, 1977.

Parkman, F. *The Jesuits in North America in the Seventeenth Century.* Toronto: 1899.

Parsons, G.F. *Arctic Suburb: A Look at the North's Newcomers.* Ottawa: Indian and Northern Affairs, 1970.

Patterson, E.P. *The Canadian Indian: A History since 1500.* Toronto: Collier-Macmillan, 1972.

Richardson, B. *Strangers Devour the Land.* Toronto: Macmillan, 1975.

Sawchuk, J. *The Metis of Manitoba.* Toronto: Peter Martin, 1978.

Sealey, D.B. and Lussier, A.S. *The Metis: Canada's Forgotten People.* Winnipeg: Manitoba Metis Federation, 1975.

Smith, D. *Occupational Preferences of Northern Students.* Ottawa: Indian and Northern Affairs, 1974.

Smith, D. *Natives and Outsiders: Pluralism in the MacKenzie River Delta.* Ottawa: Indian and Northern Affairs, 1975.

Sommerlad, E. and Berry, J.W. The role of ethnic identification in distinguishing between attitudes toward assimilation and integration of a minority racial group. *Human Relations,* 1970, *23,* 23-29.

Stymeist, D.H. *Ethnics and Indians: Social Relations in a Northwestern Ontario Town.* Toronto: Peter Martin, 1975.

Trigger, B.G. *The Children of Aataentsic: A History of the Huron People to 1660.* Montreal: McGill—Queen's University Press, 1976.

Vallee, F. *Kabloona and Eskimo in the Central Keewatin.* Ottawa: Canadian Research Centre for Anthropology, 1967.

Washburn, W.E. The Moral and Legal Justification for Dispossessing the Indians. In J.M. Smith (ed.), *Seventeenth Century America.* Chapel Hill: University of North Carolina Press, 1959.

Watkins, M. (ed.) *Dene Nation: The Colony Within.* Toronto: University of Toronto Press, 1977.

Waubageshig, The Comfortable Crisis. In Waubageshig (ed.), *The Only Good Indian.* Toronto: New Press, 1970.

Wuttunee, W. *Ruffled Feathers.* Calgary: Bell Books, 1971.

Name Index

Subject Index